MAKING SENSE OF MYTH

Making Sense of Myth

Conversations with Luc Brisson

GERARD NADDAF
WITH LOUIS-ANDRÉ DORION

McGill-Queen's University Press
Montreal & Kingston • London • Chicago

ISBN 978-0-2280-2070-7 (cloth)
ISBN 978-0-2280-2071-4 (paper)
ISBN 978-0-2280-2072-1 (ePDF)
ISBN 978-0-2280-2073-8 (ePUB)

Legal deposit first quarter 2024
Bibliothèque nationale du Québec

First published in French as *Entretiens avec Luc Brisson: Rendre raison au mythe*, interviews with Louis-André Dorion, Liber 1999

Printed in Canada on acid-free paper that is 100% ancient forest free (100% post-consumer recycled), processed chlorine free

Funding for this book was provided by the Faculty of Liberal Arts & Professional Studies and Office of Research Services of York University.

Financé par le gouvernement du Canada | Funded by the Government of Canada | Canada | Conseil des arts du Canada | Canada Council for the Arts

We acknowledge the support of the Canada Council for the Arts.

Nous remercions le Conseil des arts du Canada de son soutien.

McGill-Queen's University Press in Montreal is on land which long served as a site of meeting and exchange amongst Indigenous Peoples, including the Haudenosaunee and Anishinabeg nations. In Kingston it is situated on the territory of the Haudenosaunee and Anishinaabek. We acknowledge and thank the diverse Indigenous Peoples whose footsteps have marked these territories on which peoples of the world now gather.

Library and Archives Canada Cataloguing in Publication

Title: Making sense of myth : conversations with Luc Brisson / Gerard Naddaf with Louis-André Dorion.

Other titles: Conversations with Luc Brisson

Names: Naddaf, Gerard, 1950- author, interviewer. | Brisson, Luc, interviewee. | Dorion, Louis-André, 1960- author, interviewer.

Description: Includes bibliographical references and index.

Identifiers: Canadiana (print) 20230561829 | Canadiana (ebook) 20230561888 | ISBN 9780228020707 (cloth) | ISBN 9780228020714 (paper) | ISBN 9780228020738 (ePUB) | ISBN 9780228020721 (ePDF)

Subjects: LCSH: Brisson, Luc—Interviews. | LCSH: Myth. | LCSH: Plato. | LCSH: Philosophy. | LCGFT: Interviews.

Classification: LCC B398.M8 N33 2024 | DDC 184—dc23

This book was typeset by Marquis Interscript in 10.5/13 Sabon.

To humanity and its enduring myths,
which have made us who we are

Contents

Acknowledgments

This book has been a labour of love. Over the years it has taken on many different dimensions, expanding and morphing into the multidisciplinary project you see before you. Nonetheless, Luc Brisson was always the publication's main protagonist, catalyst, and guide. A special thanks to Louis-André Dorion for initiating the original conversations twenty-five years ago.

Above all, I'd like to thank Luc Brisson – a dear friend, colleague, and mentor – for hosting me on several occasions during my research trips to Paris to discuss the translation, participating in a series of interviews, and reviewing countless versions of the manuscript.

I'd also like to express my appreciation to Liber, the Quebec publisher, for giving me permission to translate the original conversations. As well, I'd like to thank the three anonymous reviewers for their valuable suggestions and insightful comments.

My thanks to the physicist and science historian Norman Sieroka for reviewing my translation of the section on the big bang and contemporary physics in part 3. I am especially indebted to Richard Allen, who read and edited numerous drafts of the translation, notes, introduction, and afterword, and who never tired of offering me generous and perceptive comments.

I'd like to thank my editor, Khadija Coxon, for shepherding me through the various stages of publishing the book with McGill-Queens University Press. Further, I'd like to acknowledge the generosity of York University, and in particular the Faculty of Liberal Arts and Professional Studies, for several research leaves and grants over the years connected with this project.

Finally, I'd like to thank the Awards to Scholarly Publications Program and the Federation for the Humanities and Social Sciences for their generous publishing grant.

MAKING SENSE OF MYTH

Introduction

ORIGIN OF THIS PROJECT

Luc Brisson is a leading anthropologist and historian of antiquity (notably of philosophy and religion), and one of the foremost specialists on Plato (427–367 BCE). In some respects, Plato is to philosophy what Jesus is to Christianity.[1] For Plato, it's reason and not faith that is king, and the spell of Plato for many is as powerful now as it was twenty-five hundred years ago. Plato's dialogues have been translated into dozens of languages, and millions of copies are sold every year; and it is he who coined the word "myth" in the sense in which we use it today. It's a primary tenet of these "conversations" that we're all products of myth, that it's impossible to escape them, which raises the question of how we can best live with them if some myths don't tolerate others, which is largely the source of conflicts within ourselves, and, of course, within countries and among countries. But there's much more to these conversations. They narrate the life of Luc Brisson, who was born into a modest family in a deeply Catholic and closed Quebec in 1946 and rose to the top of the French intellectual hierarchy, grounded as it is in a rigorous meritocracy. The title of these conversations, "making sense of myth," offers both a philosophy of myth and with it a philosophy of life. Indeed, to make sense of myth is to make sense of life, and in this respect myth is inescapable! Along the way, these conversations offer some penetrating insights into Quebec society past and present, and into many other societies as well, the United States among them.

In this introduction, I want to explain how I took on this project. I want to put into context the origin and meaning of myth, which is otherwise lost in time.[2] I'll be using copious notes so the general reader can, hopefully, follow any technicalities, and this will also be the case for the afterword and the conversations themselves, which are divided into four parts. I'll also describe in some detail the notion of myth as Brisson understands it and some insights into the importance of Plato for non-specialists.

One theme I'd like to highlight is that the reader – although this is somewhat unintentional on the part of Luc Brisson himself – will get to see the formation of the individual behind the theory; indeed, individual and theory are inseparable. In my opinion, witnessing the formation of the individual behind the theory is the exception rather than the norm in most disciplines, including philosophy.[3]

I've known Luc Brisson as a friend and colleague for over forty-five years. It was Pierre Hadot,[4] with whom I had recently begun studying at the École Pratique des Hautes Études (EPHE) in Paris, who introduced us.[5] The first volume of Brisson's Platonic bibliography (*Platon 1958–1975, Lustrum* 20 [1977]), which he had taken over from Harold Cherniss,[6] had just appeared in print, and Hadot thought he'd be a perfect contact and adviser for me to work with as I began a thesis on Plato under Hadot's supervision.

As it turned out, Brisson and I were both Canadian, he a Québécois and me an anglophone Nova Scotian but with maternal Acadian roots stretching back to 1632. We bonded, and after a number of meetings Brisson convinced me that Plato's *Laws* would be a good dialogue to work on because it was relatively unknown, compared to other Platonic dialogues. I opted to work on the theology of the *Laws*, Hadot agreed, and off I went. After completing my thesis at the EPHE, I then pursued my doctorate at the Sorbonne. Hadot and Brisson were co-supervisors, although Hadot was listed as my primary. I worked closely with both of them for over eight years, but my relationship with Brisson was far more than academic. We became close friends, and have remained so ever since.[7]

Although Brisson and I shared many personal stories about our respective Catholic upbringings, travels, world views, and research, it was only after I read his conversations with Louis-André Dorion[8] around twenty years ago, with the captivating title *Rendre raison au mythe* (Making sense of myth), that I discovered a new dimension of which I had previously been unaware, or at least had never put into context: the correlation between Brisson's fascinating insights into myth and the role of the Catholic Church in his upbringing, and, of course, in the formation of Quebec society.

But the conversations are about a lot more than this. While the unifying theme is "making sense of myth," Brisson proposes nothing less than a philosophy of myth, of life, inspired by the insights of arguably the greatest and most influential philosopher and mythmaker in Western culture, Plato. Since myths define in large part who we are as human beings, past and present, I'd like to begin with what we should understand by the term "myth" in the context of these conversations.[9]

WHAT IS A MYTH?

For Brisson "myth," a transliteration of the Greek *muthos*, has several interrelated facets,[10] but he employs it first and foremost as Plato describes it – that is, to refer to a traditional story passed down orally from one generation to the next, through which a community preserves its "memory" of its past and articulates its values and sources of knowledge. Plato saw these stories, especially when the main actors were gods, as largely fictive – which explains "myth" in the sense of a fictive story, the sense in which most people understand it today.[11] As Brisson observes, Plato's use of "myth" is both descriptive and critical. A myth, for Plato, is a traditional story, but he applies a value judgment with respect to another kind of discourse he considers superior – namely, philosophy.[12] Nonetheless, Plato also recognized the formidable power of myth for the vast majority of people, and he thus saw a reformed myth or mythmaking as a key to reforming society, moulding through myth the souls of future citizens from birth in order to create a more "ideal" society in time and space. Plato was the first to *consciously* do this.

Plato also provides a paradigm of myth and mythmaking that is among the most famous in Western culture, the Atlantis myth. It's so persuasive that generations of scholars, dilettantes, and enthusiasts have been stubbornly searching for the "lost" civilization.[13] Myths commonly speak of events that took place so long ago that they cannot be verified by the listener.[14] But myth also has a performative function: the power of language to control the individual within the group insofar as the makeup of each individual follows the rules admitted by the group. From this perspective, there is a fine line between the natural and the social. This will emerge in a powerful way in the course of the conversations as a means of understanding contemporary society and as an antidote to its constraints.

When the performative function of language is linked to corresponding actions, then the word "ritual" is appropriate. In English, this term is often used to refer to a prescribed order for the performance of religious services, which, etymologically, is not unconnected to the meaning that implies a lawful and regular order of a norm (related to the Sanskrit *rta*, "visible order"), all of which are grounded in myth. But ritual and its correspondence with myth is lost in time. Until recently, it was unclear what came first, the ritual or the myth.[15] Strictly speaking, there is a difference between narrating a myth and acting it out (that is, at the level of imitation or mimesis). At some historical point, they were inseparable. The ritual brings the myth to life, executes it so to speak. There is then a *literal* return to the primal event, and, by definition, the participants see the story as literally taking place, so that imitation becomes reality.[16] Rituals are so ingrained, so *natural* to those performing them, that nothing short of a revolution can unseat them, and even then, they're replaced with competing rituals, competing myths, competing ideologies, competing masters of truth.[17] This revolution is what fascinates Brisson. What is it that makes one want to substitute one ideology or myth for another, often violently in the name of reason – a reason, Brisson insists, that is also grounded in myth, though not in the eyes of its proponents?

The origin of myth, in Plato's sense of a traditional story, is lost in time. Ethnologists, cultural and evolutionary anthropologists, and the like do not know of a non-literate culture that does not practise "storytelling."[18] Indeed, storytelling may be as old as language itself;[19] in fact, it's necessary for cultural and social evolution, and, by extension, survival. In this regard, myth has a socio-biological function.[20] Since storytelling fosters social co-operation and threatens norm-breakers with punishment, it can be seen as one of the initial paths humans trod before organized religions developed with more complex societies. Of course, religions are grounded in myth and storytelling. In this case the primary actors are gods along with the people who interact with them.[21] But there may have been thousands of generations before organized religion occurred, if storytelling among the Ju/'hoansi tribes (mentioned below) is any indication.[22] Richard Wrangham has argued, persuasively in my opinion, that the discovery of fire would have led to language, and that the culture around the campfire would have instigated storytelling, which would have initially been grounded in a more primitive form of language before it became genetically coded.[23] Brisson doesn't discuss these more distant precursors to myth and storytelling; my point here is, and will be, to introduce the general reader to the anthropology of myth and storytelling in the evolution of humanity.

THE SPELL OF PLATO

But let's return to Plato. There is more published on Plato every year (around three hundred and fifty scholarly articles and books annually) than on any other philosopher, ancient or modern.[24] Unsurprisingly, Plato's works have been translated into dozens of languages, including Chinese, Japanese, Korean, and Hindi.[25] There are many millions of copies of Plato's works sold each and every year.[26] Indeed, it's difficult to escape university – and not just in the humanities – without having been exposed to Plato in some form. Plato's *Republic* is arguably the most influential political treatise ever written, and his *Timaeus*, the first creation story to mathematize the universe, was the main competitor with Genesis. And for those who have never read, or even heard of, the *Republic* or the *Timaeus*, they most certainly have heard of Atlantis, a Platonic invention, and an integral part of both the *Republic* and the *Timaeus*.[27]

The British mathematician and philosopher Alfred North Whitehead (1861–1947), best known for his work in mathematical logic and philosophy of science, made a famous claim that "The safest general characterization of the European philosophical tradition is that it consists of a series of footnotes to Plato."[28] Plato is certainly a towering figure in Whitehead's own work. Indeed, the *Timaeus* presages for Whitehead the giants Newton and Einstein. The German physicist and noble laurate Werner Heisenberg (1901–1976) argued that modern physics has decided in favour of Plato's cosmological account in the *Timaeus* that the smallest units of matter are not physical objects in the strict sense but forms or ideas that can only be expressed in mathematical language.[29]

The first volume of Austrian-British philosopher Karl Popper's famous *The Open Society and Its Enemies*, considered by *The Guardian* newspaper to be one of the top one hundred non-fiction books of all time, is entitled *The Spell of Plato*. Popper (1902–1994) argues that most of Plato's interpreters throughout the ages have been seduced somewhat by his magnitude and literary power.[30] If Heisenberg's primary focus was Plato's cosmological account in the

Timaeus, Popper was referring first and foremost to Plato's political works, and notably the *Republic*, which is about a lot more than politics, just as the *Timaeus* is about a lot more than physics. In fact, not only are politics and physics inextricably linked for Plato, but myth is omnipresent in both fields. Plato insists that his cosmological account can only be a "likely story" (*eikôs muthos*), because we were not there to witness how it occurred, and he would consider all contemporary cosmological accounts, including the big bang theory, to be no more than "likely accounts," although the evidence may suggest that some are more likely than others. Brisson has devoted several books and numerous articles to putting this into context and arguing why Plato is correct. It all comes down to myth. Reason, myth's nemesis, must nonetheless return to myth. This theme will be one of the driving forces of these conversations. As for the political treatise in the *Republic*, which resurfaces on numerous occasions in these interviews, the philosopher's reason could never be successful in creating an ideal society without using myth to mould the souls of the inhabitants from the earliest age.

Some readers who may be most familiar with the philosopher kings (and queens) of the *Republic* may be surprised to learn that Plato jettisoned them in his final dialogue, the *Laws*, and replaced them with the "the rule of law" as the best form of constitution, another Platonic first. According to Plato, every law, and the law code itself, must be prefaced with a preamble to explain the spirit behind it. These preambles are meant to persuade the citizens in a manner reminiscent of a myth. Laws become akin to incantations, spells, and are meant to be hard to escape. They will be set to music and even danced to. It's also in the *Laws* that Plato offers the first *arguments* (*logoi*) for the existence of God. For Plato, God (or *nous*, referring to mind/reason) and nature are intimately connected. These arguments are meant to be part of the finest preamble of all.

Let me note in passing that there is an interesting correlation between Plato's notion of the rule of law and what some members of the Supreme Court in the United States, and notably Justice Neil Gorsuch, characterize as originalism – the position that in its decisions the court should follow the *original*, and thereby fixed, meaning of the relevant passages in the Constitution.[31] This is precisely what Plato advocates in the *Laws* – a dialogue with which Gorsuch, with a DPhil in the philosophy of law, is no doubt familiar. Plato, for his part, sees the laws and the law code as dispensations of reason (*nous*), which is the divine spark within us. In sum, the legislator draws inspiration from reason and observation, which includes a historical analysis of the situation. And, once legislated, the law code is to become as immutable as the motions of the celestial bodies, which in Plato's eyes are themselves gods and constitute a model to follow.[32] The framers of the Constitution were first and foremost children of the Enlightenment, and as such were grounded in *secular* reason. But Jefferson and others knew their Greek and Latin, and saw the culture of the Greeks as a *sine qua non* of a cultured person. They knew their Plato too.[33]

It's important to note that reason for Plato is the ultimate God; this is, of course, the antithesis of the Judeo-Christian God, which, ironically, *seems* to be what inspires many of the Catholic justices of the Supreme Court in the United States. Interestingly, all nine of the current justices claim to be members of the Judeo-Christian faith (for its part, Canada has in recent years nominated justices of other religions and/or cultures to its own Supreme Court). It's surprising to those in other liberal democracies the degree to which the notion of God is still largely reflective of Judeo-Christian values in the popular mind in the United States, and, I assume, among the members of the Supreme Court.[34]

Some of Brisson's arguments and insights in the conversations on the differences between the Judeo-Christian and Greek notions of God may come across as provocative for some and refreshing for others. And as Brisson reminds us, it's the fear of death that makes the Christian promise of salvation a driving force behind its popularity from antiquity to the present. It's the antithesis of the intellectual rigour of the Greek philosophers, who, ironically, provided the primary source of the philosophical concepts used in Christian, Jewish, and Islamic theology, of the notion of theology as a "rational" discourse (*logos* as reason) on God and not just a discourse on God (*logos* as speech). It's remarkable that in the highly religious culture of the United States, the preamble to the Constitution begins with "We the people," without any reference to God.[35]

Given that a third of Canadians claim to be atheists or agnostics, and that two-thirds feel that religion plays a less important role in the country's affairs than it did even twenty years ago,[36] it comes across almost as paradoxical that the preamble to the *Charter of Rights and Freedoms*, which became part of the *Canada Act* in 1982, reads, "Whereas Canada is founded upon principles that recognize *the supremacy of God* [my italics] and the rule of law ..."[37] There can be little doubt that the god in question is again the very Judeo-Christian

God with whom the current majority of Canadians would hardly identify, not to mention the fact that the majority of those who have immigrated to Canada since the *Charter* was enacted are not Christian.[38] Anyone working in the Platonic tradition will see, of course, the Platonic correlation between God and the rule of law. Plato's notion of God is, if I may, refreshingly different, as we'll see in more detail further on. But they're both, as are all gods past and present, creations of myth.

Most readers will be familiar with the expression "Platonic love" (*eros*), but some may be unfamiliar with its intricacies or the rationale behind it. One of the catalysts behind Brisson's own love of Plato in his youth was his introduction to the famous dialogue in which the notion first appears, the *Symposium*, which consists of a series of competing discourses by prominent individuals on eros or love.[39] This dialogue will play a prominent role in these conversations on several occasions. Unsurprisingly, perhaps, dual sexuality or bisexuality (the two terms used synonymously here) will be seen from a new perspective; indeed, the very origin of the phenomenon will be seen in light of one of the famous discourses on love in the *Symposium*. But there is considerably more on dual sexuality in these conversations. Some of the more challenging parts of the conversations present Brisson's brilliant insights following a structural analysis of several traditional myths related to dual sexuality in his own research, summarized in context in part 2. Readers will learn that the nature of dual sexuality is inseparable from the concept of God in many creation and cosmological myths, including Yahweh in Genesis. In these prominent myths, the first God, the generator of all things, is both male and female, but also its own mother, wife, daughter, and so on. The intricacies are fascinating and yet largely commonsensical.[40] Brisson also provides some insights into Greek monism, and how we get a plurality from one, which is at the foundation of Western philosophy. An important question is at what point does reflective self-consciousness emerge to account for reasoning behind the formation? In other words, when does a theogony become a cosmogony, or when does what Lévi-Strauss characterizes as a subconscious phenomenon become conscious – that is, self-conscious of what's happening below the surface to give it more of a reflective generation? It's about the evolution or genesis of the self or person on which I'll have considerably more to say in my afterword in the context of myth.

A movement that Brisson gives special attention to is Orphism, which many will connect first and foremost with the myth of Orpheus, armed with the conscious power of music and song, descending into Hades to bring back his beloved Eurydice. But this is late. It's the Orphic movement that originated around the same time as the birth of philosophy that can be as intriguing and fascinating as the origin of philosophy itself. Orphism was a religious movement that was radically opposed to the blood sacrifices of traditional religion, promoting vegetarianism, reincarnation, and initiation instead.[41] It's also one of several Greek religious movements from the same period that *invent* new myths to overcome death. Meanwhile, any new religious movement must construct a new cosmogony or world order to account for the new belief system, and Brisson provides several penetrating insights into why these new cosmogonies unfold as they do. These are also competing myths, newly contrived stories that are part of a new awakening, analogous to Pythagoreanism, which emerges around the same time, but with a mathematical twist. As such, they will have a profound impact on Plato's own cosmological account, and hence on the history of science and the scientific method.

One of the most famous antitheses in philosophy is the opposition between myth and reason (*muthos/logos*). One of the driving forces and insights behind Brisson's philosophy of myth is that reason, rooted in myth,[42] always returns to myth, as if it's dependent on myth for its very existence. Brisson dedicated a book to this topic, aptly entitled *How Philosophers Saved Myths*. This volume covers the period from the birth of philosophy to the discovery of the Americas. The book is intimately connected with the invention of the interpretation of myths,[43] which is, in large part, what the allegorical method is all about: you can make a text say anything you want it to say.[44] But it's also about making the wisdom of the ancients, considered as "divinely inspired," compatible with modern theories. Meanwhile, Brisson's own philosophy of myth also covers why even contemporary science must return to myth because the premises it works with are, like those of myth, unverifiable. Thus, in *Inventing the Universe* (1991), Brisson and F. Walter Meyerstein argue that the gap (or the *irrational hiatus* as they call it) is so deep that no immediate data originating in the sensible world can modify the fact that the theory itself is always based on an ideal construction, on a set of irreducible and indemonstrable axioms that are pure inventions of the human mind accepted only on the basis of the operational argument "it works." Whence the book's opening sentence: "To know the universe is to invent it."

Interestingly, Plato's allegory of the cave in the *Republic* (514d–518c) is, strictly speaking, not an allegory but rather an imaginative description of the ascent of the human mind from ignorance to knowledge and of the fate of those who dare to leave the cave. It's as meaningful today as it was then.[45] It will resurface during these conversations with Brisson's own novel insight. And how can one ever forget Plato's thought experiment in the Gyges's ring episode in the *Republic*? What indeed would we do if we were provided with a ring that would make us invisible? Would we act as a tyrant with an uncontrollable urge to fulfill our egotistical passions, or would we use it in the pursuit of goodness? While there is a sense in which, for Plato, we are all responsible as individuals for who we are (recall the Socratic "know thyself"), it's the state, he argues, that should dictate the norms of behaviour and provide an educational cursus to achieve them, and myth plays a fundamental role in this development. While the notion of the individual, as we'll see in the afterword, first appears in ancient Greece with the emergence of conscious reflexivity, humans were still understood as socio-centric creatures with competing notions of virtue or excellence. Meanwhile, Brisson is quick to remind us that by using the soul rather than the body to define who we are, Plato provides a role for women that makes them *equal* to men. This is an argument, if one is needed, that women shouldn't be defined by their maternal roles, as using their bodies to define them would suggest, which was the norm in ancient Greece and still a cliché for many even in Western liberal democracies.

LIVING A MYTH AND A PROTAGONIST IN THE MAKING

This introduction may so far give the impression that the conversations are first and foremost about Plato. This isn't entirely the case. While the spell of Plato informs this dialogue in important ways, and can often be found hovering in the background, it's very much about Brisson making sense of myth, and describing a life lived according to this theme. One of the most important subjects in the conversations is, in my opinion, the awakening of consciousness – that is, the point at which one becomes conscious of what is happening in one's life, of what kind of education or myth one is being exposed to, or, better still, have been captivated by. As I noted above, for Plato myth is a form of manipulation, a kind of noble lie.[46] Brisson's own narration begins with a genealogy providing a background to his early and subsequent life. This, too, is very Platonic, as origin myths begin, of necessity, with genealogies in some form.

There are many elements that define, in Brisson's view, who he is and what he will become. The rural world and an intimate family portrait provide a consistent, but conflicting, setting.[47] Nothing, however, plays a more fundamental role in his narration than the Catholic Church. Indeed, Brisson provides a lucid historical analysis of why the history of Quebec society is inseparable from the history of the Catholic Church in Quebec, and the correlation is a perfect paradigm of myth and mythmaking. Ultimately, Brisson wants to explain how his work on myth corresponds to a life that began in myth, the myth of the Catholic Church in Quebec. But we soon see that his theory of myth and its practical application is relevant to each and every one of us *without* exception.

Meanwhile, Brisson reminds us that the church recruited its future janissaries by taking gifted children from poor rural families and retaining only those who could pass the rigorous intellectual, psychological, and even physical examinations imposed upon them. Brisson's account is riveting. Since an education in view of the priesthood was the only way for gifted children from poor rural families to get formal and classical instruction, and since Catholic families saw the priesthood as a considerable honour and calling, few failed to acquiesce when the church came knocking. Indeed, every facet of the francophone educational system in Quebec was Catholic, and it was virtually impossible to escape the spell of the church without being ostracized, and here, too, Brisson captures our imagination with pertinent lived accounts. The myth in which Brisson and his peers were raised was all-encompassing, the focus was, as in Plato, on controlling the soul (the seminary had directors of conscience), and one popular maxim in the seminary was that "an independent mind is the enemy of obedience." Brisson makes the insightful observation that this explains why knowledge was devalued in francophone Quebec, and why Quebec was so far behind before the Quiet Revolution.

While Brisson richly describes the torment of an eleven-year-old "handicapped" child being torn from a loving family, he also makes the extraordinary claim that both he and his parents deceptively took up the challenge, knowing full well that he would get a good education but not become a member of the clergy. So, the young Brisson played the myth wisely, tolerated the intolerable, because he had a conscious end in view. The result was indeed, to Brisson's mind, a first-class education in the classics and mathematics and a thirst for knowledge, a desire to discover the world that had until then been closed to him.[48]

We are given an account of the collapse of the Catholic Church and "traditional" francophone Quebec society following the Quiet Revolution, which, of course, was anything but quiet. Brisson describes it in terms reminiscent of the Russian or French Revolutions insofar as the resulting social change was mesmerizing (clergy changing from cassocks to jeans almost overnight). We thus find a young man escaping the insular world of the seminary and then exposed in France in 1968 to a revolution. The new masters of truth, he observes, replaced the myths of the Catholic Church with those of Marxism, based now on "reason" but no less grounded in myth, and no less horrifying, as he confirmed through his travels to the Soviet Union. His critique of the French intelligentsia blinded by Marxism is all the more engaging in that the rural lad had just arrived in France, the paradise of his dreams. A house of cards built on lies – noble for some, less so for others!

Brisson provides an overview of his undergraduate and graduate studies, first in Quebec and then in France, and how he ended up doing his doctorate on Plato's *Timaeus* (Brisson 1974). He offers a vivid description of his first encounter, in a graduate course, with the French meritocracy, but also insights into his introduction to the trailblazing work of famous linguists, anthropologists, and historians of religion and mythology who were to define the direction of his work. I'll describe each of these individuals in context in a series of footnotes, as well as the elite French school system of which Brisson is both critical and admiring.

It's really in part 3 that the conversations come to focus on Quebec and questions of identity. They also provide insights that are invaluable for those trying to understand Quebec as a distinct society. But the conversations also offer historical background to Quebec's controversial Bill 21 (2019), on the laicity of the state, even though the original edition was published over twenty years ago.[49] While the spell of myth is omnipresent here, Brisson teases this out on more of a world scale in part 4. The consequences of the *Canadian Charter of Rights and Freedoms* for a Québécois sense of identity are discussed in some detail in part 3 (and again in my afterword), where they are compared with what Brisson insightfully sees as the instruments behind Quebec's previous identity and the French language's status as the "new" pillar of collective identity in a world where English has become the international lingua franca. He also has some discerning and surprising observations on the consequences of English for international scholarship. Of course, there is also Québécois culture, which is remarkably distinct from the rest of Canada. Also driving a sense of alienation is the perception of a lack of acceptance by the rest of Canada.[50] I'll have more to say on this in the context of "social" groups that feel alienated in many societies, including Canada and the United States. In the case of the latter, this alienation is, in large part, a major factor behind the dangerous political turmoil engulfing the country.[51] But is it a question of myth or rumour? This is a difference that will resurface in the context of these conversations.

Another surprise is the exchange with Dorion on why Quebec independence will never happen; it's a mirage, although its threat is cleverly maintained. There is also the important consideration that what Canada is missing is a founding mythology that could bring the two sides together.[52] Brisson also claims toward the end of this section (the conclusion of the original edition) that he is a bit stateless as a product of his history. In other words, the myths that have shaped his identity, including every facet of his education, have rendered him a citizen of the world, rather than of any one place. And this world is a kind of cosmopolis of the type we find in one form or another among Greek philosophers. Indeed, Brisson sees Greek philosophy as a model he tries to emulate.

I try to tease out Brisson's theory of myth in more detail in part 4, which aims to delve more deeply into the man and his work. Here, we find that his productivity goes back to his life in the seminary, and that his preference for working in teams is connected with his childhood. In conjunction, he provides a digression into individuality and originality as a kind of mirage: they're always grounded in the work or lives of others. It's not unlike the position adopted by the late French philosopher Bruno Latour, for whom historical advances in science are always governed by contingency and debate. Meanwhile, I ask Brisson to address the enormous number of foreign students he supervised without compensation, which runs contrary to the norm in the French system (as well as elsewhere), and his answer offers further revelation of the kind of person he is and his attitude to money. In sum, there is a Socratic twist. We also discuss his success in publishing pocket-book editions of Plato's dialogues, the most popular in the francophone world with over a million copies sold. We also discuss recent innovations in publishing and the ever-changing trends in Platonic scholarship. I ask him to discuss how his own interests in Plato have developed since the interviews with Dorion were done, the fundamental differences between the Greek and Judeo-Christian notions of God, and the repercussions of these perspectives for what it means to be human. Brisson provides a stimulating overview of the differences that should leave no one of good faith indifferent. The notion of faith is, in fact, a key that we all deserve to reflect on, and Brisson offers an insightful analysis of why and how the notion of faith (*pistis*) in the Greek and Christian traditions are so different. Much is dependent on the attitude toward death, which Brisson reminds us has been and remains a catalyst for coming to terms with our humanity. This fear, according to Brisson, accounts for the success of Christianity. Brisson also addresses the difference between myth and rumour to show how his theory of myth differs from that of another distinguished French scholar, Marcel Detienne.

It's the final section of part 4 that brings together the whole. Myth, as Brisson understands it, comprises stories that give us our identity; they're a way of *unconsciously* (until Plato) controlling the individual within the community to which he or she belongs. As such, myths are creators of the self, of one's identity. The notion of individuality is a kind of mirage; it's as if there is no self independent of one's larger group or community. From this perspective, myth, as Brisson understands it, is a phenomenon that few have given any real thought to, and yet it's a key to understanding what it means to be human, and to the future destiny of humanity itself.[53]

Part One

BORN IN SAINT-ESPRIT, QUEBEC

LOUIS-ANDRÉ DORION: Luc Brisson, you're one of today's preeminent specialists of the work of Plato and of the Platonic tradition in antiquity. Your publications are acclaimed around the world, and they win admiration for their scope, rigour, and depth. A few numbers will provide some sense of their abundance: you have published thirteen books and more than seventy articles, and you have collaborated on ten collections. This is a considerable body of work, and it's not yet completed since you're more productive than ever and you do not seem to want to retire anytime soon.[1] Now, your work is rather unknown in your native Quebec, whereas you stand at the forefront in the field of the translation and interpretation of the dialogues of Plato. How did it happen that you devoted your life to the study of Plato and of the Platonic tradition? Why should people today be interested in Plato and in Greek philosophy more generally? These are two of the questions that I'd like to take up with you in the framework of these conversations, to which you told me that you would like to add a certain autobiographical twist. Why do you feel that this is necessary?

LUC BRISSON: I must be very clear on what I understand by "autobiographical." I don't want to make it "the story of my self," as Saint Augustine and Rousseau do in their *Confessions*, for I have lived quite an ordinary life from the human perspective. That said, it's impossible to understand what I did if one doesn't have an idea of the context in which I lived my first years and how my studies progressed before

I left for France. My decision to practise philosophy, as well as that of studying Greek religion, derive from fortuitous experiences that I had at school and at the seminary in Quebec in the fifties and sixties. My life at the university, the direction my thinking was taking, and the political struggles in Quebec at the time were determining factors in my decision to leave Quebec to pursue my studies in France rather than in Germany, the United States, or England.

LAD: Let's begin, then, at the beginning. I believe that you've done a genealogy.

LB: In fact, I only had to complete the one that my grandfather started. My extended family, which is large, derives from two Brissons, who were born in Montreal. One of them, Ambroise, lived in Saint-Jacques, a village first settled by Acadians – we're not ourselves descended from Acadian roots – at the end of the eighteenth century, after having stayed in L'Assomption. The father of these two Brissons was a French soldier, Nicolas Brisson, who came from a village not far from Nancy in France.

Nicolas Brisson was born in August 1733 and joined the Royal Army in 1755. We're not sure why he joined, but it seems that the family was quite poor. He arrived in Quebec in July 1755, and as a soldier in the French army, it's possible that he saw action in the Battle of the Plains of Abraham in September 1759 as well as other military engagements. He was in Montreal in September 1760, when the French surrendered the city to the British. Taken prisoner, he was sent back to France with his battalion.[2] In Montreal, Nicolas Brisson had lived with Marie-Josephte Pesant. They had two children, Nicolas-Jacques and Ambroise. Although Nicolas and Marie-Josephte were living together as husband and wife, they were not legally married, because simple soldiers were forbidden to marry. Their marital status caused some confusion when Ambroise was baptized, for the priest first wrote "legitimate child" before crossing it out and writing "natural child" in the church register. When Nicolas was sent back to France – along with the French troops, Quebec militia, and even civil servants – the two boys remained in Montreal with their mother, who, after the legally required seven-year delay, entered into a second, and this time properly legal, marriage. Nicolas was discharged from the army in 1768 in Corsica, which belonged at the time to Genoa, but for which the French provided the police and the army. He never returned to Canada.

The priests of Saint-Sulpice gave Ambroise Brisson a plot of land from the considerable amount that they owned at the time. This branch of the Brisson family remained in Saint-Jacques, which helped my grandfather in easily tracing our family tree to Montreal, and it helped me, in turn, to trace the family to Badonviller, a village close to Nancy. Indeed, the French army maintained in its archives, which in the 1970s was located in the castle of Vincennes, a card of every soldier since 1716. This was a way of preventing desertion, which affected nearly half the soldiers.

Both in Saint-Jacques and later in Saint-Esprit, we lived in the French, and Catholic, *Québec profond*.

LAD: You were born in Saint-Esprit, a village north of Montreal in the region of Joliette.

LB: I was born on 10 March 1946 in the home of my maternal grandparents, with whom my parents were living at the time. It was a Sunday. My mother, Cécile, went to Mass that morning and I was born near midday. Because she shared in the collective anxiety of Québécois mothers of the time, who believed that their children, if they died before being baptized, would spend an eternity in Limbo, she requested that my father, Fernand, promptly take me to the church to have me baptized that very afternoon.[3]

My mother's fear had a determining effect on me. My maternal grandmother asked that I be given the first name of one of her own sons, Luc, who had died of a heart attack before his eighteenth birthday after having saved on a very hot day his two brothers from drowning when their raft capsized on the river that ran through the village. My brother, who was born shortly after me, was given the name Maurice, which was the name of another of my grandmother's sons, who also died early, this time of an infectious disease, diphtheria. In one way or another, this heroic and mythical eponymy influenced my character. The transiency of human life constituted a basic reality for me. Very early on, I felt a kind of "saviour" complex, which was expressed in a sentiment of great responsibility to others that was sometimes hard to bear. My grandmother never stopped talking to me about her deceased son Luc, who had saved his brothers.

LAD: What was Saint-Esprit like at the time and how has it changed?

LB: Saint-Esprit is about twenty kilometres from Terrebonne and Joliette. It's still an agricultural village, the last farmland before the Laurentian Mountains. It's at the intersection of the roads – that is, of the lines or concessions leading out to the farms.

The village itself had a population of about fifteen hundred: artisans, merchants, day labourers, and retired folk. One could also find various establishments that interested farmers: the general store, grocery stores, the hotel – that's to say, the tavern – a bank, a credit union, the doctor, who also maintained a pharmacy with basic necessities, a notary's office, and the church, which at the time was served by a priest and a vicar. Founded at the end of the eighteenth century, Saint-Esprit was a typical village in the Montreal region. When I was born, right after the war, there were still restrictions on sugar and chocolate. A surprising detail is that the time in the village was not the same as in the surrounding countryside (which was less than four kilometres away), since the latter continued to live under daylight savings time.

There are two differences between the Saint-Esprit of the fifties and the Saint-Esprit of today: one has to do with the standard of living, the other with the disappearance of the village infrastructure. At the time, we were self-sufficient. Cars and trucks were a rarity. There were numerous artisans and two flourishing businesses: a slaughterhouse and a sawmill.

The village changed in relation to the evolution of agricultural work. Up until around the sixties, agriculture was traditional. We mostly cultivated tobacco, wheat, and hay for cattle feed. Then, farming methods changed radically with land irrigation, and especially in terms of subsidies for milk production, which helped farmers considerably. After irrigation systems were installed, the cultivation of tobacco, the quality of which wasn't very good (it was only pipe tobacco), came to an end. I still retain a vivid memory of the strong fragrance of the tobacco that was being cured in the village barns. It was pressed into bales at the end of December. Meanwhile, animal husbandry increased, and truck farming appeared and developed. Farmers, protected by crop insurance and supported with subsidies, became richer. This economic transformation was in sync with the political transformation of Quebec. The village was now open to the outside world, and contacts with Montreal were not only possible but quite frequent. There was a train that left from Saint-Jacques, and a bus from the village centre.

There remain very few families today who lived in Saint-Esprit when I was a child. The members of these families grew older and disappeared. Saint-Esprit became a kind of distant suburb of Montreal. At the beginning of the fifties, bread and milk were delivered by horses that pulled carts attached to skis in the winter and wheels in the summer. People got together at the general store and met at the tavern. Now they go shopping in Joliette or even Montreal, and consult with the doctor elsewhere, etc.

LAD: You emphasize the precarious material conditions of those times. Was your family of a particularly modest class?

LB: My father was a baker and we depended on his salary. I didn't like Fridays. On that day, my mother was particularly anxious since she worried that my father might bring home his final paycheck. That being said, if we were less rich than others, our standard of living corresponded to that of the majority of the village. A great precariousness thus ruled the day, due essentially to material and sanitary conditions. In many houses, there was only one source of water, the kitchen sink. All the rooms were heated by a wood stove, even in the winter, when it was twenty or thirty below Celsius (or from four to twenty-two below Fahrenheit). The chimney pipe radiated heat into the house. I can still see the red elbows of the pipes that I watched at night when I couldn`t sleep. When a snowstorm started, my mother turned off the wood-burning stove since she feared that a chimney fire would break out – something that happened quite frequently. Nearly every year, fire destroyed a poorly constructed wood house. When this happened, the priest allowed people to work on Sunday. Solidarity demanded that the entire family be welcomed into one or two houses. The wealthiest paid for the construction materials, and anyone who was able worked on building a new house and/or donated furniture, utensils, maintenance materials, and so on. This is one of the most admirable things from this period.

In cold weather, we slept fully clothed, and several times during the night my mother would get up to check that everything was well. We used the same wood-burning stove in the summer, even though it was very hot. This is why summer kitchens were so important. There were no indoor toilets. Instead, there was an outhouse in the backyard. There were no indoor bathtubs either. Daily life wasn't easy, for you had to survive on your own. My mother raised chickens and sold the eggs. One of my single aunts had a large garden and cultivated fruits and vegetables, which she gave us. At the end of the summer, my brothers and I spent entire days preserving the fruits and vegetables. At the end of autumn, potatoes and carrots were buried in sand in the cellar under the house for winter. Sometimes, my mother bought a side of veal or pork that we kept in the summer kitchen so the cold would preserve it. It was a question of spending as little as possible.

That's what the material conditions were like. But worse than these, there was an almost complete lack of major medical care. In the village, we were lucky to have two doctors. There was a young doctor who was efficient, dedicated, and who would come to make house calls even if one were unable to pay. But in the case of a serious accident or illness, death was the usual outcome. It was almost impossible to transport people to the hospital quickly enough. Moreover, there were very few hospitals, and even those were far away and poorly equipped. At any rate, there were minimum payments; and most couldn't even afford those.

LAD: You were the first of a family of six children, which wasn't, at the time, a large family.

LB: Yes, indeed. One of my uncles had fifteen children, of which fourteen survived. Another uncle had twelve, of which eleven survived. This latter uncle, Gérard Vézina, was my mother Cécile's brother; he married my father's sister Laurence. The first eight children of this family were all daughters, and I think of them as sisters. In my own family, the first four children were boys. I therefore lived in the context of a very large family.

Fernand, my father, was born in June 1925; he was only nineteen years old when he married and about twenty when I was born. My mother, who was born in September 1921, was about twenty-five when I was born. As I mentioned, my parents were living with my maternal grandparents at the time, and I was born in their home. Some time later, my parents moved elsewhere, and during my entire childhood my father worked in a bakery right across from our house for a rather meagre salary, which was to pose a problem for my studies. My brothers and sisters were all born shortly after me: my brothers in 1947, 1950, 1953, and my sisters in 1956 and 1961. My two sisters were born around the time I was leaving home; I never knew them well, which is quite sad.

My mother belonged to a family that was one of the founders of Saint-Esprit at the end of the eighteenth century. My maternal grandfather, Maxime Vézina, was a descendant of the family that had founded the parish in 1790. Moreover, it was on a plot of family land that the parish church was built. Maxime was the youngest of a family of four children, three of whom were boys. According to tradition, being the youngest son, he inherited the homestead. Also according to tradition, the oldest son was able to study and became a doctor. He was the father of Medjé (a pen name) Vézina, the poet (*Chaque heure a son visage*, 1934) and journalist (notably, at the popular magazine *Terre et Foyer*), who was a friend of Gabrielle Roy and especially of the journalist and novelist Adrienne Choquette, the author of *La nuit ne dort pas* (1954). This cousin of my mother, often mentioned by my grandmother, always constituted a reference point for me, despite the fact, I admit, that I never gave her collection of poems a careful reading.

My maternal grandmother was the daughter of a doctor who had died young and poor after contracting blood poisoning while doing medical research on the cadavers of people who suffered from malformed bones (the lower limbs). Of his twelve children, only three girls survived, one being my grandmother, who was then raised by her aunts in Saint-Esprit. Her first love was her cousin, but he was committed to the priesthood, became a monsignor, taught philosophy at a seminary in Joliette, and was, for quite some time, a well-known figure in the nationalist movement in the region. She ended up marrying my grandfather, who owned a large amount of land, but who had hearing problems. This prevented me from having a close relationship with him. My maternal grandmother played a significant role in my life. She was a woman who was frail, gracious, and very kind. For me, she represented the world of culture. It was with her that I first heard about literature and history, and also with her that, once I was able to read well enough, I read over the newspaper (she was one of the few in the village to receive them). For me, reading has retained the taste of the cookies that I munched as I flipped through the newspaper, while glancing from time to time at my grandmother's serene, bright face as she bent over her sewing.

My father, Fernand, was, as I mentioned before, originally from Saint-Jacques, a village around ten kilometres from Saint-Esprit. My paternal grandfather, Joseph Brisson, lived an uncommon life, and this is important as it explains a lot about me. Born in July 1894, Joseph married in 1922. His wife gave birth to three children – the first in June 1923, who was born prematurely and died soon after, the second in June 1924 (my aunt), and the third in June 1925 (my father) – but she died in August 1925, a few months after the birth of my father. My grandfather thus raised his children alone, as he tended to his land. He tried to make ends meet, but, overworked and without enough money to pay for a farmhand, he sold his land in July 1930. He left for Montreal, leaving his daughter in a convent in Saint-Jacques and my father first with friends and later in an orphanage. It was around that time that my father had an operation on his neck, which was only partially successful; he lost a certain amount of movement in one of his arms. This, coupled with his myopia, later made him unfit for military service, and it also made it difficult for him to find work. After some odd jobs, my grandfather found work as a gardener at the Hotel-Dieu, the famous hospital connected to the convent at the time, which was fairly self-sufficient in food production. In September 1938, however, a nun who had just been employed as treasurer wanted to fire the garden staff, including my grandfather. So, he decided to leave for Abitibi-Témiscamingue, a remote region in the southwest of Quebec, where clerical propaganda in favour of colonization encouraged all those who had financial problems to settle. He therefore left with Fernand, my father. There, on the night of 3 December 1938, a fire in a metal drum that was being used for heating spread and destroyed the house. Having lost everything, my grandfather returned with his son to Montreal. He then reconnected with his daughter, who he had previously hoped would join him in Abitibi. Having used up all of his own resources, he had to appeal for help. His brother-in-law, the brother of his deceased wife, who was the priest in Lanoraie, asked him to come work in a factory there as an odd-jobber.

This priest was an unconventional character. He didn't much respect established rules. The following anecdote sums him up. Once, while I was a passenger in his car, we approached a fairly dangerous crossroad, and he didn't stop. I yelled at him to stop the car, and in a calm and serious manner, he said, "Luc, a priest never stops, you should know that." He was a hard worker and equally hard-headed with members of his family who were less well-off than he was. But his demeanour also served his parishioners well. He respected the will of the church, which supported co-operatives. In one of the parishes that he oversaw, he encouraged the members to raise chickens to oppose industrial meat farming and to open a bottling factory to oppose Coca-Cola. All this is still there. He was also an enlightened individual. Despite belonging to the church, he always expressed his liberal convictions (red, as one says) during the reign of Maurice Duplessis.[4] In August 1939, the same priest was chosen to practise in Saint-Esprit, and he asked my grandfather to go along with him. Thus, after spending a few months in Lanoraie, my grandfather moved to Saint-Esprit with his two children.

After a short stay in a high school in Ottawa, my father returned to Saint-Esprit to help his father and the priest – that is, before working for the village baker in the summer, for in the winter he worked as a general labourer for one of my uncles at a logging camp. It was during this time that he met my mother; they married in May 1945. After living for a time with my mother's parents, where I was born, and then with my paternal grandfather, my mother and father rented a house that was situated right in front of the bakery, as I mentioned.

I evoke this past to show to what degree I identify with my paternal grandfather. Like him, I'm totally indifferent to the places where I live, completely indifferent to possessions, to social relations. I'm a fatalist, while somehow managing to remain an optimist; it's a question of surviving in a hostile environment that can have in store the worst surprises. My grandfather died happy at the age of ninety-two. He was always well-groomed, always looked proud, and managed to remain generous and dignified despite his poverty. On New Year's Day, for instance, he always prepared a meal for the families of his daughter and son, and he had a gift for each of his grandchildren. I still get emotional at the memory of his traditional benediction before moving to the table at New Year's dinner. That being said, it's no secret that he and his children lived a life of poverty; and this poverty explains why my father didn't go far in school. I never saw my grandfather or my father do anything bad toward one another, or even say anything bad toward anyone else.

LAD: If I'm not mistaken, I believe all his children attended university.

LB: Yes, despite his personal intellectual limitations, my father was always very happy and proud that his children were able to study. He was also happy that my mother was able to study before her marriage at the convent in Saint-Esprit and at the high school in Saint-Jacques, an institution that gave young women an education of the kind that allowed them to maintain a household and to fulfil the roles society expected of them. My mother would have liked to continue her studies to become a teacher, but circumstances did not allow this.

LAD: Your father was a baker. Did you also try your hand at this?

LB: Not really. My father was very proud of his job and didn't want to share his secrets when it came to the art of making bread. But when my studies allowed it, during breaks and on the weekends, I helped him with everything else. This consisted for the most part of moving sacks of flour, wheelbarrows full of wood for the fire, and other odd physical jobs, both during the preparation of the dough and after the bread was baked. I did this mostly at night. During the day, I helped my uncle, who also worked with my father, with deliveries – at the time, we delivered bread door-to-door because most people did not have a car.

Very early on, then, I did manual labour. I think I liked it because it allowed me to relax; it's one of the only things that leaves me with a clear head. Then again, in this kind of work, the penalties are immediate. If the dough isn't well-prepared, it doesn't rise, bakes poorly, and has to be thrown out. If you don't have a good contact with your client, the client leaves, and the competitor makes the sale. In the intellectual world, on the other hand, you must sometimes wait five, ten, or even fifteen years before knowing where you stand. Finally, I'd like to add that when you begin to make the dough, you must be certain to put it in the oven at such and such a time; any delay makes the entire operation impossible. This is how I learned to respect appointments and due dates.

ELEMENTARY SCHOOL

LAD: You completed your elementary schooling in Saint-Esprit. What memories do you have of that time?

LB: At the time, the Catholic Church controlled the public services in Quebec: the hospitals, the education system (primary, secondary), the seminaries, and even the universities. The chancellor of the University of Montreal, just like the one at the University of Laval in Quebec City, was an archbishop. The chancellor named the rector, who was also an ecclesiastic, until 1965; that year, the first layman, Roger Gaudry, received the posting. He was appointed by Cardinal Paul-Émile Léger.

In Saint-Esprit, elementary school was already much the same for girls and boys, but the village schools were not coeducational. There was a "convent" run by nuns for the girls, and for the boys a school directed by religious brothers, who were not ordained and who had less education than the priests.

During the time of my mother and father, the situation was different from today. Boys left school very early on to work. In contrast, young girls were sometimes sent to what we called "family institutes" – that is, institutions where the sisters taught future wives the basics of maintaining a house and how to fulfil the demands necessary for daily life. Overall, women were, at least in the countryside, better educated than men. My mother knew how to read, write, count, fill out forms, and take care of the budget. My father left all of those tasks to her. The fact that women were better educated than the men, who were only asked to work, explains why Quebec at this time was a kind of matriarchal society.

I completed first grade in the "old school," which was located in a large wooden building. The classroom was heated with a wood stove that the students had to fill during the classes. The building still exists, but it has been turned into housing now.

At the time, the student population was very large – it was the baby boom. With the exception of first grade – because it was there that we learned to read, write, and count – classes were grouped two by two all the way to ninth grade. In general, the eighth- and ninth-grade classes were a "warehouse" in the sense that school was mandatory until the age of fourteen, even for those who were not continuing their studies. During planting or harvest, attendance was sparse. The boys were allowed to work on the farms. In fact, education stopped in the seventh grade with the elementary school diploma. That diploma was necessary if one were to be employed or to continue on with one's studies. I started off in a school that was very poor from a material point of view, but in second grade I found myself in a new school, one that was better equipped than the majority of people's houses. For instance, there was hot running water, a central heating system, and a gymnasium.

LAD: Was school a happy time for you?

LB: From a cultural perspective, yes. I always enjoyed reading and learning. My mother never taught me to read. Since my two brothers were born very shortly after me, this didn't leave her much time. But from a social point of view, I found the experience very hard. From their earliest years, the bullies imposed their law. In addition to being timid, I also had a sort of physical disability – I wore thick glasses and had a problem with balance. This prevented me from participating in sports and from being able to fight back.

From my first days in school, I found myself in trouble with the teachers because I could never repeat what they wrote on the blackboard. They initially thought I was just disinterested. I can still picture them hitting my head against the blackboard. But they quickly realized that I had quite a severe visual impairment. The brother even apologized for his brutality, which wasn't so bad. A few weeks after the beginning of class, I found myself wearing a pair of very thick glasses. For a child at this time, in a farming environment, where physical strength and success in sports really mattered, this was an insurmountable handicap. From that point of view, I always had trouble in school, precisely because I wasn't aggressive enough or athletic enough. To fight this deficiency, I protected myself by using my intellectual abilities. I began to do the homework of those who requested it, and went so far as to make intentional mistakes in each case to cover my tracks. And whenever there was an oral examination, I transmitted the answers that I found faster than others to as many as possible. Because they could count on me in this respect, they left me in peace. I paid a kind of intellectual ransom. Once these school problems were resolved, I was quite happy in primary school.

LAD: Teaching was also the responsibility of religious brothers. What about religion?

LB: As far as elementary school is concerned – it will be something quite different in the seminary – I found the brothers to be tolerant. Religious problems in the village were under the direct responsibility of the priest, whose action wasn't restricted to moral issues but also extended to economic and political ones. If someone did something scandalous – say, by drinking too much or cheating on his wife – the priest denounced him from the pulpit on Sunday, and the person was ostracized. If someone didn't receive communion, it would be useless for him to try to borrow money from the bank, and especially from the credit union. And when such people died, they were buried outside of the cemetery on unconsecrated ground!

This was also the case for suicides, which were quite numerous in our village. If a girl became pregnant, she was forced to keep the child even if this caused her insurmountable difficulties, and she was subject to finger-pointing. I could keep going with these examples. From this perspective, it was really very difficult. The priest was even in charge of the birth rate. My mother once told me that she was visited by the priest, who said, "Listen, Cécile, it's been three years since you've had a child, what's going on?" This was his role. To maintain both the French language and Catholicism in a region where the "English" created the Township of Rawdon, the birth rate had to stay high! In my opinion, it's the dramatic decline in the French-Canadian birth rate that contributed to the failure of Quebec independence. However, the brothers, for their part, did the minimum on the religious side. We did have religious instruction, but it was like what we would have received at home. My parents respected appearances, but neither cared much about religion. They attended Mass like everyone else, and they received communion like everyone else.

One thing I remember is that we regularly participated in First Fridays Devotion. Thus, every first Thursday of the month, to earn a plenary indulgence – that is, a remission from all the "temporal punishment" that our sins deserved even if they were pardoned after confession – we went as a group to confession, in order to receive communion the next day. Fairly often, this just ended in a good laugh. During confession, we spoke very loud, so that everyone could hear us. Even bets were made: the one who admitted the loudest to committing the most horrible, but unlikely, sins (adultery, for instance), won a few dimes. In elementary school, we prepared ourselves for First Communion and Confirmation. These were important times both personally and for the community in general. It was an initiation, a ritual, like the ones in primitive societies.

After our First Communion, around the age of seven, we became, of course, altar boys. We had to serve Mass each in turn dressed in our soutanes and surplices during the High Masses on Sundays and holidays. When it was my turn, my father would wake me up at six in the morning. In winter, I left the house hungry because I had to fast for communion. It was dark and I trudged through fresh snow that no vehicle had time to flatten down, to arrive at church around twenty past six in the morning. The nun who attended to the sacristy would yell at me because the bottoms of my pants, wet from the snow, were going to wet the soutane. I served Mass for young girls in the convent at six thirty in the morning, and again at seven for the parishioners, who consisted mostly of elderly ladies. I received five or ten cents per

Mass. I couldn't eat until about eight in the morning, and I had to be at school a half hour later. But, outside of these services, religion was no more a part of my life than it was for society at large.

The fact remains that the influence of the church was very constraining. Here is an example. One morning during a second Mass, I was assisting the priest during communion and holding the paten – the small plate that you placed under the chin of the one receiving communion. By mistake, I wasn't able to prevent the sacred host from falling from the mouth of an old lady. The nun placed a rosary around the host, and after the mass forced me to remain with her. She picked up the host with gloves, and washed the floor with a cloth, and then threw everything (the gloves, host, water, and cloth) in the furnace that barely heated the church. One can see that belief in transubstantiation was strong. During the consecration, during the mass, the bread and wine truly became the body and blood of Christ.[5] Following this incident, I left directly for school, hungry.

Church on Sunday was mandatory for everyone. The men had to take off their hats to enter the church, while women had to wear a hat or a veil. My mother and one of my aunts resisted this. For the sermon, the priest commented on a verse of the Bible using out-of-date language. But sometimes things livened up. The priest would denounce someone who was drunk, or who had committed adultery, or disobeyed other of the church's moral regulations. It was often juicy! My father rented the third bench from the balustrade near the pulpit. He dozed off during the service, including the sermon, and only awoke for the consecration or when told to kneel or stand. He was more interested in the church square, where everyone met and exchanged news. For most, social life was restricted to this perimeter. The parishioner who didn't go to confession or didn't take communion at Easter was banished from society. They couldn't borrow money from the credit union. Whoever resisted, claimed to be an atheist, or committed suicide, was buried outside the cemetery. When the Municipality of Saint-Esprit administered the cemetery, a strip of land had to be purchased around the consecrated area to include the graves of those who were buried outside of it.

There's another event that should be mentioned. Every weeknight, Québécois families were invited, if not obliged, to get on their knees and recite the rosary as a family under the direction of the cardinal from Montreal, Paul-Émile Léger, who recited the rosary on the radio. This is indicative of the degree to which the church intruded into daily life.

LAD: There were just the same a number of collective religious high holidays that instilled religious principles deeply in peoples' minds.

LB: Firstly, I want to clarify this point: I never believed in anything personally. For me, religion was always something social, and it was this aspect that always fascinated me and that led to my studying the religious practices of ancient Greece and Rome. From this perspective, religion is an instrument for social cohesion. It's also a way of denying that time is passing, for, within the context of the liturgical year, the same rituals are performed by everyone every year. There was, indeed, one year that repeated itself indefinitely. This idea really affected me, the idea that a rite could, to a certain extent, affect the passing of time.

Every year saw the renewal of the same cycle of festivals, ceremonies, and celebrations. We lived to the rhythm of the liturgical year, which did not correspond to the official civil year since it began with Advent, four weeks before Christmas. On Christmas Eve, everyone reunited for midnight mass. We listened with emotion to "Minuit Chrétien" (the origin of the popular anglophone Christmas song "O Holy Night") sung by a parishioner with a thundering yet trembling voice. Then we gathered with family for the Christmas Eve party. After that, there was Lent, then the Holy Week, and then Easter. Lent was very strict. My mother would weigh the food we ate.

Celebrations for Holy Week were very grand and touching as well. On the Thursday, the town gathered at church after the evening meal, for it was a question of re-enacting the final hours of Christ that corresponded with our supper. There was the washing of feet, during which the priest washed the feet of certain parishioners; this may seem ridiculous, but I think the act really materializes Christ's humility. Then we would remove the linen that covered the altar, as you would take the tablecloth off a table. This gesture re-actualized the stripping of Christ that took place during the Passion. Friday was even more dramatic. We re-enacted the death of Christ, almost as if Christ were just a person from our town. The church almost looked like a mortuary. All of the statues were covered with purple cloth. It was a day of fasting and abstinence. There was no Mass, but we re-enacted the Stations of the Cross at the end of the afternoon as darkness was approaching. Then came the adoration of the cross, followed by communion with hosts consecrated on Holy Thursday. On Holy Saturday, there were prayers in the morning; then, during the night, the town gathered again in the church as it fell into darkness. Sometime after midnight, a paschal candle announced and materialized the resurrection of Christ. Bells, silent since Friday, chimed loudly. Easter, which coincides more or less with the arrival of spring, was always a fabulous time for me, even outside of church activities. It's a time of year that has always deeply affected me. The smell of the humid earth rises once again, and you know that the snow will soon disappear.

There was also the Procession of Corpus Christi. All of the town followed the priest, who carried the holy host, a consecrated host in a monstrance beneath a richly decorated canopy, all the way to the altar. The canopy was built and decorated with flowers and branches in the preceding days by the children with the help of my uncle, who was a carpenter.

I also recall one ceremony during which a new priest was being ordained. At one moment, dressed in the most beautiful sacred vestments, he lay face down in the central aisle of the nave that was inundated with light. This posture illustrates the priest's submission to the church and was typical in such ceremonies.

LAD: In retrospect, how would you describe your elementary schooling?

LB: Reading, writing, and mathematics were taught above all else. We were also taught history and geography and, I'm not exactly sure how to explain this, a very peculiar kind of religious education – something that fluctuated between morality and civics. The religious instruction the brothers provided was infused throughout the curriculum. Even history was integrated with religious education – a history of Quebec, where the accent was on events of a religious character (the martyrdom of Brébeuf, Mary of the Incarnation, etc.),[6] and world history, where religion was also given a priority. Religious education, strictly speaking – that is, preparation for First Communion, for Confirmation – the priest came to give once a week.

From a purely technical point of view, compared to European standards at the time, especially England and France, the education I received in Saint-Esprit was very poor. But perhaps this is too harsh. Now that my anticlericalism has softened, I think the brothers did a pretty good job. We learned to read, write, and do mathematics in a systematic way and at least as well as the rest of the population. Even if they were sometimes stubborn, stupid, and violent, the brothers really did take care of us; they knew each of us very well and had frequent contact with our families. They didn't react like civil servants who fulfilled their duties without an element of humanity and without giving a second more than required by their contractual agreements. Finally, it was not a competitive system. Students were indeed classified and graded, but most students did not even realize that they could continue on with their studies, so competition was non-existent – it wasn't even mentioned. Overall, I don't think there was anything shameful about the system, although I wouldn't want to return to it. At least, it filled a social role.

The brothers as a community were paid quite little by the school board – something that created a lot of tension and political divisions in the town. But they still managed to maintain glimmers of French culture in an impoverished milieu. In spite of all the grief, we have to remain grateful.

LAD: On two occasions, you finished two grades in on year: fourth and fifth grade, and sixth and seventh grade. Was this kind of accelerated learning common?

LB: No. I was an exception. But, like I said, classes were always split classes, with the same brother teaching the two grades by turns. It sufficed to be attentive to follow the teaching in the advanced class and to do the exercises that were required. Because I was already doing the exercises and the homework of the other boys, it was not really a huge effort for me to skip grades. At the time, I never forgot anything I heard or saw; this meant I was a good learner, but psychologically, it was very tiring. Also, the acceleration of my studies only aggravated my problems with bullies. I quickly found myself with classmates much older than me and, indeed, older than they should have been considering the grade. In seventh grade, for example, many students were already almost full-grown men. They were already interested in girls and had a physical presence that even intimated the teachers.

LAD: Did the decision to continue your studies just come naturally?

LB: No. Things were much more complicated than that. The church recruited most of its clergy from rural, relatively poor, and uncultured communities like mine. At the end of sixth or the beginning of seventh grade, representatives from the bishopric (clerics from Saint-Viateur) came to each town to give students intelligence tests in order to determine if they were fit to continue their education in the seminary. In our region, the seminary to train secular priests was located in Joliette. It was Monsignor Papineau who organized the bishopric at the time, and I distinctly recall passing the test in the basement of the church. Although my parents received several letters from the bishopric in Joliette requesting that I attend the seminary, there were financial difficulties. In the countryside, the seminaries only took in boarding students, and the seminary in Joliette cost sixty dollars per month. Everything was included – classes, lodging, and food. But my father's salary was only thirty dollars per week. If they had enrolled me, my family would have run out of money halfway through the month.

My mother therefore refused, but my father was determined that I somehow continue my education. One of my mother's brothers, who lived in Saint-Jacques, raised a family of twelve children, five of whom were in the Congregation of the Blessed Sacrament – three priests, one brother, and one nun. Two of the priests offered my parents a space for me in their seminary for thirty dollars per month. My parents readily accepted.

For the first two years of my studies at the Terrebonne seminary (1957–58 and 1958–59), my mother received some help from a cousin of my maternal grandfather. This lady, who had no children, worked at the National Bank of Canada and managed to convince the manager to allow my mother an advance payment during the hardest months of the year – the winter months. My parents began to repay the bank at the end of winter and continued until June. During the summer, business improved somewhat because of a little tourism, and my parents were able to reimburse the bank, which then provided an advance for the following winter months. This lasted for two years. At the beginning, I was the only one in my family to pursue any higher education. This made me feel quite guilty. The situation improved with the establishment of the Ministry of Education in 1964. In the early 1960s, we could already feel that things were about to change.

LAD: Without this help, your parents would have never been able to put their six children through school.

LB: It would have been impossible. My one brother, who closely followed me, had a fairly difficult and chaotic experience, which caused him to lose two years. My other brother began his studies in high school shortly after the establishment of the new Ministry of

Education. We were then able to get student grants, and during the summers we all worked on a dairy farm. In my case, I worked for at least three years delivering Coca-Cola.

LAD: Did the fact that your father was a baker rather than a farmer – a job that would have required another kind manual labour – favour your pursuit of higher education?

LB: Without a doubt. Like I said previously, children in the eighth and ninth grades were often absent to help with agricultural work. But I believe it was also, and especially, the will of my parents. My mother was prevented from realizing her dream of becoming a teacher because of the length of time it would take. Moreover, she was a woman with family obligations. My father, for his part, was in contact with the public, and he very much admired well-educated people. He was honoured that his oldest son was able to go to high school and attend the seminary.

SEMINARY

LAD: For your parents and yourself, was attending the seminary essentially synonymous with pursuing a religious vocation?

LB: No. Not for me, and not for them either. And it was this conviction that enabled me to survive in the seminary. My mother and father wanted me to attend the seminary because, at the time, it was the only way for a poor but bright kid from a modest family to study. There were no other choices in Quebec.

I therefore entered Saint-Tharsicius Seminary, of the Congregation of the Blessed Sacrament, in Terrebonne in 1957. Saint Tarsicius was a young Roman who was entrusted with the sacred relics (the consecrated hosts) kept in the catacombs during the persecutions that took place under Valerian in the third century. He was to transport them to Rome. He was intercepted on the Via Appia by Roman soldiers who interrogated him and asked why he kept his hands so tightly crossed on his chest. He refused to talk and died from blows given by the soldiers while keeping the Holy Sacrament next to his chest. His statue was in the entrance hall to the seminary, and I believe it's still there even though the seminary itself has since been turned into the Collège Saint-Sacrément, a private institution. Light rays emanate from the chest of this pious image.

LAD: He's even called the first martyr of the Eucharist.

LB: Exactly. That's why Saint Tarsicius was the model for the community. The Congregation of the Blessed Sacrament was a mixed order, both active and contemplative. The perpetual adoration of the Eucharist, of the sacred host, continued twenty-four hours a day, with all the religious members taking turns every hour.

LAD: The students too!

LB: Certainly, the students as well. At the seminary, we had to adhere to an association of contemplatives where a sort of competition took place to see who could remain before the Blessed Sacrament the longest. When I reread the texts from the beginning of the church, I find the same rivalry concerning the merits of this test. You can therefore understand why Saint Tarsicius was the very symbol of the community founded by Pierre-Julien Eymard – originally a Frenchman from La Mure, in the Alps, who was once an apprentice to Rodin, the famous sculptor. Rodin in fact made a bust of Pierre-Julien Eymard. An official copy is still found in the chapel of the Saint-Sacrément high school.

LAD: According to the regulations of the Saint-Tharsicius Seminary in Terrebonne – at least according to the document that you've retained – "the main purpose of the Seminary is to recruit children who meet certain conditions and who exhibit signs of a divine calling and to develop in their souls a faith and love to the Most Holy Sacrament and to train them in His service." Or again, "The Seminary is not an open college for any student simply wishing to acquire a classical education. Its sole purpose, rather, is the spiritual and intellectual formation of young men destined for the priesthood and religious life, especially in the Congregation of the Most Blessed Sacrament." And a little further on, "However, the Seminary does not require a formal lifetime commitment to the Holy Sacrament. Rather, it merely asks its students with any serious interest in the priesthood and religious life to explore the vocation and to be faithful and join, if such is the will of God." The ultimate end of the seminary leaves little doubt in my mind. Wasn't there a kind of duplicity on your part?

LB: That's quite correct. But how could I have done otherwise? Before I even entered the seminary, I remember very well that the director of the seminary asked me if I wanted to become a priest. I answered "yes" without hesitation, and I still don't feel any remorse or regret.

LAD: That's almost Julien Sorel in *The Red and the Black*!

LB: Yes, except that in Quebec, there was "the black" (the church), but not "the red" (the army). In any case, the die was cast. I accept the charge of duplicity, and it's something that has always been on my mind. But it must be said that the Fathers of the Blessed Sacrament had the opportunity to do the sorting. There were few who actually remained in good standing during the six years of classical studies, which had the following nicknames: Latin, Syntax, Method, Versification, Great Literature, and Rhetoric. When I began my studies, we were divided into two classes with between fifty and sixty-five new students in each. By my last year there were less than ten of us remaining. The majority of the students were from very poor areas. By attending the seminary, they contracted a debt. At the age of thirteen or fourteen, they were forced to make a choice that would affect the rest of their lives. Those who really believed in what they were doing were distressed once they realized they had doubts or could not handle the stress. I know of many overwhelming stories, but I prefer to keep silent out of respect for those who were victims. I'll cite only one well-known example, that of Louis Dantin (1865–1945), who lost faith during his novitiate in Rome but was ordained a priest in Saint-Sacrément and lived in Montreal. He was also the mentor of Émile Nelligan (1879–1941) and provided the preface for the first edition of his poems. What allowed me to survive was really my intention to continue my classical studies in a seminary, although I was not a believer, because that was the only place I could materially afford to do it.[7]

LAD: Leaving the orders aside, did you have an idea of what you wanted to do?

LB: No. The only conviction that always motivated me – and this is already very Platonic – is that the life worth living is not one tied to material possessions, but a spiritual existence of some kind, or in my case, an intellectual life. I quickly realized, and one didn't have to be very smart to see, that the Christian dimensions that permeated the spiritual and intellectual spheres in Quebec were particularly constraining. From the moment I became aware of my physical inferiority, I was left with but one way to resist: to believe that "the real life was elsewhere," that it was in culture, in intelligence. On this level, I had a great deal of facility, and I tried to camouflage my potential in order not to become a circus animal.

I was always fascinated with mathematics. A simple calculation or a demonstration of geometry were, in my eyes and from an intellectual point of view, much more satisfying than any of the twaddle that the priest would sell from his pulpit. I excelled in mental calculations, even long and relatively complex ones. And what were the priests asking me to believe in? As for a "sacred history," most mythological narratives analyzed by Claude Lévi-Strauss, for example, appear to be models of simplicity and rationality. And love? The kind given to me by my parents was sufficient for me.

LAD: What were your feelings about being at the seminary seven days a week?

LB: In 1957, I was eleven and a half years old, but most of my peers were thirteen or fourteen, and so physically much bigger than me. Some of them also had psychological problems that I never suspected. My difficulties in adapting were further exacerbated by the fact that between the beginning of September and the end of June, we only had a few days vacation for Christmas. Visits to the parlour were rare. I had never left my home before the seminary, and I suddenly found myself cut off from my family and from my community, ten months out of the year. It was like being in prison. In this new world where discussions were usually settled by fighting, I didn't carry much weight. My physical inferiority was a chronic problem; I usually ended up losing my glasses. Since the days were long and hard, I was forced to construct my own system of protection.

The dormitory was divided into two parts – one for the older students, and one for the younger. In the centre, there was a row of wash basins with only cold water. At five in the morning, an electric alarm rang, and when it was not working, a bugle. You had to jump to your feet and yell, "*Deo Gratias!*" If we didn't wake and get ourselves ready quickly enough, the prefect of discipline punched the beds with his fist, so it was better not to be there. One got cleaned up and dressed in uniform: white shirt, red tie, blazer with crest, and grey pants; it might seem classy, but in fact we were relatively dirty and dishevelled.

Then we went down to study for an hour – before eating, of course – and then to Mass. During Mass we had to take communion – a fundamental detail. After Mass, we went to the refectory. They gave us chicory coffee, in which there was often small stones, with stale bread. There was also butter, canned beef, and cereal. Most of the time, there was also some thick, grey porridge. After breakfast, we were required to do the "job." You don't know what it is? Since the seminary was very poor, all tasks and cleaning were done by the students themselves. Some of us were in charge of cleaning the gym, and others maintained the sporting grounds or the ice rink. Because the prefect of discipline did not much like me – he considered me an "intellectual" – for a long time I had the job of choosing the squad cleaning the toilets (though in principle duties were supposed to be rotated two or three times per year).

LAD: It was the worst of all the jobs.

LB: But positive for me! For in such a militaristic environment, only those who were good at athletics could make it to the top of the social hierarchy. Now, since the seminary was poor, most of the sports equipment was in bad shape. To get hold of the better equipment, you had to be the first to arrive at the equipment room after completing the job. The athletes quickly realized that my squad finished before the others, and our sector was closest to the equipment room. This meant that they all requested to be in my squad so that they could have first pick of the best sports equipment for the day. Moreover, I put the best equipment aside for them the night before, and if there was more cleaning than anticipated, I stayed behind and finished it myself. Otherwise, as soon as the athletes in my group had finished, if it was well done, I let them leave in advance without respecting the order that everyone had to stay put. It was in my interest to do this for it benefited the prefect of discipline's favourite students. In turn, this protected me both from the prefect and from those who could make life difficult for me. You can see the perversity of the system.

After finishing our work assignments, we had a short break and then classes started. Around noon, it was Angelus, like at six in the morning and six in the evening. Then we ate. Then we had to do more sports, which I absolutely hated. In the afternoon, the classes resumed. In the middle of the afternoon, around four o'clock, we had a kind of snack – usually a slice of bread with either molasses or applesauce.

After the snack, we had either classes or a study period. Then came daily adoration of the Blessed Sacrament (around 5:45) or vespers. Then we ate and had more sports. After this recreation, we had an hour to study and then we went to bed, the youngest at 9:00 and the oldest at 9:30. On Saturdays, when the prefect of discipline left for the weekend, we had to be in bed by 8:30 p.m., even in the month of June, when it was still light out, and on Saturday we heard people assembled in the city hall playing music, having fun, etc. Friday, Saturday, and Sunday were all similar.

LAD: What I gather from the notes you retained is that the discipline of the seminary did not really suit you.

LB: The shock was actually very painful. Until the end of Syntax, my marks were relatively low. Actually, I was warned about the consequences of poor performance. Then my grades improved. I attribute my poor performance to a psychological shock, to the difficulty of living in such a constrained universe. The military aspect of daily life was only reinforced by the prefect of discipline, who in his youth had been a member of the cadets, a kind of paramilitary organization for young men. He established rules in the seminary that were inspired by those found in all military schools. In this system, the authority was as absurd as it was ever-present and effective. If the warden came across someone alone in the hallway, he punched him or kicked him without warning or justification. It was absolute arbitrariness. When we played hockey, the warden would sometimes ask a player from the team he was coaching to injure a player on the opposing team. He loved collective punishment. He'd wake us up at four in the morning, including in winter, and have us run until we fell from exhaustion. He liked self-accusations too. When a serious problem occurred, he would bring together all the seminarians and demand that they publicly admit what they had done; otherwise, everyone would be punished. Those who admitted were humiliated. I'm sure that some of those who did admit were not guilty, but simply exasperated. Can you now understand why the Red Guards never inspired me? Nevertheless, for expressing this sort of opinion, I was considered "reactionary" at the time!

LAD: According to the rules of the seminary, all authority comes from God: "The regulation is the expression of the will of God over you." Similarly, rule 61: "The ambition of the seminarist will be to obey perfectly any requirements of its regulation and any order of his superiors and masters, as they're the most certain expression of the will of God." Finally, rule 85: "All owe to the Father Prefect the most perfect obedience and absolute respect. He must be spoken to with humility, to receive the good grace of his warnings and to consider him as invested with the authority of God to help them become, later, men of duty, character, and religious perfection." Your superiors represented the will of God and the authority they exercised there emanated from Him. Was this really how they presented themselves?

LB: Yes, absolutely. This kind of authority was even more terrifying than the military kind insofar as the latter only dealt with our bodies, which only last a few decades, whereas divine authority concerns the life of the soul for eternity.

There was constant interference. Every morning, we had to go to Mass and take communion. Now, for communion, we had to be in a state of grace. Anyone who had committed a mortal sin (masturbation and even "bad thoughts" were considered mortal sins) was forced to confess. Anyone who confessed too often was naturally viewed with suspicion. He would quickly find himself in a dilemma. Either he would be expelled because he could not control his sexuality – for a poor young man, being expelled meant having to find a job immediately – or he would take communion in a state of mortal sin and commit a sacrilege. In this case, eternal damnation was inevitable. In short, the physical life and the spiritual life were always bound together in a dynamic that involved both body and soul. This put unbearable pressure on us, and it was the prefect of discipline who ultimately held all the cards. I don't blame him entirely – some amount of injustice and violence always comes with the exercise of authority. But I cannot forgive him for his excessive militancy and especially for the pleasure he took in humiliating and punishing us.

For the longest time, I hated this prefect. Then, after talking with others, I realized that there were many problems, and I came to understand that his job was fairly awful: maintaining order with more than one hundred students between thirteen and twenty years of age, day and night, ten months per year. He had to do this on his own, and so it's not surprising that he regularly left on weekends. His two major problems were the same as those of many of the priests in our seminary: women and alcohol. I emphasize this because usually the first thing that comes to mind is homosexuality. There were no problems with homosexuality between our priests and the seminarians. Two brothers, who didn't make the same vows as the priests and who performed administrative and maintenance tasks, were still feared because some seminarians thought they had disturbing sexual behaviours. And each time problems of this sort emerged between seminarians, they were immediately expelled. On the other hand, alcohol and women remained major problems, and not just for our superiors, but to a lesser extent for us too. How is this the case? Occasionally, we had to provide some services for a sports centre in Terrebonne: put chairs into a room or store them somewhere, turn a basketball court into a handball court, etc. All group activities took place outside of the seminary and involved compensation. The prefect of discipline had his – to be doted on, and we had ours; we were all able to drink beer, to smoke, and to meet young girls.

LAD: One regulation says this too: "Obedience meets his enemy in an independent mind and in a lack of respect for authority. To guard against these two vices, the poisonous fruit of pride, the seminarians will remember that the Holy Spirit teaches through the words of Saint Paul, 'there's no authority except from God' [Rom. 13:1]; and it's written in the Holy Gospel, 'Whoever listens to you listens to me, and whoever rejects you rejects me, and whoever rejects me rejects the one who sent me'" [Luke 10:16]. It's incredible to me that an independent mind and a lack of respect for authority would be placed on the same footing. You'd be hard pressed to find anyone today who places an independent mind and a lack of respect or insolence on the same footing, and to present an independent mind as the fruit of an empoisoned pride.

LB: Everything was based on the rejection of the independence and freedom of the mind. Why did our seminary education end with Rhetoric, the sixth-year classical studies? To keep us protected from two years of philosophy, lest we turn away from becoming priests! We had to go to the novitiate to learn to pray and obey. Independence was simply seen as tantamount to a lack of discipline. Among the priests of the Blessed Sacrament, there were many stories of this kind: if a priest was interested in French literature, in Greek, in Latin, or whatever else, he was sent to Latin America for five years to learn to obey *perinde ac cadaver* (as if it were a question of a corpse). In sum, one applied to the students the regulation of the members of the community relative to the mind and conduct.

The regulations certainly didn't favour personal research in a specific area; moreover, intellectual research in itself was treated with the greatest suspicion. I believe that the mediocre performance of Quebec in this area can be explained, in large part, by this distrust, which dates back far into the past. Knowledge was always devalued as a threat to power, whatever the power.

LAD: From this point of view, in what way was your seminary different from other classical institutions and colleges of the time, especially from those run by Jesuits?

LB: In every way! The Jesuits, those from Brébeuf or from Saint-Marie, didn't really pressure their students to become priests. Certainly, they hoped that some would, but they were also well aware that many would go on to become lawyers, notaries, doctors, engineers. Unlike the Jesuit colleges, the seminary only had one vocational goal for students. Also, in the Jesuit colleges, study was encouraged as a good in itself. For the Jesuits, this was one way they could be sure to have an influence in society. This may have been a cynical attitude, but it was nonetheless an effective one. We were the janissaries of the church. The janissaries were the elite soldiers of the Turkish infantry, part of the sultan's guard. We shouldn't forget to mention that these soldiers were children stolen from families of Christian farmers (Orthodox in this region) to be raised in the Muslim religion and in absolute obedience for Turkish power. We were torn from our communities to become managers of the church – our futures defined by the problems of the church.

LAD: Is it true that the Terrebonne seminary was one of the most extreme?

LB: Yes. Actually, even other seminaries of the same diocese were more liberal – the one in Joliette, for example. There was the prefect of discipline, of course, but also – and this is something I learned much later – the poverty of the establishment. The director had made a catastrophic real estate blunder.

The seminary agreed to exchange land for buildings that were never built. And the court case that was destined to recuperate the land was not only lost, but it also cost the community a considerable amount of money. This explains the chronic lack of funds, and it was aggravated by the fact that half of the seminarians didn't pay tuition. In principle, there was at least enough for us to eat – meat, milk, vegetables, canned food, etc. All, or almost all, of this food was given to the seminary by a local supermarket, but it consisted of products that were damaged or beyond their expiration date. Moreover, food preparation was not done with care and the food tasted terrible. Sometimes we would even go without fresh food because there was no cook or because of a lack of money. We would find on the table cans of meat and bland bowls of applesauce to eat. After meals of this kind, fights would break out. For hungry teenagers, it was the only outlet. And we were so isolated!

LAD: For students of the classics and rhetoric, there was, in September, a so-called retreat. What was that exactly?

LB: It was an extraordinary event! It happened outside of the seminary, which already presented a certain interest. It lasted a week and ranged from mid-September to mid-October. It consisted mainly in lectures on various topics. Well, usually the same two topics: sexuality, that is to say, masturbation and girls as representing mortal dangers to the vocation, and obedience. We had returned from summer vacation – a period of perdition! – and it was best to put a quick stop to any attachments that had begun over the summer. I remember a retreat when we were taken to Saint-Jérôme, a wealthier institution. Instead of our two favourite themes, sexuality and obedience, all of the lectures concerned death and hell. A priest, with an intimidating morbid expression, spoke to us in complete darkness as he stood in front of a coffin placed in the middle of the room, surrounded by candles in all four corners. For an entire week!

LAD: This is a lot like the famous religious retreat in Joyce's *Portrait of the Artist as a Young Man*, where the rector paints a graphic picture of the punishments of sinners in hell. It's absolutely terrifying.

LB: The Irish and the French Canadians share a great number of traits – both the best and the worst of them!

LAD: How did the holidays go?

LB: Vacations lasted two months. To reduce contact with the outside world, the priests asked us to spend a month helping at a summer camp at Saint-Emilie-de-l'Énergie – a camp in a forested area north of Saint-Esprit. I never went. Instead, I helped my father in the bakery. I disliked sports and nature too – the mosquitoes, rain, mud, wind, field mice. And before I forget, there's another thing I must mention. At the beginning of summer vacation, we were required to pay a visit to our parish priest, who, at the end of the holidays, had to send the director of our seminary a report concerning our moral conduct over the summer.

LAD: The seminary also had a spiritual director. What was his role?

LB: I prefer the title "director of conscience" – it seems more eloquent and more precise. Even your conscience didn't belong to you! Daily activities were controlled by the prefect of discipline, and our thoughts by the director of conscience. To bring in a book that was not in the seminary library, a student needed to get the signatures of a priest in the seminary and his director of conscience. And when the prefect of discipline saw a student with such a book, he checked it to see it had the required signatures in it. I was fortunate that my spiritual director was not too demanding. I did well and he did not question me much. He seemed to think I was fine and signed a report that said, "Luc is doing very well, his soul will be saved, etc." The salvation of the soul was inseparable from daily discipline. At every moment, eternity was at stake.

LAD: From the fact that the seminary represented a total institution – a totality whose constitutive parts were closely connected – you seem to conclude that a young believer was subject to constant terror.

LB: Yes, it's for that reason that I never stop saying that the only way to survive was not to believe. The reasoning is really quite simple. In what did the religious phenomenon consist? In the negation of the death of the individual! Only human beings seem to have this worry. In order to deny death, Christianity, like many other religions, wants to shift the problem. Our bodies will die, but our souls will live on for eternity. This introduces a major new problem. Eternal life can be full of hope or despair. The fear of time is transposed to eternity. Everything changes in scale. Everything becomes absolute and infinite. Hence, there's constant anxiety for those who believe that the meaning of life can switch from one side to the other, for all of eternity.

Believing is to condemn oneself to perpetual terror. If one was damned, it was for eternity. To have received communion in the state of mortal sin, because one masturbated, one had to suffer for eternity, far from one's family and friends. And this, without any chance of redemption. When you think about it, even for an instant, it's terrifying. I recall what the priest said to us in primary school. Imagine a dove skimming across the Himalayas once every hundred years. When the Himalayas themselves disappeared, eternity would not have yet even begun! There was such a disproportion between the sin and punishment! That being said, the system the church promoted could only lead to this conclusion.

I became aware of this in October 1956, when I was ten years old. One day after school ended, around 4:00 p.m., I saw someone from the village give a ride on the back of his motorcycle to a young guy I knew. I greeted them and started walking home, taking the usual route. When I arrived at the centre of the village, I noticed a crowd. An accident had happened. The young man who was riding on the back of the motorcycle was unconscious, his leg torn off by a car that had hit the motorcycle. After several days in a coma, he died in the hospital. I was told that the priest said to the mother of the blessed, "Madame, let him die. You will meet him again in heaven." I then understood that the main task of the priest was to make the parishioners accept physical death, or rather, to occult it by interpreting it as the beginning of another life. This physical death really upset me because it suddenly struck someone so young. Before this young man, a boy and a girl in our village had died accidentally: the first was crushed under his father's tractor in 1953, the second was hit and killed by a car at the age of sixteen the following year. For a small village like Saint-Esprit, this was a lot. I still see this young girl "exposed" in a coffin with white satin lining, surrounded by flowers, wearing makeup; a faint peach fragrance floating in the room. Death still has for me the odour of a soft and fading peach.

LAD: You seem to think of religion very negatively. Yet, the church and its organization is one thing, God is another. One may very well reject the church and its institutions while remaining deeply and sincerely a believer. Awareness of the artificiality and the deceptive or illusory nature of the institutions of the Church does not necessarily mean loss of faith.

LB: Assuming that your position is defensible, and that one should distinguish between God and His church, why is it necessary, to be saved, to fulfil rituals that can be characterized as "obsessional," and especially to obey rules established, irrespective of when, by men with more than doubtful morality? And why should we fear the worst during this earthly life while waiting for this other life that might just be an eternal punishment? I don't think I have ever had faith, but the drama that I just evoked constituted for me the point, absolutely, no return, for it made me conscious of the foundation of faith itself: the fear of inevitable death.

Why not accept the human condition and its limits, why not accept death in its brutality, even sometimes in its horror? Anyway, even if, for one reason or another, in one way or another, there's another life, this should not interfere in our lives here on earth and should not interfere in our relations with others. It's hard enough to figure out how to live, given all the suffering and violence around us. The fear of death, as the ancients correctly understood, is pure illusion to the extent that, before death, we do not know what it is.

LAD: But here, you're reiterating the argument of Epicurus. You're not at all a Platonist.

LB: Plato admits the survival of the soul after death, but in the context of a system of retribution that teaches that an individual's soul passes, after cycles that last ten thousand years, from one body to another according to its merit; a man can become a woman or an animal, even the most insignificant animal. I find this quite beautiful and reassuring, for the world of the living must be respected in its entirety, and it gives a picture in human or animal form of the value of individuals. The body reflects the state of the soul. After each cycle, everything begins again from the start. There's nothing definitive, nothing eternal. This doctrine of the survival of the soul thus remains quite primitive and thus a long way from what I was taught. The church used Plato much more than he inspired it.

Very early on I understood that religion was a spectacle, a stage. Humans are the only living beings conscious, and afraid, of death. To overcome this fear, we play theatrical roles for which eternal life is the fundamental issue. I refused to enter into this game and spent much of my time watching others play out their roles. Indeed, religious practice is a merciless exposer of the interior of a human being. It reveals our basest desires, terrors, obsessions, and unsuspecting sentiments. The soul of a believer is laid bare, as it will be at the last judgment; nothing can be hidden.

This deeply interested me. Obviously, I had to play the game to a certain extent – hypocritically. You know that in Greek, *hypocritês* means "actor." I simply had great clarity in the face of the illusion that society transmitted. A life was imposed on me that I had not chosen. But it was the mandatory passage to achieve liberty such as I understood it, the liberty to live a spiritual life grounded in intellectual work. For me, it was the only possible life. And I was prepared to pay dearly to achieve my goal.

LAD: You alluded to the library a little while ago. Did it have extensive holdings?

LB: The library was not well-endowed. Most of the books were donated. One of the priests, fascinated by the new educational method, worked very hard to make it into a pleasant space. I have very fond memories of him. He was very eccentric, and the students ridiculed him. Moreover, from the time I took over the bookbinding department as my "job," after being assigned to the toilets for a very long time, I had direct access to books without needing anyone's permission. I loved the task of bookbinding because through it I rescued old and damaged books otherwise destined for the trash. The bookbinder takes a book in his hands, takes it apart completely, and puts it back together again, giving it a new cover and especially a new life. It's touching especially when you love books.

LAD: During your six years in seclusion, did you experience much of the outside world?

LB: Hardly at all! Newspapers were banned. If you were caught with a radio, you could be expelled. Television was banned until the last few years I was there. We watched *Father Knows Best* (a program endorsing the role of authority) for half an hour on Sundays – unless a hockey playoff was on at the same time. I hated it. We did watch a few movies – cowboy movies where there were no women; films with Laurel and Hardy that I adored. We also put on plays. But generally, we were truly cut off from society. We were removed from the world. We were reserved for the exclusive service of the church. Among the Jesuits, things were very different.

LAD: But these years were decisive for the history of modern Quebec: the last re-election of Duplessis in 1956, the death of Duplessis in 1959, Paul Sauvé and his famous "from now on" (1959), the short-lived government of Antonio Barrette, who was incidentally the provincial representative of Joliette – he must have been appreciated in the region although he was held in ridicule elsewhere in the province – not to mention the election of Jean Lesage in 1960.[8] What did you know about all of this?

LB: The priests presented the election of Jean Lesage as the invasion of Québécois society by evil. It was as if it was the Devil himself who had taken power in Quebec. They probably anticipated the radical changes in the world of education that were to come.

LAD: In 1962, Jean Lesage was re-elected after one of the ministers, René Lévesque,[9] convinced him to run his election campaign on the theme of nationalizing electricity.

LB: All of this was lived out like it was a catastrophe, a real earthquake. And I think from that moment on, the priests of the Blessed Sacrament knew that it was over, that the world was "becoming dark," that it was dissolving like a sugar cube in water. But neither I nor my comrades could really understand the issues. I saw very well that the priests in the seminary were panicked, stunned, and terrified, but I didn't understand why as I didn't have any point of comparison.

LAD: Let's talk more about your studies. Your classes were fairly traditional – French, English, mathematics, history, geography, and Latin. For Greek, you had to wait a few years, correct?

LB: No. We started learning Greek in the class on syntax during the second year of our studies. It wasn't actually included in our report cards, but it was a way to evaluate students, and even to get rid of some.

LAD: Were there any teachers who deeply affected you?

LB: Yes, there were several. But it wasn't like public school, where teachers had a determinate effect on students' futures. We didn't receive an education to acquire competency in subjects sanctioned with diplomas. We were there to become priests, the managers of the church. Latin and Greek were the preferred tools of the priesthood. The New Testament, which includes the Gospels, is in Greek, and all the prayers and Mass itself were in Latin. Latin and Greek were more than mere intellectual performances, they were also signs of a religious vocation. They also used Greek to "test" the seminarians during the second year. It was a way to eliminate some. French was considered a working tool and not really a means of evaluating students academically. It was intended for preaching and for administrative work. Don't forget that public records (births, marriages, deaths) were kept by the village priests. There was no provincial register of civil status.

LAD: But weren't there any teachers who loved Greek and Latin in themselves?

LB: Yes, but only during the final years, in Great Literature and in Rhetoric. The Greek and Latin teacher was excellent. He had a master's degree from the Catholic Institute of Paris. Also, he was very cultured and an aesthete. He had many personal problems, though, always of the same sort. The French teacher was also exceptional, but less gifted than the Greek and Latin teacher. He adored French literature and knew how to transmit his passion. He had a master's degree from the University of Ottawa, with a thesis on Félix-Antoine Savard's *Menaud, maître-draveur* (Boss of the river).

LAD: And the authors? Did you study the great Greek and Latin authors?

LB: In Latin, it was Cesar and Ovid, for their Latin is generally easy. But I adored Horace, Sallust, and Tacitus. I didn't like Cicero, though the style, I have to admit, is admirable. But I hated his judicial rhetoric – founded on lying and focused only on victory at any cost. In Greek, we started with Lucian. His Greek wasn't that difficult since it was not his first language. It wasn't too controversial and there wasn't much sexual innuendo. But pretty soon after, our teacher had us reading Xenophon and Homer, then the tragedies, which we had to learn by heart. I thus learned several pages of *Oedipus the King* by Sophocles. But the revelation for me was Plato. The end of the *Symposium*, obviously expunged of all of its homosexual allusions, the defence of Socrates by an inebriated Alcibiades, which we translated in Great Literature, remains for me the summit of literature. I've never read anything more beautiful. Even thirty years later, I still get emotional in translating this dialogue.

LAD: Why did you complete the last two years of your classical/standard course, Philosophy I and II, at the Sainte-Thérèse Seminary?

LB: According to the priests of the Blessed Sacrament, the only question worthy of being asked in the Rhetoric class was that of vocation. Of course, it was always implicit, but there the question was posed more forcefully. The student was cornered. For after the Rhetoric class, the school curriculum was not complete and so we couldn't enroll in university. For those who wanted to continue, there were two possibilities: enroll in an institution with higher fees or do the novitiate, where we had to wait two years before taking Philosophy I and II. At the noviciate, one learned to pray and obey. One had to wear a cassock, with white near the heart, the symbol of the Fathers of the Blessed Sacrament. You had to spend two years in Quebec City, in a house set deep in a large park, praying and practising spiritual exercises. It was only after those two years that you returned to Montreal and did Philosophy I and II. There, at the "scholasticate," the residence of the religious community that played the role of grand diocesan seminary, you took the first vows (poverty and obedience – chastity came later). One was then enlisted, and all that was left was training in theology.

In my case, it was agreed from the month of January, at home, that I'd make a request to attend Sainte-Thérèse. But the last weeks in Rhetoric in Terrebonne were horrible. The director of conscience kept calling on me to measure the size of my cassock; they were absolutely sure that I'd go to the novitiate in Quebec City. When it became clear that this was not the case, all the students were called into the meeting room. All the clergymen were in the front row. They called me to stand before them, not to be insulted, they said, but so that they could remonstrate with me. It was shameful to leave the institution that gave me so much. I was a traitor, ungrateful. They demanded a full reimbursement for each of the years I spent in the seminary. Put in a stranglehold, my parents were forced to suspend for several years their payments on the purchase of the bakery.

Finally, I left. I was free! My health was not deplorable. I had an impressive education in French, Latin, Greek, and even in mathematics. Six years spent in "prison" only reinforced my determination. I'd live the life I'd choose, whatever happened. I had already paid enough.

I detested that incarceration that kept me cut off from my family, from my community, from society, to turn me into a manager of the church. But my hostility faded in time, a bit like the sea smooths a rough rock. The French of Quebec survived because the church trained them. The church protected itself in the same way the Turkish sultan did, by establishing a personal guard or an army of elite soldiers – by taking the children from civil society, isolating them to train them, and then returning them to civil society, where the lack of affection and the toughness of the life that they were exposed to during their adolescence doomed them to the two problems I mentioned: women and alcohol.

That being said, one cannot forget that for the majority of us poor, bright kids, becoming part of the clergy was a huge social promotion. Priests were on the top rung of the French-Canadian social hierarchy, followed by notaries, doctors, and lawyers. In any kind of a reunion, it was usually a priest who presided. For a child coming from an impoverished milieu, to become a priest provided access to parts of society that would otherwise be off limits. Also, despite their problems, the priests of the seminary were always available, contrary to contemporary teachers, for whom teaching is most of the time a profession that often exasperates them – and you can understand why! We must also remember that the priests at the seminary were not paid. This enabled a poor society, as was the case in Quebec, to provide a level of education to members of society who were particularly deprived. But at what cost!

LAD: Was the Sainte-Thérèse Seminary very different?

LB: It actually wanted to become the University of Quebec. It presented itself like an American college. It was a school with money. We were able to leave on weekends, we had our own bedrooms and could close our doors whenever we pleased, and television was accessible day and night. We had enough to eat, and it was usually quite good. An education from this seminary allowed one entrance to university. It was really only a seminary in name. There was a chapel, certainly, but it wasn't obligatory to visit it.

LAD: It was part of the spirit of the times. There was a breath of fresh air! It was in tune with the Quiet Revolution. Those years saw a lot happen.

LB: Yes, a lot was going on. In November 1963 President Kennedy was assassinated in Dallas. We spent many hours in front of the television watching the story unfold. It was a tense atmosphere. We didn't understand the motive and we didn't know who was responsible. We feared another world war.

I was also exposed to the political problems in Quebec. We had Raymond Barbeau, the son of Victor Barbeau, as our French teacher. He was the founder of the Alliance Laurentienne, the first independence movement in Quebec. Raymond Barbeau was a bewildering and fascinating person. He went to Paris to complete his doctoral dissertation on Léon Bloy, a French writer with a flamboyant style of writing. Bloy was also an unorthodox Catholic who believed that the Holy Spirit, identified with Lucifer, would begin his terrestrial reign in the year 1900. The event would be announced by the appearance of the Virgin Mary in Europe. You have to reread Bloy to really appreciate the beauty of his words in service of total deliriousness. When Raymond Barbeau published his thesis, this made him a pariah in the francophone world. The Christians were horrified and the atheists were shocked.

He was always formally dressed when he taught his courses. His oral expression was superb and his written expression impeccable. He considered it a grave error to forget to dot ones i's or j's. I maintain a serious respect for the French language because of the terror he instilled in me during the first semester. To this day, I expect others to have the same kind of respect for their mother tongue.

Raymond Barbeau kept to one topic. I think he believed that the Holy Spirit would return to earth and that humanity should prepare itself for this grand event. He had immense intellectual rigour and showed very strict discipline regarding his body and his habits. Vegetarianism and naturalism were the rule, drinking and smoking were forbidden! He would not bring children into a world full of debauchery. His Alliance Laurentienne was supposed to represent a prelude to a better future, where human beings could attain dignity, epiphany, and the manifestation of God in the Holy Spirit.

At the time, I found this utterly delusional. I'm even more convinced of this now, especially because of all of the horrors committed by various sects. But I can't help but have a kind of admiration for Raymond Barbeau's eccentricity, which at the time must have demanded an incredible emotional and intellectual investment.

The same year, in 1962 or 1963, Pierre Bourgault, who had recently been appointed as the director of the Assembly for National Independence, came to give a speech. It was quite the event. Bourgault was impressive with his reddish-blond hair, white skin, and blue eyes. His presence literally heated the room. It was fascinating when he spoke of broken dignity, ridicule, conquest, political injustice, and revenge. But all of it was essentially emotional. He offered no rational argument. It was more like a howl of pain: Pierre Bourgault felt the "pain of Quebec." In the auditorium, everyone felt the emotion except me. My recent experiences made me view things differently. During the six years that had just passed, I didn't suffer at the hands of English Canadians, I suffered at the hands of the church in Quebec. It was being argued that this manipulation was the consequence of the defeat of French forces in North America as well as the attitude of English leaders. This was true in part, but only in part. For the Catholic Church had found it in its interest to become the managers of this urgent historical situation. It had monopolized a lot of powers, and this for more than two centuries.

More generally, I think the deeper feelings awakened by Pierre Bourgault were similar to those described by Marcel Mauss and Lucien Lévy-Bruhl. Individuals define themselves in relation to the group to which they belong. A group gains recognition and respect when people desire to belong to it, and those who desire membership perform various actions toward that end, including those of gift and counter-gift, as described by Mauss.[10] But we could just as well connect this search for recognition to the importance that victory takes in a particular sport. In this context, we can see that the individual expects to enjoy this pre-established recognition by being connected with the group.

It is evident that the francophone community in North America did not feel recognized and respected by the anglophone community. That being said, it has to be admitted that such a lack of recognition was felt even more keenly in France by the Bretons, the Corsicans, the Basques, and even by those who feel connected to the Occitan language. The lack of recognition in Canada was mostly a consequence of the radical isolation in which the French community had survived, and which had also caused considerable delay in many areas of social development. Faced with this situation, two positions could be adopted: one of confrontation, held by those supporters of independence, or one of prudent and lucid, but real, co-operation, which is what I preferred. However, in order for this to work in an atmosphere of mutual respect, such a co-operation demands a strong sense of belonging but also, and especially, a high birth rate, sustained and effective employment in all areas, and an excellent level in the handling of the French language. All this exceeds sentiment; it requires effort, much effort!

Moreover, from a strictly personal standpoint, I had survived six years of confinement in a seminary. I was finally free, I could not bear to be told what to do, what to think, and what to say, as was the case with the Catholic newspaper *L'Action catholique* (1915–62),[11] in order that a cause be triumphant, whatever the cause, including the survival of French Quebec through political independence. I was for a French Quebec because French culture is truly my "country." However, political independence did not seem to be a necessary objective, and, more important, it seemed to me to be far too negative. I wondered why the quality of life, language, and culture were not ends in themselves, and why they had to be absolutely subordinated to a political solution that took the form of political independence. We were returning to a new kind of isolation, secular this time, based on language alone.

LAD: At Sainte-Thérèse, you began your first steps in philosophy. What did the teaching consist of?

LB: It was a methodical philosophy program: logic, physics, metaphysics, and ethics, on the model of medieval scholasticism. In fact, the Thomism that Leo XIII promoted as the philosophy of the Catholic Church reigned supreme, even in physics. We were told that modern discoveries amounted to little compared to the intuitions of a thinker like Thomas Aquinas. In fact, we were taught the Thomism that prevailed at the Catholic Institute of Paris, where our textbooks were from. It was a Thomism mixed with Cartesianism and especially neo-Kantianism. We had a professor who was approaching retirement age who gave us essays to write on the papal encyclicals and the priestal letters of Bishop Léger, the archbishop of Montreal. The courses on the history of philosophy were superb! Terms of abuse were hurled against various philosophers: Hegel's thought had no more consistency than the fog that absorbed the heat of the sun over Heidelberg in the early morning; Kant was a Pietist who deserved to be blacklisted (he was still on the Index when I attended the University of Montreal); Renan had died on the toilet, an appropriate death for an atheist, etc.

UNIVERSITY OF MONTREAL

LAD: Did these condemnations incite you to consult the works of these philosophers to see precisely what they were saying?

LB: No, but it did disgust me just the same. The only one I really enjoyed studying was Nietzsche. I had read, in translation, Heidegger's *Holzwege* (Off the beaten track) as well as his article on Nietzsche's contempt for Plato. This interested me very much and made me want to learn more about Plato. But, remember, at that time, I did not intend to study philosophy, but rather mathematics, pure mathematics. But I was not permitted to enroll in the sciences section at the seminary at Sainte-Thérèse and, therefore, the Department of Mathematics at the University of Montreal. My capabilities in mathematics were sufficient and my marks well above the average, but I had never had access to physics and chemistry at Terrebonne because the seminary was too poor to build labs.

So, I was then convinced to enroll in philosophy, where I could study logic and attend mathematics classes. The only thing that made me not choose mathematics was writing. I always wanted to write, not so much because I cared about eloquence or style, but to communicate ideas. I was also, by then, very attached to the ancient languages of Latin and Greek. When I was asked to write papers on historical subjects, I'd always choose to write on texts written in Latin or Greek.

LAD: In September of 1965, you enrolled at the University of Montreal. What were your first impressions?

LB: This was the first time I lived in Montreal. For the first time in my life, I was in a coeducational environment. It was also the first time that I found myself in the midst of Quebec's political problems – the University of Montreal General Students' Association was very active. At the time, I remember well, there was the Vietnam War, the Front de Libération du Québec (FLQ). I didn't have much money, which meant I wasn't really able to enjoy the big city.

LAD: You completed your BA and MA in three years, though they usually take five to complete. Why the rush?

LB: At the time, in theory, a BA took three years, and a MA an additional year, so four years in all. My goal was to leave Quebec as soon as possible, so I tried to work as much as possible. Why this urgency? I don't know how to explain it simply. Everything really goes back, in part, to my time in Terrebonne, of finding myself kept away from the world, isolated, locked in. It stirred up a desire to go anywhere, but far away. Of course, things had changed considerably by then, but it was not enough. The problem was more individual than cultural. I wanted to reach the summit in the area I had chosen. That is also why I decided very early on to give up mathematics. University was like a waiting room. During the first months, I realized that I could leave if I was at the top of the class, and to do that required working in a single area. And then, mathematics would have cut me off from reading, and especially writing. Now as far as writing and philosophy are concerned, I had the impression that it was strictly impossible to do something really exceptional in Quebec, which had just awoken from its "dogmatic slumber" and was now rubbing its eyes.

LAD: Isn't this a demonstration of ... pride?

LB: You talk like the provincial community of the Fathers of the Blessed Sacrament. Yes, it was a form of pride, but I don't see why this desire to achieve excellence is reprehensible. I think if I had chosen mathematics I'd most probably have remained in North America. I'd have gone to the United States. But insofar as I wanted to write and do philosophy, I was well aware that it was impossible to continue in Quebec. In order to obtain a doctorate, we were advised to leave.

You should know that at the time the University of Montreal didn't have a Department of Philosophy as such, but a Faculty of Philosophy, which was directed by a Sulpician,[12] and included both a Department of Philosophy and a Department of Psychology. The Department of Philosophy, for its part, was headed by a Dominican. The Sulpicians raised the money – although they were ruined in 1967 – and the Dominicans brought the brains. The Faculty of Philosophy was a pontifical faculty. The pope had a say with respect to both the teachers and the programs. The archbishop of Montreal was his representative; moreover, the archbishop was the chancellor of the university. And since the Department of Philosophy was headed by a Dominican, we were taught Thomism. Saint Thomas had belonged to the community of Dominicans. They read the Greek authors based on an interpretation from the Middle Ages, and they read modern authors from a Thomistic perspective. For example, courses on Heidegger offered an interpretation of Thomistic philosophy. When I arrived, the majority of the professors were clerics. The only one who wasn't was Vianney Décarie. Mr Décarie became the first director of the new Department of Philosophy when it was established in 1967. This was the context, and it seemed obvious that we could not do anything worthwhile in Quebec, at least at a high level. I should also add that in the mid-sixties, things were moving at a lightning pace. For example, when I arrived, during the first year I saw teachers wearing cassocks in September. In the month of December, they were in jeans, and some already had ...

LAD: ... a woman?

LB: Yes. In the meantime, Mr Décarie became director of the department, and then everything changed. He brought in secular teachers like Paul Lacoste, Charles Taylor, André Gombay, etc. And he invited several European professors: Paul Ricoeur, Father Jean Trouillard, Jean-Baptiste Gri, among others. All of this was like a revelation. It reinforced my desire to go abroad. There were other aspects of openness to the world that Vianney Décarie exemplified. He tried to make it obligatory to study at least one living foreign language. With this in mind, he organized language classes that were free. I had the opportunity to learn German. I completed three years of German lessons for free. I wouldn't have been able to afford them myself.

LAD: The interest in bringing in these teachers was twofold: not only did Québécois students in Montreal profit from this, but once the teachers returned to Paris, they then helped Québécois students pursue their studies in France. The exchanges were thus favourable in both directions. We received teachers, to whom we later sent our students who returned later ... except a few ...

LB: I think that was directed at me.

LAD: A wink, that's all. The political situation in the 1960s was probably also a reason to leave. It was at this point ...

LB: Unbearable! Between 1965 and 1968, the years I was at the University of Montreal, there were three big issues: the war in Vietnam, the Front de libération du Québec, and the student uprisings. I was opposed to the Vietnam War. I participated in the first three demonstrations organized in Montreal. I didn't believe in the domino theory and didn't think that the United States should intervene in a civil war. These were the only demonstrations in which I participated in my entire life.

The violence of the FLQ was much less bloody than what I later saw in Paris and in England – bombs were placed in mailboxes and in symbolic public buildings. But it was the first time that someone like me, someone from the middle of nowhere, was exposed to real terrorist violence. The violence that I had experienced before then was a form of individual expression, whereas terrorist violence takes the form of social and political action. I could never admit that in the society where I lived, groups could impose their will. This also touched the Department of Philosophy. The brother of the president of the Philosophy Students' Association was killed placing a bomb behind a factory whose workers were on strike. From that moment on, we were constantly under watch. The atmosphere became unbearable.

Regarding the student revolts in 1968, especially in Paris, well, that didn't work for me. My reaction was selfish. It's certainly not very edifying. I feared that the country would collapse and that I'd no longer be able to go. But how could I associate myself with the stupid slogans they shouted that were praising the Soviet Union and Mao Zedong? The first students that I encountered in Nanterre in October 1968 recounted the events as if they were veterans. When they told me that they were against consumerist societies, I smiled and told them that before I could oppose consumerism, I'd have liked to know it. My parents never even had a car, and we never took a vacation. I was always working. In the summer, I'd work between eighteen and twenty hours a day. We got our television quite late, we almost never went out, my mother didn't have a dishwasher or a modern washing machine or dryer. I can still see her hands covered with callouses from of all her housework. Consumer society, what was that? "Under the cobblestones, the beach?" The first time I saw the sea, and so the first time I saw a beach, was at Easter of 1969. I was in Saint-Malo in Brittany, the very place that Jacques Cartier left four and a half centuries earlier. I was twenty-three years old and I had made the journey in reverse.

These three themes, even if only one is properly Québécois, were inextricably linked: the protests against the Vietnam War were related to demands for Quebec independence, violent cleansing should encourage the birth of a new, more just society, and all of this was brought together in the American and French student revolts that wanted to change Western society by subverting the "system" and in rejecting capitalist "consumer society" in order to work for the advent of a communist society. Now, in these three movements, I encountered again what I hated most about the seminary – the need to think, speak, and act in conformity with what was expected of you. But there was a fundamental difference: in religion, there's no one who can really verify if life in heaven is truly the best, whereas in politics you find yourself confronted with results at every moment.

LAD: And were you interested in national politics, in the three Québécois "doves" in Ottawa (Trudeau, Marchand, and Pelletier), in Charles de Gaulle's visit to Quebec in 1967?

LB: Until 1968, I must confess that I didn't understand what was going on between Quebec and Ottawa at the political level, and I wanted nothing to do with it. It was only in the seventies that I began to understand what Trudeau, Pelletier, and Marchand represented.

Regarding de Gaulle, I was not in Montreal when he launched his "Vive le Québec libre!" at the end of his visit to Quebec in 1967. I was in Saint-Esprit, but I watched the event live on television. I confess that I perceived the statement as an attack, a kind of interference in a quarrel that France really had nothing to do with. Even if I were a separatist, I'd have felt a certain discomfort to receive support from a country that had done nothing for Quebec for over two centuries, and that now took the opportunity to appeal to the good memories of everyone. The most shocking thing about this "Vive le Québec libre!" was the use of the adjective "libre," or "free," and this because the same historical figure, de Gaulle, actually liberated France. I'm not forgetting the Allied forces, but it was de Gaulle who restored to France its honour. The situation in Quebec was not at all comparable to that of occupied France. No sensible and honest Quebecer is ready to equate the power of the British Empire or of the federal government to that of the Nazi Germany that occupied France. Moreover, this adjective constituted a serious injury to the courage and honour of all the countries that with their blood and their wealth contributed to the liberation of France. I understand that Canada and Britain considered this slogan a real insult.

De Gaulle said that what he said was for sentimental reasons of course (this was confirmed by those close to him), but also and above all to put Canada, England, and the United States in a difficult position. It was fair game, even if the game seems ridiculous now. France along with England are a part of Europe that is increasingly federated and, like it or not, must co-operate more closely with Canada and with the United States. Moreover, for material reasons, the feelings of France for Quebec would not last long; it's obvious that the presence of France in West and North Africa is primarily about its economic interest. I think the cultural connection holds only a small place, and I'd go as far as to say a derisory one. It's sufficient to compare the budget of the Francophonie to that of other ministries. I admire France, and I'm happy to live here. I consider French culture vital to my intellectual well-being. But I don't feel it's treasonous to remind one that the interest of France toward Quebec is first and foremost economic.[13]

The positive reaction on the part of much of the population that listened to de Gaulle's speech shows that people expected much of France, considered as the "mother country." For me, France is a cultural home, but not a political one. France is the heart of French culture, which I have always deeply loved and admired, and for which I continue to fight every day. But politically, France abandoned New France in 1763. Admittedly, it was a result of military defeat, but diplomacy could have worked things out. This abandonment was the result of a political decision. It also represented a turning point in world history. What would have been the influence of France if the French had remained in America from Newfoundland to the Mississippi for even a few more decades?[14] France has long been resigned to this loss, but not Quebec. However, we cannot rewrite history. And in the actual state of things, I believe that the cultural identity of Quebec is better assured within a country like Canada that extends from the Atlantic to the Pacific and has maintained a real independence with regard to the United States. The political independence of Quebec would lead to the breaking up of Canada, which would disintegrate into several parts (one of which being Quebec), whose territory would remain perhaps extensive but whose economy would remain weak. American power would encroach somewhat mechanically, like a huge planet exerts an irresistible force of attraction on the smaller masses that lie within its vicinity. We'd be the Cajuns of the North. This is not exactly a very attractive picture!

This is what I came to understand during the seventies. Quebec had an alternative: either live up to the myth of liberation that would take us back, politically, to relying on our "mother country," or stay with North America in spite of everything. Trudeau chose the second option. This was also my choice. You don't return to your mother's womb, even collectively.

LAD: Were you taken with the charm of René Lévesque?

LB: I always was very much moved by René Lévesque. I liked his persona ever since *Focal Point* began to be televised in 1956, I think. I was still a little boy. When I could, I'd go watch the program at the house of one of my uncles. It was, if I remember correctly, at the beginning of the sixties.

LAD: What did you think of Québécois culture at the time, notably the writers, singers, and artists?

LB: I knew very little of them. I liked a few poets (Alain Grandbois, Jacques Brault, who taught us at the university, Gaston Mitron), and some writers (Gabrielle Roy, for example), but I didn't much care for many contemporary writers, for I couldn't stand *joual*, not for reasons of language purity but just because I couldn't read this gibberish. I also read some political works (the *Parti pris* review, and Pierre Vallière's *White Negros of America*). I didn't really like theatre and I hate going to mass spectacles to watch a singer or a sporting event. I didn't read newspapers, but I watched television and I also listened to the radio.

Just the same, I want to add something about politics and my relations with Quebec. I never had the opportunity to exercise my right to vote in Quebec; there were no elections between 1966 and 1970, and when there were, I was already in Paris. It was hard for me to be directly interested in politics. But this disinterest was short-lived. I received my French citizenship in 1987, but I maintained my Canadian citizenship as well. I began voting, and I urge my children to vote as well. Since large numbers of young people rarely vote, their demands are neglected. In the final analysis, I never really felt like a complete citizen in Quebec, for I lived in seclusion for too long. I now feel free to express my opinion without imposing it on others. I say what I think and I'm careful, as many others have been and continue to be, in expressing an unbridled feeling of power.

STUDYING PHILOSOPHY

LAD: Returning to your interest in Greek philosophy, where do you think it comes from?

LB: I'm very interested in Greek philosophy because I studied Greek for a long time and was also touched by Plato's works. But it was very difficult for me to get interested in Aristotle because Thomas Aquinas sucked him dry.

What I've just said about Aristotle is extremely simplified, and it's false when applied to philosophy at the university level, but at the high school level, where we got exposed to philosophy for the first time, it's strictly true.

At the Institute of Medieval Studies, first Paul Vignaux and then Raymond Klibansky gave courses on Aristotle that were free from the influence of Thomism. And especially Vianney Décarie, who had published his book *L'objet de la métaphysique selon Aristote* (The object of metaphysics according to Aristotle) in 1961, provided us with a unique perspective on Aristotle inspired by the work of Jaeger and Cherniss. In 1962, there were also the two theses published by Pierre Aubenque, *Le problème de l'être chez Aristote* (The problem of being in Aristotle) and *La prudence chez Aristote* (Prudence in Aristotle). They were inspired by Heidegger, but in a reasonable way. The immense success of these two books eclipsed all the other books on Aristotle written in French, even those of Vianney Décarie and Jacques Brunschwig. Nearly forty years later, I'm not sure that this eclipse helped the study of Aristotle in the francophone world. Although I regularly reread the works of Pierre Aubenque with pleasure and admiration, I still think that on the question of being, Décarie was right. The object of metaphysics is indeed the realm of divine being understood as "separate" being.[15]

My prejudice against Aristotle was due to the Thomistic interpretation popular at the time. This influence was much too strong for me to engage in research on Aristotle. It took another generation, your own, in order to be totally free from Thomism.

LAD: There's a famous statement from Pico della Mirandola that Pierre Aubenque placed at the opening of his *Problème de l'être chez Aristotle*: "Sine Thomas, Aristoteles mutes esset" (Without Thomas, Aristotle would remain silent). It took another generation before Québécois students could finally study Aristotle himself, independent of Thomism or another religious or theological attempt at "recuperation." I therefore understand the circumstances that the rejection of one suddenly led to the rejection of the other. That said, if you will allow me, there's nonetheless a paradox here: turning your back on Aristotle for religious reasons, you threw yourself into the arms of Plato, who is far more religious. The religious dimension plays a considerably greater role in Platonism than in Aristotelianism.

LB: Yes, of course. But the following caveat must be made. To make a place for philosophy, Plato was a radical critic of the myths transmitted at the time by the poets, but no one described better than he the religious experience of his contemporaries, and the decisive influence of religion on them and even on philosophy. For my part, even if I've rejected religion as a life experience, I've been fascinated by the obsessional and highly ritualized behaviour that it implies, and I wanted to understand why philosophy has always been in solidarity in one way or another with religion. I need a framework of this kind to live, but as a spectator. And I find this attitude much more in Plato than in Aristotle.

LAD: And as regards other philosophers, where are your preferences?

LB: Medieval philosophy, as historical production, interests me a lot; on the other hand, I've considerable difficulty in appreciating German philosophers, with the exception of Kant. Moreover, it was Charles Taylor who taught the course on German philosophers. It was at a very high level. He also gave lectures on Hegel, on the *Phenomenology of Spirit*, which is one of the most beautiful "novels" ever written. The chapters on the master-slave relationship and on Greek tragedy are really impressive. But for me, it's a metaphysical novel, it's not philosophy.

LAD: What do you mean?

LB: I've never embraced the idea, as Hegel and Marx do, that history is teleological, and that things must happen the way they do. In a chapter in *Philosophie grecque*, I noted that the Christians lived according to this idea. But they won, not the Marxists! That being said, the *Grundlinien der Philosophie des Rechts* (Elements of the philosophy of rights), a series of notes from classes taught by Hegel, seem decisive to me. We find there a philosophical description of the modern society in which we still live.

LAD: What about what we call modern philosophy – that is, Descartes, rationalism, and empiricism?

LB: We had a remarkable class on Descartes that was taught by Paul Lacoste, who later became the rector of the University of Montreal. There were also courses on Locke, Hume (whom I liked a lot), and Hobbes. It was André Gombay who taught us these authors from an Anglo-Saxon perspective, which was disconcerting but nonetheless interesting. The problem was that André Gombay, who taught at McGill, Charles Taylor, who was deeply involved in the New Democratic Party, and Paul Lacoste, who was absent most of the time, were not easily accessible. They rarely gave courses and did not supervise students.

As far as contemporary philosophy goes, it was totally haphazard. We were taught Heidegger, but only because we were supposed to be convinced that he didn't say anything different from Thomas Aquinas. I really disliked phenomenology. We were taught Husserl in order to study Merleau-Ponty or Heidegger. Paul Ricoeur gave classes on Husserl, but from a very different perspective that was terribly hard to follow insofar as we hadn't read the German texts. In phenomenology, awareness and acts of consciousness take place in a vacuum. All of this seemed vacuous to me and not very useful. I'm probably too simplistic, but I believe that consciousness cannot be described without an object or another subject, much like an electric current needs to encounter resistance to produce heat.

Sartre was considered to be very dodgy. I always thought of him as a writer and not as a philosopher. I really enjoyed *Nausea* and *Words*. The rest I didn't much care for, and I found his plays too mechanical and schematic. When I read *Being and Nothingness*, Sartre appeared to me to be a kind of vulgarizer who took great delight in making thoughts obscure by using abstruse language. On the other hand, I found *Nausea* to be a fundamental work of the first order. And *Words* is a work of exceptional quality. That said, Sartre was mostly known at the time for his political positions, which seem even more laughable now.

LAD: What about psychoanalysis?

LB: We were taught Freud and Lacan. I didn't read much by Freud, mostly his later works, the more speculative ones on Moses, Leonardo da Vinci, *Totem and Taboo*, and *Civilization and Its Discontents*. Among the true psychoanalytic works, I think I read *The Schreber Case* and *Three Essays on Sexuality*. I had a certain admiration for Freud, but I didn't care for Lacan. I thought his views on linguistics and his grammatical contortions were ridiculous.

LAD: What did you think Nietzsche, the third "Master of Suspicion" after Marx and Freud?

LB: There were no courses on Nietzsche. He was read through the commentaries of Heidegger. I very much liked *Thus Spoke Zarathustra*, but as a literary work. I never particularly liked the idea of Nietzsche's Overman. His philosophical ideas seem both naive and grotesque to me. Nietzsche draws out the most extreme consequences of the modern predicament where the subject constitutes an object and claims his autonomy without noticing that it's all a function of prejudice. Those who have made the assumption of realities in themselves (akin to Platonic forms), did not do so out of hatred of the sensible world, but to give the world we live in enough stability to become the subject of speech and thought.

LAD: Did you do other readings that you now find particularly influential?

LB: At the time, I read a lot. This is not true today. Sartre said, I think, that "when we write, we no longer read." When I was at the University of Montreal, I was very interested in French literature. I read all of Proust, for example, and I reread a good part of Flaubert and Maupassant. I also read a lot of English and American literature, notably Conrad, Graham Greene, and more recent authors like Kerouac. But if I have to pick my all-time favourite, it's definitely Faulkner. Having said this, during my university years I was more interested in anthropological works: those most notably of Lévi-Strauss, and earlier writers who concerned themselves with religious anthropology, notably Marcel Mauss, Lévy-Bruhl, Jane Harrison, and

Malinowski. In short, I liked those authors who thought of religion as a spectacle, as a representation that society gives of itself.

LAD: Always, then, this conception of religion as an instrument of social cohesion, of domestication of life and time. I'd have thought your interest in the anthropological approach to Greek religion, and even to philosophy, went back to your years in Paris, while you were attending the seminars of Jean-Pierre Vernant, Marcel Detienne, and Pierre Vidal-Naquet. But let's return to Lévi-Strauss and the influence of his work.

LB: The *Mythologiques* were finished when I was already in Paris, but the first two volumes, *The Raw and the Cooked* (1964) and *From Honey to Ashes* (1967), I had already read in Quebec. Before this, I had read *Tristes Tropiques* (1955), *Structural Anthropology* (1958), and *La Pensée sauvage* (The savage mind, 1962). These books had a profound impact on me. I thought Lévi-Strauss's analysis of myth was extremely original, even if I couldn't exactly follow his method because I found it both too mechanistic and too sophisticated. But the recognition that Lévi-Strauss discovers in myth a rational foundation that allows for societal organization, to make sense of our place in the universe, to make sense of ourselves without the force of a church or a constituent body of representatives, to offer an explanation of the passage of time, and therefore death – all this represented for me an exceptional advancement. Lévi-Strauss no longer derived his set of concepts from the philosophical context, but from social context. A community gave itself, somewhat unconsciously, the instruments that enabled it to encounter what it considered reality, where reality is but a habit of custom, and as I never tire of saying, maybe even a bad habit. In reading Lévi-Strauss, I had the impression that I understood Québécois society and that I understood myself.

The social cohesion and the inclusion of a human group in nature require a particular mythology that is all the more effective in that the technique it employs is grounded in the human psyche. It's not at all obvious that a human group can survive without mythology in a hostile natural environment.[16] The biological survival of the human individual occurs through inclusion in a group whose cohesion depends on its capacity to represent itself at the level of its imaginary.[17] I found the same theme in Plato: a rationality that tries to make a conscious endeavour to renounce myth, and yet is incapable of abandoning it. First, we try to eliminate myth, second, we use it, and third, we try to find a balance. I think Plato's procedure can be described as such. The critique of myth ends with a return to myth.

LAD: Given your interest in anthropology, it's quite surprising that the topic of your master's thesis didn't move in that direction: "Le non-être comme autre dans le *Sophiste* de Platon" (Non-being as otherness in Plato's *Sophist*). We find ourselves here in full ontology, in full metaphysics. Where is myth, religion, and the representations that the society makes of itself?

LB: My master's thesis was part of a strategy. I wanted to get it out as quickly as possible and I wanted to demonstrate that I had mastered the material I was being taught. I therefore knew Plato, I mastered Greek (there were many Greek quotations), and I was interested in all the ontological questions that we covered at the university. Also, I had already begun to work on the *Timaeus*, which would become the theme of my doctoral dissertation, the central point of which remained the famous section of 35a–b, on the constitution of the world soul, where the world soul is constructed by a demiurge from being, sameness, and otherness.

LAD: In sum, "Le non-être comme autre dans le *Sophiste* de Platon," announces the topic of your doctoral thesis: "Sameness and otherness in the ontological structure of Plato's *Timaeus*."

LB: Yes, but the *Sophist*, whose general sense depends on one's interpretation of the *Parmenides*, played a role just as important in the history of philosophy in general as in the analytic interpretative movement regarding Plato. This interpretive movement took off after the Second World War under the impulse of Gilbert Ryle and John L. Ackrill at Oxford. Ackrill considered that the *Parmenides* marked the abandonment of the doctrine of separate intelligible forms by a more reasonable Plato, who now interpreted the forms as concepts. The *Sophist* was thus considered the first attempt to develop an analysis of the proposition in terms of predication. This new current of interpretation was in opposition to the traditional one that saw in the *Sophist* a partial solution to the problem of participation in that Plato, by introducing the five kinds (Being, Motion, Rest, Sameness, Difference), could show how the forms considered separate intelligible realities could entertain relations with one another. In another context, Plotinus found in these great kinds the categories of the intelligible world.[18]

That said, when I arrived in Paris, my thesis proposal was worked out and my bibliography was ready. My master's thesis was just a preliminary work. It was the *Timaeus* that really interested me.

LAD: The *Timaeus* is the dialogue of Plato's that was the most likely to interest you insofar as it provides the largest variety of seemingly opposing themes. On one hand, the hyper-rationalization of the mathematization of the universe, and, on the other hand, a para-scientific reflection on the importance of myth, without forgetting that the dialogue itself is presented as a myth. Can one say that the *Timaeus* is a representation of a sort of survey of Platonism?

LB: Yes, and also a survey of all of my preoccupations. The *Timaeus* was for a long time the only work on the creation of the universe to compete with Genesis. During the Middle Ages, some philosophers, including those of the school of Chartres, tried to show that the two texts were saying almost the same thing. Moreover, it's in the *Timaeus* that we find the oldest version of the myth of Atlantis.[19] We can therefore understand the importance of this dialogue in the history of thought. For most people, however, it's the *Republic* that represents the best of Plato's thought. This substitution is due mainly, I think, to the fact that science now offers us alternative narratives regarding the origin of the universe that seem more complete and convincing. It's precisely this vision of things that Walter Meyerstein and I have tried to challenge in *Inventing the Universe*.

APPENDIX ON THE MASS IN QUEBEC AND ITS MYTHICAL ANTECEDENTS

Mass was mandatory on Sunday but optional during the rest of the week. Normal people had to do their Easter duties – that is, to confess their sins at least once a year and receive communion during the Easter Mass. If one didn't do their "Easter duties," one was excluded from the church. At the seminary, on the other hand, Mass was mandatory every day, and so was communion. This implied that we had to be in a state of grace. If not, in addition to what was already a mortal sin, one was committing a sacrilege: consuming the body and blood of Christ. This put most of us into a horrible dilemma, and one that was even more grave when considering that Christ himself was present in the form of a sacred host. Moreover, if a parishioner died without having made a confession, and without the final sacrament, he or she could not receive a religious service or be buried in the blessed part of the cemetery.

The Eucharist (from the Greek *eukharistia*, "action of grace") is a sacrament. It occupies a central place in the liturgy. It's celebrated during the Mass and constitutes its culmination. According to an interpretation from the New Testament, and in particular from the First Epistle of the Corinthians and the synoptic Gospels, it was instituted by Jesus Christ himself during the Last Supper, his final meal with his disciples. Indeed, the evening of his Passion, he distributed bread and wine to his disciples, saying, "This is my body ... and this cup is the new alliance of my blood ... so do this in memory of me." The Eucharist presents several dimensions: the action of grace and praise by God the father; the memory of the Passion, and therefore the death and resurrection of Jesus of Nazareth, who sacrifices himself for human salvation; celebration of the presence of Christ; and the sharing of bread and wine, which, during the consecration, become, for the Catholics, the body and blood of Christ offered in sacrifice on the cross and resurrected.

This latter point constitutes a serious object of dissension among Christians. For Catholics, transubstantiation happens during the ceremony: bread and wine become the body and blood of Christ, and the faithful go to consume it during communion (see the anecdote above of the host falling on the floor). The theological culmination of this doctrine is due to Thomas Aquinas, a thirteenth-century theologian. Despite Thomas Aquinas's subtle explanation inspired by the work of Aristotle, it's difficult to argue that a substance that is the subject on which the attributes of a thing are grafted can become another substance. Indeed, a non-living substance becomes a living one, while retaining its specific characteristics: the host remains white, light, breakable, etc. We find ourselves on the side of metamorphosis, of which the Latin poet Ovid provides several examples. We can understand why so many Christians have not accepted this doctrine. We're in the middle of a fairy tale where the kiss of a princess transforms the frog into a handsome prince.

This remark may come across as blasphemous, but its excessiveness highlights the paradox associated with the doctrine of transubstantiation, especially if one insists that God himself is the object of this phenomenon.

More paradoxical again, it's God himself whom the believer swallows when taking communion. This incorporation of the body and blood of Christ can be described as an act of divine cannibalism. In antiquity, several mythological texts developed the theme of the incorporation of a god. In Hesiod and Orphism, for example. But it was always a god that swallowed another god. In Christianity, it's a human being who incorporates a divine being. Once again, this may seem blasphemous, but in school we were warned never to bite or chew the host, for our mouth would then fill with blood!

By metonymy, the word "eucharist" is still used to designate the consecrated bread and wine that become, respectively, the body and blood of Christ. In a contrary sense, the Eucharist is also traditionally called the "Blessed Sacrament," but this term applies essentially to the consecrated hosts conserved in the tabernacle or exposed in a monstrance by the Eucharistic adoration by the faithful. The Fathers of the Blessed Sacrament were an order that was semi-contemplative and semi-active. They had to assure the adoration of the Blessed Sacrament twenty-four hours a day. In fact, this adoration took place during the night because during the day we had a number of other tasks to attend to. Sometimes I awoke at four in the morning to go to the chapel to genuflect in front of the monstrance on the altar. Most of the time, the young contemplative was sleeping.

Part Two

PARIS

LOUIS-ANDRÉ DORION: In 1968, you found yourself in Paris. The sixties were the great decade for Quebec students leaving for France. This is easily understandable: the decade marked the first great opening abroad, and one naturally turns toward what one thinks one knows best. Today, this is certainly less evident. The United States, England, and even Germany attract them more and more.

LUC BRISSON: For me, the reasons for choosing France were both compelling and circumstantial. Every year, Vianney Décarie invited Paul Ricoeur, who at that time taught at the University of Chicago, to give lectures in our department. I spoke to Paul Ricoeur about my desire to pursue my studies in ancient philosophy. During this conversation, he gave me the address of Clémence Ramnoux, who was his colleague at the University of Nanterre. I wrote to Prof. Ramnoux and she replied very nicely, saying that she agreed to supervise my work. This encounter with Ricoeur was decisive. But beyond that fact, France was a cultural choice. At the time, I knew much more about the history of France or England than that of Canada or the United States. French culture was the only living culture familiar to me, and I passionately wanted to experience what constituted its historic and geographic heart.

LAD: What were your feelings in undertaking this journey?

LB: I don't really know how to express it. I had made the choice to live an intellectual life. And I wanted to live this intellectual life in a French way since I was born in, and had always studied in, this culture. There's another thing that I haven't mentioned until now, but that has always constituted a problem for me since my childhood. It's a question of history, real history, one that carries the traces of the passage of time both on things and on people. In North America, whether one is in Quebec, Canada, or the United States, the absence of cultural traces bothers me. There's only space, but no history. A lot of nature but not much culture. Chateaubriand writes in his *Memoirs from Beyond the Grave*: "Nothing is as sad as the appearance of lakes in Canada. The expanses of the Ocean and the Mediterranean open the routes to nations and their shores that are or were inhabited by numerous and powerful civilized peoples; the lakes of Canada show only the nakedness of their waters that reach barren land, solitudes that separate other solitudes. Shorelines without people oversee seas without ships. You land on deserted shores from empty waves."[1]

Brute nature scares me. I have always seen it as just a fight for survival, from bacteria to the largest mammal. I imagine that even the plants compete. Man has no place in this obscure mix, whose only aim is the perpetuation of one species or another by chance and at any cost. For me, green forests are an expression, not of an infinite calm, but of a constant battle that takes place without mercy. The entire ferocity of nature is here for all to witness. I always wanted to live in a place where the city's buildings and the countryside with its cultivated land provide a permanent and concrete spectacle of a history and culture that go back centuries, if not millennia, and where even people's alimentary and culinary habits are integrated into the landscape.

I have a vital need for depth in history. My interest in ancient Greece and Rome, which is extended by an irresistible attraction to India, is connected to this need. I quenched this thirst notably with translation, which isn't a mechanical exercise for me, but rather an encounter with people who have lived a few thousand years ago and an attempt to establish between them and my contemporaries a relationship of affinity and recognition. As such, these ancient people are talking through me.

LAD: When you left Quebec, you probably doubted that you'd ever return except for short visits.

LB: No, I had the firm intention to return. The University of Quebec had been established, professors would be hired, and I also felt I had contracted a debt to Quebec society. But certain events changed my plans. I arrived in France in October 1968, with doctoral funding for four years. And eventually, a fifth year of funding! But I finished my doctorate in three years. By June 1971 I had written my seven hundred pages and defended my dissertation. When I asked the Canada Council for the Arts for my fourth year of funding, my request was denied: "But, my dear sir, your thesis is finished. The financial support is for writing a thesis and not a year's vacation." Obviously, it wasn't a question of vacation, but simply to prepare my thesis for publication. I nonetheless completed the project despite the setback.

LAD: You need to be exceptionally disciplined to write seven hundred pages in three years.

LB: Indeed! The constraints that come from within must be stronger than those that impinge from without. Someone who isn't expecting an order from anyone to go to work must establish a network of strict habits that rigorously structure his existence. I must say, however, that I always loved to work. I only become aware of who I am by throwing myself into written or oral discourse. Work constitutes for me a good outlet for anxiety. I only attended the lectures of Vernant, Vidal-Naquet, and Detienne at the École Pratique des Hautes Études (EPHE).[2] The rest of the time, I worked at the National Library from nine in the morning until seven in the evening from Monday to Saturday.

LAD: We will return in a moment to the content of the thesis and your research topics. For now, let's talk about your first impression of Paris.

LB: The dream became reality. Until then, I knew the city only through books, radio, or television. Now, I walked on the boulevard Saint-Michel and on the boulevard Saint-Germain. I could visit Notre Dame, the Sainte-Chapelle, the Louvre, etc. Each side street in central Paris had its history, whether happy or bloody: the Saint Bartholomew's Day Massacre, the Commune, etc. I contemplated those great avenues lined with magnificent seven-storey buildings made of stone dating back to the nineteenth century. I now actually lived in a world that, until then, had only been there for me in novels and history books.

Integration into everyday life seemed, on the other hand, extremely difficult, much harder than in North America. At the time, Parisians were much more arrogant than they are today. When you asked a newspaper vendor where to find such and such a monument or such and such a street, he'd answer dryly that he should not be confused with a travel guide. When you couldn't find the money in your pocket to buy a loaf of bread, you'd be yelled at. People appeared to be very aggressive. I should also say that, like most Québécois in France, I felt a sort of inferiority complex when it came to language, not to mention that I personally have absolutely no sense of wit.

Moreover, when it came to services, or standards of cleanliness, hygiene, and safety, these were well below those found in North America. I'll give you an example. I booked a room at Canada House, the dorm for Canadian students at the University of Paris's Cité internationale, in the fourteenth arrondissement.[3] A new wing was under construction, and when I arrived, in October, I found myself in a gutted house. There was no question of turning on the heat; there was no working system. At seven in the morning, foreign labourers began to work. And then, I got a shock: these workers climbed the scaffolding without helmets, wearing only sandals, and in a physical condition that seemed deplorable to me. I found it quite unacceptable. At Coca-Cola, where I worked to pay for my studies, everyone was unionized and followed rules with regard to working hours, health, and safety.

Then I rented another room in a more bourgeois area, the seventeenth arrondissement. It was nice enough but stripped of most comfort. "Turkish" toilets were on the landing, there was only one sink, and we had to ask permission to take a bath on the lower floor in the owner's bathroom (no more than once a week). But the building was well situated, the rent was reasonable, and the owners were friendly. The third year I lived at Norway House, on the same international campus I mentioned before because there was no more room at Canada House.

LAD: From a cultural perspective, how would you describe your first few years in Paris?

LB: I went to a lot of movies. I always loved cinema, but in Quebec, for purely financial reasons, I could only watch films on the television. Watching movies on the TV is of course pretty disappointing because of the size of the screen and the lack of other people. I love being surrounded by others when watching a film. In addition, I really dislike dubbed movies, because I lip-read. And lastly, films shown on television are interspersed with so many commercials that it's unbearable. Paris is the film capital, not only for contemporary film production but also for film history. At the time, small viewing rooms were numerous and inexpensive. When I'd leave the National Library, or again on Sundays, holidays, and even sometimes during the week for lunch, I saw many films, especially American films, those featuring Humphrey Bogart or comedians (Chaplin, the Marx Brothers, Keaton, etc.).

I also visited all the museums of Paris and toured the castles that were easily accessible by public transit. This is how I essentially passed my leisure time.

As for the theatre, I didn't often go because it was much too expensive and too little inventive. It was associated as it were with the restricted traditions of the petite bourgeoisie, in contrast to the cinema at the time (Truffaut, Kubrick, Fellini, Godard, Rossellini, Visconti, Antonioni, Pasolini, Bunuel, Bergman, and others that I forget to mention). Moreover, I did not appreciate the new style of theatre that was trying to stage plays with fashionable revolutionary themes. They were everywhere and I couldn't stand them.

The opera and concerts were also too expensive and too elitist. With the money I had left, I used to travel, although I never really visited France.

LAD: Did you travel a lot?

LB: A lot? I don't know, but the trips I did take turned out to be significant for me. The first took place in the period from December 1969 to January 1970, thus in the middle of my second year. During the summer of 1969, I took advantage of a seat sale to return to Saint-Esprit, where I saw on television the first man landing on the moon. This is an event that will take up but a line in these conversations, but I was deeply moved, and the event continues to haunt my mind and imagination. For the first time in history, man escaped terrestrial gravity and arrived on another planet. Along with the fall of the Berlin Wall in 1989, which shows that nothing in history is irreversible, the moon landing was the most important event I ever witnessed.

But going back to my first trip. I absolutely had to visit the Eastern Bloc countries in order to understand why I wasn't able to accept and repeat the Marxist discourse that was the only one allowed in our intellectual milieu. So I went to Poland and to the Soviet Union, where I experienced the biggest revelation of my life.

At that time, as you know, in the intellectual circles that I frequented, Marxism was regarded as the pinnacle and purpose of humanity. You couldn't say anything anti-Marxist without fear of being labelled extremely right-wing. Some countries in Indochina – Vietnam, Laos, Cambodia – were at war with capitalist America. In Africa, the so-called socialist republics and/or democracies were flourishing. Latin America under the aegis of Cuba was in turmoil. Communist China was shaken by violent movements where excess seemed to have no limits. In the West, all these movements were embraced by intellectuals who prided themselves on their secular outlook. However, orthodox Marxism, militant and intellectual, looked to me just like another face of the Christian religion, even though there's a fundamental difference between Marxism and Christianity. No one had ever returned from the "other world" to tell us whether God, heaven, and hell were real. On the other hand, it was possible to verify what was happening in the communist societies, and I was absolutely committed to this verification. I therefore went to Poland and the Soviet Union.

LAD: Did you have trouble obtaining a visa?

LB: Not at all! Our small group, which included a number of Marxists, was organized by a student association, the UTO, which was also led by convinced Marxists. Moreover, for the Soviet Union, it was a godsend: Western cash and indoctrination went together! Therefore, there was no problem.

Once there, I confirmed that we were in the empire of a great lie! Not only did everyone lie, but everyone knew that everyone else lied, everyone knew that everyone else knew that they lied, and so on. It was a game of mirrors – like those you find in some chateaus or fairs – where the same image is reflected a thousand times. In the USSR, when Brezhnev took power, the deceit only multiplied.

The exchange rate at the airport established parity between the ruble and the dollar. In the street, we exchanged a dollar for seven rubles! To take a taxi, it was better to have a dollar in hand. In certain state stores, there were fabulous displays of goods, but when you wanted to buy the displayed products, there were none in stock. Inside the stores, crowds of people lined up. When asked why, they replied that they didn't know, but that since there was a line, it meant that goods had arrived and that there was, hence, something to buy.

In winter, you could buy swimming trunks, but there were no *ushankas*, those characteristic fur hats. To find what you wanted, you had to go to special stores where you had to pay in dollars. We were staying in student residences at the Patrice Lumumba University in Moscow, a university for foreign students. Patrice Lumumba was the symbol of the struggle for African liberation. In the Belgian Congo, Lumumba was eliminated by Mobutu, who assassinated him before taking power and founding Zaire. In university residences, we would often meet young Africans, most of whom spoke French or English. While Marxist ideology explained that racism arose out of economic reasons, and that the cause was capitalism, these young Black men told us stories of everyday racism, which seemed worse than what we knew in Europe or North America.

Finally, you were forbidden to leave Moscow, forbidden to go to the monasteries that still stood in Sergiev Posad (at the time, Zagorsk). To go to Leningrad, we had to take the night train so that nothing could be seen. The guides were supposed to know the official slogans by heart, but they recited them incorrectly and without conviction. This was all well-known, of course, but to experience this directly and, especially, to imagine that the intellectual elite of the Western countries, the intelligent, educated, and well-travelled elites, were proposing such a lie as a model – didn't they speak of a "third" road in France? – left me speechless.

Deception made giving meaning to the everyday difficult since it made reality too random, too elusive. That the intellectual elite in France propagated this lie despite being well aware of what was happening there from André Gide's *Return from the USSR* (1936) – that was for me like receiving an electric shock. I became from then on totally incredulous at what was being said in France about the countries of Eastern Europe.

That being said, I found the Russian people admirable and very much like us. I now realized that the classical music played over the radio in Quebec was very often Russian. We visited the famous Hermitage Museum in Leningrad. The old Leningrad was very touching, with its pastel-coloured Italian palaces that on summer days were reflected in the water of the canals. We were there at the beginning of January. At this latitude, the sun only lights the city for a few hours a day. The rest of the time, it was dusk, but somehow the snow made it luminous. And then something distressed me deeply, the cemeteries. For the sake of propaganda, they took us to visit those victims of the Second World War who are buried near Leningrad. It's unforgettable. Unforgettable.

LAD: Why for propaganda?

LB: To show us the atrocities committed by the Germans. But the effect was really a thousand times more potent than what the guides intended. They didn't even need to speak. It was enough to see graves where dozens of corpses were stacked. These common graves seemed to go on for infinity. In Leningrad, commemorative plaques were everywhere: "Here, two hundred and fifty people were massacred on this day at this time." At the museum, we were shown paintings at which a German soldier had intentionally shot. This really upset me. We were taken there for propaganda reasons, but the propaganda was just a ridiculous mask compared to the screaming face of reality.

In Poland, the Soviet Union's satellite, traces of occupation were obvious and endless. I only saw Warsaw. At the end of the war, the Soviets, who were on the other side of the Vistula, allowed the Germans to destroy the city to get rid of insurgent nationalists. At the time, the Poles had rebuilt the downtown with some success. However, the new city architecture was atrocious, especially crushed by this monstrous, monumental, and grotesque Palace of Culture and Science. One wonders how the dream of a political utopia could lead to such nightmares in architecture.

LAD: Your fears were reinforced?

LB: Yes, they were, but I was unhappy, because Marxism was considered to be scientific in contrast to religious superstition. Because I am a Platonist, I cannot flout reason. I think it suffices that man knows the good in order to do it. The Marxist claim or "scientific" claim appears to me to be an absurdity given everyday experience. But I do think that those who devote their lives to thought can rationally determine where the good resides, and in so doing, are able to realize/achieve it.

Now, the intellectuals have in the century that is now closing [i.e., the twentieth century] held positions and supported regimes that caused millions of deaths, not to mention the suffering and the destruction. Why is this the case? Should we not admit, as the Stoics taught us, that even reason can be perverted by the passions, and thus that there's nothing in man that is naturally good and inherently reasonable, including, and especially, reason itself? Rather, I think that far too often we cover what is shameful with a cloak of "reason."

LAD: In June 1970, the year you visited Eastern Europe, you also visited India.

LB: It was monsoon season. I wondered by what miracle we managed to land the plane right in the middle of the storm. On the runway, there were several inches of water, and it was necessary to remove your shoes. We visited northern India – Bombay, Delhi, Benares, Srinagar, and Nepal. It was very stressful when it came to issues of safety and comfort, but on the human level it was quite extraordinary.

It was the time when, after the Beatles in 1968, the hippies went to India to smoke marijuana and hashish. I was very attracted by the strange mixture of religion and socio-political structure that had hardly evolved in two thousand years. I was surprised to see a traditional social organization based on a rigid hierarchy in an enormous continent that was a practising democracy and industrializing despite its poverty and all kinds of other problems. Here yet again I was plunged into the past, much more profoundly than in Europe, where it's hard to go further back than the Middle Ages. And I wanted to see this land where Sanskrit continued to be spoken by several million literate people.

As a foreigner in India, you're immediately confronted with the structure of the caste system – that is, groups that define themselves by rank in a system organized around purity (from *castus*, a Latin term used by Portuguese missionaries to describe the social organization). Eating habits, social relations, everything is determined by the caste to which one belongs. That said, we must also take into account the Muslims, Sikhs, Buddhists, Jains, and many other social and religious groups that abound in this reservoir of a billion human inhabitants. I was fascinated by the Hindu religion, where everyday religious practices and norms are embodied in society, family, work, and relationships with others. At the same time, Hinduism also offers the possibility of an experience that transcends all these, in which all social life is an illusion compared to the Absolute – an experience that allows the individual freedom from material bonds and contingencies. Such an attitude is very surprising and corresponds in part to what one can imagine of certain aspects of Greek and Roman religion; it constitutes a powerful antidote against the monotheistic religions founded on books and oriented toward individual salvation, that is, personal immortality.

LAD: For many Westerners, no doubt – for me anyway – India represents absolute otherness.

LB: Not for me. And I'm not going to make any apology for either the poverty or the Hindu religion or Buddhism. In India, living conditions are appalling for tens of millions of people: the selling of infants, child labour, prostitution, the use of all kinds of handicapped beggars to obtain money, corruption at all levels, and so on.

From what I remember, the suburbs of Bombay greeted the morning smelling of the sewage. The outskirts of Delhi and other major conurbations were not much better. But then in Benares, I saw the funeral pyres on the banks beside the muddy waters of the Ganges. Entire families watched the bodies being burned, and they did not seem in the least dismayed. In this I encountered something deeply human, truly natural.

On one of these mornings, with the glow of the funeral pyres shining through the mist, I'd love to have my ashes scattered in the Ganges – with no hope of reincarnation, of course.

In our own society, death constitutes a vanishing point. We avoid talking about it, and yet, by its very absence, it dictates much of our behaviour, in particular the actions of those who propose or impose a religion.

Where is a society going that can't look death in the face and consider it as a normal phenomenon, necessary and natural? That aims to prolong life even under the most deplorable conditions? That puts an end to humanity itself?

I suspect that whoever believes in reincarnation is led to respect nature as he respects the human species; for him, the animal world is a part of the human species.

LAD: You also visited Egypt, another country with a deep history.

LB: Yes, in January 1971. It was the last trip that I took before my doctoral examination. It was several years after the Six-Day War – June 1967. Nasser was in power, and the United Arab Republic, the result of the union of Syria and Egypt, was on its last legs. The Soviets, who were completing the construction of the Aswan Dam, were everywhere. The highways were often closed because the fighter-bombers were using them to land. Given the situation, hotels rented luxurious rooms for hardly anything. This was the Egypt of Nassar who took Gaddhafi (then unknown) in his arms and shook his hand.

I travelled from Beirut with an inspector (and her daughter) for the French secondary school system. It was then that I heard, for the first time, about the atrocious civil war in Lebanon that was approaching. During this trip, I was amazed not only by ancient Egypt but also by the modern Egyptians, who lived with dignity in the difficult conditions caused by the lost war; they remained calm, although one would imagine them as fanatical and thirsty for revenge. It was a Muslim country, but at the time women were not veiled. In fact, some young women were dressed in jeans. I hope that Egypt will one day overcome the problems that hold it back.

At the time, there were virtually no tourists. There were only a handful of us visiting the Temple of Philae, the Colossus of Abu Simbel, the Valley of Kings, the Valley of Queens, the Valley of the Artisans at Luxor, the Temple of Karnak, and all the other wonderful places of which people so often speak. In Cairo, accompanied by a police officer, we even visited the Jewish ghetto and its synagogue.

LAD: Before we get back to Plato, to philosophy, and to your work, one last question about the Parisian intellectual climate. Your doctoral years correspond to a period of great upheaval in Paris.

LB: Althusser had already written *For Marx* (1965), *Reading Capital* (1965), and *Lenin and Philosophy* (1969), and his influence was still very strong at the École Normale Supérieure, where he both taught and lived.[4] Lacan's *Writings* was published in 1966 and the publication of his *Seminars* followed. The fervour he generated was almost ridiculous. An entire nebula of "intellectuals" gravitated around this Freudian-Marxist or Marxist-Freudian centre: Philippe Sollers, Julia Kristeva, and the collaborators of *Tel Quel*, including Barthes, who published *The Empire of Signs* in 1970. Lyotard tried to summarize all of this in *Discourse, Figure* (1971). Deleuze reflected on representation in *Difference and Repetition* (1968) and *The Logic of Sense* (1969). Derrida was interested in the relationship between writing, ethnocentrism, and logocentrism in *Grammatology* (1967), *Writing and Difference* (1967), *Speech and Phenomena* (1967), which were then still much discussed.

I stayed completely away from this intellectual hotbed. The only exception remains Foucault, for whom I had and continue to have a genuine interest and admiration: *The History of Madness in the Classical Age* (1961), *Words and Things* (1966), and *The Archaeology of Knowledge* (1969) are important works for me. Everything else seemed to be a synthesis of Marxist propaganda and psychoanalysis of the third or fourth rate, a hastily improvised tinkering to respond to what was fashionable. The only thing holding it together, in defiance of any connection with reality, was flashy rhetoric in the service of nimble intellectual gymnastics.

Philosophy, completely impregnated with rhetoric, was no longer distinguishable from literature, and it could be likened to these two gems of French culture: haute couture and haute cuisine. The same splendour, the same brilliance, but also the same futility, the same vanity. The question is whether philosophy can continue to ape high culture.

Fortunately, Clémence Ramnoux introduced me to two authors who have greatly influenced me: George Dumézil and Émile Benveniste. She had been a pupil of Dumézil in the fifties at the EPHE, a relationship she acknowledges in the preface to *Le grand roi d'Irlande*, a collection of stories, poems, and legends of Ireland. Dumézil was a specialist in a multitude of Indo-European languages (Sanskrit, Avestic, Greek, Latin, Celtic, languages from different countries in the Southwest of what was then the Soviet empire, and so on).[5] He wanted to show that Indo-European mythology was, mainly, governed by an ideological structure, and served one of three functions reflecting the world view of the Indo-Europeans: juridical and religious sovereignty, military power, and material prosperity. It's easy to understand the interest of such a process for the study of ancient Greece. In traditional Greek mythology, there remains almost nothing of this tripartition. Curiously, the only theoretical work that promotes this ideology of social organization is Plato's *Republic*.

Émile Benveniste began his career in 1929 as a philologist and an Iranist. His linguistic studies covered the entire Indo-European realm. He very much inspired Dumézil. He's the only linguist of this century known to have excelled in comparative grammar as well as general linguistics and who was able to open a dialogue with philosophy, notably in a 1958 article that questions the linguistic origins of Aristotle's categories. Clémence Ramnoux had us read and do a commentary on the text.

Reading Dumézil and Benveniste nourished my interest in mythology and led me to India and to Sanskrit, which I studied for eight years, from 1976 to 1984, taking two courses per week. I studied Sanskrit for two reasons: in order to pursue studies in the tripartite function, and to try to better understand Greek and Latin grammar. In both cases it was well worth the effort. If I wasn't held back by my neurosurgery in 1985, I'd have most certainly continued.

LAD: Is it true you no longer study Sanskrit today?

LB: Yes, for personal reasons. In 1984, I had a serious neurological surgery that interrupted my work and my research. Also, I was short on time. If these things hadn't happened, I'd have certainly translated certain chapters of the Ramayana for the Pléiade edition. The abandonment of this area of research was truly heartbreaking for me.

LAD: But you didn't stop your research on tripartition?

LB: No. I continued to write from time to time on the topic, notably when I was working on the subject in the context of the *Republic*, where the social group is divided into three functional groups: producers (farmers and artisans), guardians (soldiers), and leaders (philosophers). The tests to which the future guardians are subjected represent a tripartite function similar to what we find in medicine: medicine practised through medication (third group), through the knife (the second group), and through incantations (the first group). The examples are, in fact, numerous.

Perhaps Plato's views on social and political organization were inspired by his visits to certain cities in southern Italy and Sicily around the time he wrote the *Republic*. Cities with Pythagorean influence were colonies of the Dorians, who were the most traditional and conservative group of the Greek world, whereas Ionia and Attica, from which we have the essential texts of Greek literature, evolved more quickly. This explains why the traditional mythology of ancient Greece conserves so few traces of functional tripartition even though Plato writes the only theoretical account on the theme in the Indo-European world.

LAD: Now we've gone too far. Let's move back a bit. You didn't have any difficulty getting your thesis project on the *Timaeus* approved by Professor Ramnoux?

LB: No. She pursued the same sort of work with regard to the Presocratics. She alternated her research between Heraclitus, Parmenides, and Greek mythology – that is, Hesiod and the Homeric Hymns that we encounter in *La Nuit et les enfants de la Nuit* (Night and the children of night) and *Mythologie ou la famille olympienne* (Mythology or the Olympian family). I was required to read these as well for my thesis. That being said, my intellectual background was quite different from hers. I wasn't interested at all in psychoanalysis, and I didn't think highly of Gaston Bachelard, whom she adored through her personal connection. Also, her perspective was much more phenomenological than my own; it was more literary and poetic. She gave the impression of wanting to enter into the game, to participate in the events; I always remained outside the texts, considered as objects, and always privileged the differences instead of resemblances. She was aware of my reasoning from the beginning. I still remember the end of those afternoons when I'd arrive at the avenue de Breteuil to discuss a chapter that she'd already have in her hands. It was on the top floor, at the end of a badly lit hallway. Professor Ramnoux read everything I brought to her very quickly and her remarks were always insightful.

Clémence Ramnoux was a remarkable person. She was born in 1905 and trained at the École Normale Supérieure in 1927, where she became friends with Simone Pétrement and Simone Weil.[6] These are the first three women in France who were both students at the École Normale Supérieure and received the aggregation.[7] She taught philosophy at a high school until 1958, at which time she joined the university after having defended her *doctorat d'état*. Her main thesis was on Heraclitus, and her complimentary thesis, *La Nuit et les enfants de la Nuit*, was on Greek mythology. Between 1958 and 1963, she taught at the University of Algiers and in 1965 at Nanterre. She stayed there until 1975. She lived through many important historical events – the Second World War, which she mentions in her preface to her dissertation on Heraclitus, the war in Algeria, where she was involved in the closing of the Faculty of Philosophy, and the events of May 1968. She was a woman with a real political sense, a Gaullist committed to solving problems in Nanterre. At the time, she acted on behalf of the minister of education, advocating for the interests of students and teachers. At our first encounter, she asked me never to visit her in Nanterre.

LAD: Why? The events in May had pretty much petered out.

LB: Yes, but in taking the train to Saint-Lazare station, you had to get off at Nanterre La-Folie. The name "La Folie" designated a luxurious country house of the type that rich people built in the Parisian suburbs, like La Folie Méricourt. But everyone interpreted the phrase as "Crazy Nanterre." The university was built on a decommissioned military site, which still retained its high concrete walls. It was bordered by a real slum – shacks made of recycled sheet metal and corrugated cardboard. When you stepped off the train, the first thing you saw was a semicircle of blue riot police buses. On each side of the railway, there were the most amazing, fragile buildings. Finally, you saw muddy fields, devoid of trees and grass. Fights broke out regularly in academic buildings, tables and chairs were thrown through the windows. Riot police would arrive, they'd stabilize the situation for a moment, and then leave. If a foreigner like myself was arrested during one of these disruptions, he was put on a plane and removed immediately.

Ramnoux thus suggested two alternatives: first, she invited me to the seminar she organized on Saturday mornings in the cellars of the Sorbonne (called the "Indians"), which her doctoral students attended; second, she suggested that I take courses at the EPHE, because she admired the work of Pierre Vidal-Naquet, Marcel Detienne, and Jean-Pierre Vernant. At the time, they all taught at the EPHE, which was, comparatively speaking, a very quiet environment. The sixth section of the school was housed in a magnificent mansion in the seventh arrondissement on rue de Varenne. It was not necessary to prepare a thesis to attend the EPHE. To obtain a student card, it sufficed to show that you attended a certain number of classes by signing a school register during each seminar. I treasure this card as one of my most important keepsakes.

LAD: You therefore didn't yet know Jean-Pierre Vernant, Pierre Vidal-Naquet, and Marcel Detienne?

LB: No. As Jean-Pierre Vernant was living in the suburbs, Clémence Ramnoux suggested I first meet Pierre Vidal-Naquet, who lived on rue du Cherche-Midi in the sixth arrondissement, in the heart of Paris.

LAD: And how did this first meeting go?

LB: We were surprised by one another. Pierre Vidal-Naquet has usually a scruffy look, except when he appeared in court as a witness or as an accused! At this time, his political convictions and his work as a journalist made him an active Trotskyite militant. His appearance and impassioned behaviour, mixed with uncommon intelligence, immense generosity, and an incredible aggressiveness, baffled me. He had never encountered a pure Quebecer before me, and he could not understand how a young man who spoke French with such an accent could be interested in Plato and ancient Greece. Mostly, he was fascinated by my rejection of the dogmas of the Catholic Church, and both amused and irritated at the same time when I compared the Catholic dogmas and attitudes to the slogans and jargon of the Communists. Of course, he understood my rejection of orthodoxy, but he hardly liked me speaking ill of the European Left.

LAD: What was your relationship like?

LB: It has always been passionate. He was delighted to see me attend and even participate in his seminar, but he could hardly bear my opposition, or even the reservations that I expressed subtly. The slightest deviation provoked confrontation that was often intense. In spite of this, we stayed very attached to one another, even though we rarely see each other now [Vidal-Naquet died in 2006]. I can say that Pierre Vidal-Naquet is the most unbearable man I have ever met, but the most indispensable. I wouldn't be the same if I hadn't met him, if I didn't spend time with him. Also, the personal tragedy that he lived as a child, persecuted as a Jew from a family fully assimilated, which is elucidated in his *Mémoires*, helped me understand and share the pain and experience of those who remain outside of a culture they admire and serve. The Jewish experience is the paradigm of the living experience in France, by any first-generation "foreigner," including myself.

LAD: How did the first few courses go?

LB: At the time – that is, after the student revolt of May 1968 – there were seminars but no classes. Of course, in practice, this means nothing! So I went to the seminars that Clémence Ramnoux conducted on Saturday mornings in the cellars of the Sorbonne. At the first meeting, she introduced me to the other students in attendance, some of whom were considerably older than me and who were all students at the École Normale Supérieure, the elite of the university, who were all destined for brilliant careers even if not high-paying ones. Mme Ramnoux asked me to make the first presentation, and I couldn't refuse. So I prepared a presentation on the famous passage from the *Timaeus* (35a–b), which describes the composition of the world soul by the Demiurge. And quite naturally, during my presentation of the text, translation, and commentary, I mostly talked about Cornford, an Englishman, and Cherniss, an American, who had invited Mme Ramnoux to pass a semester at the Institute for Advanced Studies at Princeton. Hence, the first question was, "Why didn't you mention Léon Robin or Jean Wahl?" It was then that I realized how insular the French university had become.[8] But I must confess that this was not the case for the EPHE, which, with celebrities such as Claude Lévi-Strauss, Raymond Aron, Roland Barthes, and others, was very open-minded. Anyway, the discussion ended on a subtle but insistent proposal: when you return to your fields of snow in Quebec, don't forget to mention the good authors.[9]

This experience of cultural arrogance forced me to re-evaluate myself. Very quickly, I realized that, with regard to Greek and Latin, the languages in which one reads the philosophical works of antiquity, I was much better prepared than those around me. Most had only two or three years of Greek. They could at best check the French translation. Very few knew English well, which cut out two-thirds of the secondary literature on any subject. Finally, while I had thought that all French people spoke German fluently, I realized that this was not the case, though there were a few rare exceptions. I gained confidence knowing I had studied Greek and Latin for more than ten years, English was a natural language, and I got along well in German.

The only area where I felt unease was in the handling of spoken language: the French spoken by others was more flowing, richer, and better structured. That being said, after spending some years in France, one comes to realize that this facility is often illusory, in large part due to the fact that, more often than the Québécois, the French resort to idiomatic expressions and mannerisms, which certain comedians, especially Raymond Devos, mock in a fantastic way. Speech is much more cultivated in France, and this is seen in the spirit of competition that prevails in both the professional and the academic worlds. In France any position or promotion is subject to competition. And, in the context of a competition, the quality of one's oral expression plays a determining role, and even modifies to some extent the written expression. The French are thus trained from an early age in a more precise, clear, and orderly elocution. But this virtue also has its dangerous points, and for me anyway, it's just annoying. As in Byzantium, where, they say, it was impossible to buy a fish without getting into a theological discussion, so it's hardly an exaggeration to say that in France it's difficult to buy bread or order a coffee without getting into verbal sparring. Sometimes this becomes burdensome and even ridiculous. In my area, it's often a handicap. I'd even say that this facility, this pleasure one takes in speaking and writing, has destroyed a good part of French culture. Since I've been dealing with international relations, I often hear, during talks given by the French, remarks delivered in a low voice, such as "rhetorical" or *viel Rhetorik*. The desire to shine and be seduced by words leads, more often than not, to making verbal facility the first priority and to considering the transmission of information, the understanding of a text, the expression of a profound thought or powerful sentiment, to be secondary.

LAD: Returning to your doctoral dissertation, did you discuss who would make up your thesis committee and panel with Professor Ramnoux?

LB: Yes, but the discussion didn't take very long. Ramnoux wanted Vernant and Vidal-Naquet to be on the panel, but Vernant wasn't available. She also considered getting me elected to the Centre national de la recherche scientifique (CNRS), if even on a temporary basis. She thought the only other group at the CNRS I could get elected to, and the only other person who could participate in the committee, was Jean Pépin, who also worked on ancient cosmology. This explains why Jean Pépin, whom I also knew from elsewhere, was a member of my committee.

LAD: Your election to the CNRS was therefore not accidental?

LB: No. Mme Ramnoux was very uncomfortable, as she explained at the end of the oral examination. She thought that my thesis didn't correspond to a French *doctorat de troisième* cycle. That's why she tried to transform my thesis into a *doctorat d'état*. The election at the CNRS would provide me with the time to revise it accordingly.[10]

In France, at the time, there were three types of doctorates. A university doctorate was purely honorary; it was completed in a year or two but didn't allow you any access to a teaching position. The postgraduate (or third cycle) doctorate was completed in four years, giving one the right to teach in a high school or as an assistant in a university. In principle, it was the equivalent of a PhD, but was very often considered, at least in France, as only slightly more advanced than a master's thesis, insofar as it was only the prelude to a real doctorate, a state doctorate. A state doctorate was the equivalent of a "masterpiece" for the craftsmen of the Middle Ages. It was the only degree that granted one access to a university career. It was completed over a long period (five years minimum, and between fifteen and twenty years in general) under a supervisor who had reached the age of fifty. Throughout this period, one was under the leadership of that supervisor, and, as an unwritten rule, was forbidden to publish anything other than what was reported to the supervisor. In principle, a state doctorate included two doctoral theses: a main thesis of several hundred pages, and a less ambitious complementary thesis. Both theses had to be published before the defence. By 1968, only the main thesis was necessary, but it became, however, more and more voluminous. It wasn't unusual for a thesis to comprise a thousand pages. It's obvious that for a foreigner like me, it was impossible to think of taking on anything more than a doctorate of the *troisième* (or third) cycle. Mme Ramnoux tried every means to change my registration from a *troisième*-cycle doctorate to a state one. If the application had been accepted, I could have completed a state doctoral thesis by 1973. But the Ministry of Education and the Department of Doctoral Studies from the University of Nanterre – which, it must be said, conscientiously fulfilled their tasks – did not agree to Mme Ramnoux's request.

LAD: How did the defence go?

LB: It took place in Nanterre, a place I had rarely visited. There were maybe seven or eight people in the room (and I'll note in passing that oral examinations are open to the public). It was a nice day. The weather was lovely, but, more important, there was no picketing or student violence. The door of the tiny room where the oral examination took place was left open because it was so hot. Jean Pépin was the first to speak. Clémence Ramnoux spoke at the end, but she said very little because, as soon as Pierre Vidal-Naquet spoke, everything took off.

Things were not going too badly, at least until he brought up my interpretation of the cosmological myth of the *Statesman* (268–74e), which had already raised lively discussions in his own seminars, and on which he also wrote an article that was very critical of my view.

The discussion grew heated. We were speaking so loudly that the students who passed by in the hallways actually came in to see what was happening. The room filled up quickly, and pretty soon the entire hallway was blocked. Everyone wanted to attend a thesis defence where everyone yelled at each other! Despite the events of May 1968, the students still showed considerable respect and deference toward professors. After about a half hour of animated discussions, Ramnoux, who was delighted, took the opportunity to say that since the public attendance was so high and because circulation in the hallways was actually becoming difficult, she would restrict her remarks to just five minutes. The deliberation ended quickly.

In 1985, I defended my *doctorat d'état*, based on my research publications, in rather fantastic circumstances. My oral examination again took place at Nanterre. The day it was to occur coincided once again with another of those "wildcat" strikes that shut down Parisian public transport, without notification and leaving only minimal service. Not only was the subway not running, but the streets were paralyzed with traffic. Getting to Nanterre required enormous patience and unrivalled imagination. The examination finally began even though certain members of the committee had not yet arrived. Such was the case with Pierre Vidal-Naquet, who arrived well after the start. His entrance was remarkable.

He was infuriated with Hélène Ioannidi, my collaborator for the Platonic bibliography, who was present in the room, because she didn't pick him up in the taxi! Out of all the interventions from the members of the jury, it was the comments from Vidal-Naquet that made, once again, the greatest impression on me. He made the harshest criticisms, but he was the one who gave my work the most sincere and heartfelt praise.

TRANSLATIONS AND BIBLIOGRAPHIES

LAD: When we look at the totality of your research in Greek philosophy since 1974, we see that there were several themes that have remained constant: the absence of Aristotle and the omnipresence of Plato and Platonism, a sustained interest in everything that related to myth and to the relation between myth and philosophy. If you had to, what would you say was the Ariadne's clue, the main theme, that guided your work since 1974?

LB: From the perspective of civil society, one could define me as a historian of philosophy whose main interests lie in Plato and Platonism. But I think that this doesn't quite capture the reality, for the following two reasons.

The first is that I believe that human beings are defined by what they do, in the largest sense of that term. An expertise that cannot be an object of study does not have enough existence to become an object of either thought or discourse.[11] Thought objectified in speech remains the only way for a human being to transmit and communicate information.

The second reason relates to the topics under consideration. The work that I pursued in whatever domain was always anchored in my personal experience.[12] More precisely, I wanted to respond to the following question: Given that tradition imposes boundaries, which allow a community to self-identify and to self-define, how is it that an individual or a group can come to change tradition in the name of an intellectual demand that we have called, since Plato, "philosophy"?[13] It's the magnitude of this questioning of tradition by reason that I never ceased to challenge, ever since my childhood and adolescence in a Quebec shaken by a crisis that led it to question its ties to Catholicism.

But to respond to your question more concretely, my work on the history of philosophy began with my thesis on the *Timaeus* and continued with the Plato bibliography, for which I brought out an updated volume once every five years (see below), by translations of Plato's dialogues, and by writing several chapters of a history of Greek philosophy.

I began with the French translation of Plato's works in the collection of GF [Garnier-Flammarion] paperbacks by Flammarion. In this collection, I translated the *Letters*, the *Phaedrus*, the *Timaeus*, the *Critias*, the *Parmenides*, the *Crito*, and the *Apology*. I completed the translation of the *Symposium* in 1999, of the *Statesman* and the *Laws* (with Jean-François Pradeau) in 2006, and of the *Écrits attributés à Platon*, that is, the works of Plato that are disputed, in 2014. All of these translations are annotated and prefaced with an introduction. I was also the general editor for Flammarion of the complete works of Plato in one volume in 2008.

The translation of the *Symposium* deeply affected me, and not only because the dialogue is very beautiful. It was also because my passion for the work of Plato really took off when I first read Alcibiades's praise of Socrates in that dialogue. That was around thirty-five years ago, when I was studying at the Terrebonne seminary.

The GF collection has been a great success, for it endeavours to bring together excellent scholarship with a low selling price. The books sell thousands of copies every year. For example, thirty-five thousand copies of the *Apology* and *Crito* sold in the first year of publication (1997), and since then they have sold over five hundred thousand copies. A student could now have a first-rate edition of these two dialogues for just twenty French francs (about five dollars today).

The beginning was difficult, however. Initially, some tried to dissuade me from taking on this project, claiming that it would ruin my scholarly career if I were to immediately publish paperback editions. At the time, it was unthinkable to publish research in paperback form. But the times have changed, for now you find in the GF series translations of ancient texts written not only in Greek and Latin but also in Arabic and Sanskrit, and so on. The first title, the *Letters*, appeared in 1987. I started the translation immediately after my neurological operation in 1984, when I was practically still in bed. At the time, my head was spinning because of equilibrium problems that made me constantly nauseated.

LAD: What was the need that sparked these new translations? How did you conceive of your work as translator?

LB: Let me make one preliminary remark. I think that the translations of Plato really transformed people's thoughts about paperbacks in France. Before then, paperbacks were a kind of inferior product. Writers, scholars, and historians wrote books, and if a book achieved success, some years later, a paperback copy was made available. But this meant the book had to be reprinted. The new translations of Plato were original, published for the first time. It was Louis Audibert who asked us, Monique Canto and myself, to start with Plato. He drew his inspiration essentially from the English Penguin series.

I accepted this project for another reason, both practical and monetary. When we teach at a university, we hesitate to ask students to purchase books that are really too expensive. I was familiar with this problem when I was at the University of Montreal, where

I deprived myself of meals to buy books, and notably, the two volumes of the complete works of Plato in the Pléiade series, which were very expensive.

On top of these practical reasons, there were cultural reasons. The necessity of a new translation of Plato in a paperback edition also responded to a cultural need that was more profound than it appears. You know very well yourself, since you teach, that students have an ever greater difficulty understanding the outdated French translations of Plato. First of all, they encounter a language problem. The French of the early twentieth century is often very difficult for contemporary students to understand. Even Léon Robin's excellent translation often becomes incomprehensible if one tries to translate it directly back into Ancient Greek. Moreover, contemporary students have not taken classical studies. Everything, therefore, must be explained to them. You can no longer, as before, propose a translation preceded by a short introduction and with minimal notes.

Finally, the translations of Plato published by Les Belles Lettres in the first half of the twentieth century and those published by Léon Robin in the Pléiade edition in 1950 were entirely French, that is, foreign scholarship was hardly cited. After the Second World War, research on Plato exploded in the Anglo-Saxon world, and that had to be taken into consideration. Finally, society changed. Let me give you an example. Before, we read the *Symposium* and *Phaedrus* by focusing on the metaphysical components, and the detailed and suggestive sections relating to homosexuality in Plato's Athens were also interpreted in this way. In other words, the clear expression of a male's desire for another male was systematically interpreted in a metaphorical fashion, that is, in terms of the seduction of one soul for another within the framework relative to education or, again, in terms of the impulse that draws the soul from the sensible toward the intelligible and the spiritual. Léon Robin, who, by the way, translated the *Symposium* and *Phaedrus* at least twice, published an excellent book on this subject in 1908, *La théorie platonicienne de l'amour*. And in 1926, Auguste Diès, who gave us excellent translations of other works of Plato, expresses in a very allusive way his frustration in trying to reduce Greek homosexuality to a simple literary or metaphorical mode when he writes in *Autour de Platon*, "It's only if it were possible to close our eyes to the undeniable sense of certain texts that we'd have no trouble seeing in the eroticism of the 5th and 4th centuries BCE nothing more than a literary mode and use of the metaphor."[14] In reading the introductions to my translations, even a superficial reader can't help but notice that my texts, which were inspired by the studies of Foucault, Dover, Bethe, and Halperin, grant an essential place to the social, ethical, psychological, and even physiological aspects of homosexuality in ancient Greece.[15] So, there were at least four good reasons to propose a new translation of the complete works of Plato.

LAD: The Plato bibliography that you have regularly published in the German review *Lustrum* (in collaboration with Hélène Ioannidi) since 1977 is another aspect of your work, obviously less recognized but nonetheless just as important. You took over for Harold Cherniss, a well-known American Plato scholar and Princeton professor who had taken on this project in the 1950s. When you took over his position, you were still a relatively unknown young doctorate. How did you gain the confidence of Cherniss and the German editor?

LB: It was Vianney Décarie who made me aware of Cherniss's bibliographic work on Plato. He later gave me his address at the Institute for Advanced Studies at Princeton. I very much admired the two volumes Cherniss published in *Lustrum*. I made use of and added to them for the bibliography of my thesis on the *Timaeus* published in 1974, and also for the bibliography I did for my state doctorate and my research project on the *Parmenides* filed with the CNRS in 1973. It was while working with these partial bibliographies that the idea to take on Cherniss's project came to me. I started this work alone, but after a few years Pierre Vidal-Naquet agreed that Hélène Ioannidi should work with me on this project. Mme Ioannidi, a Greek citizen who came to France as a political refugee to escape the Dictatorship of the Colonels (she was Marxist), was a very cultured lady but a tormented soul. Shortly after her return to Greece, after her retirement, she met a tragic end. Moreover, one shouldn't think that bibliographic work is purely mechanical, that it's nothing more than collecting information. I always conceived of a bibliographer as a cartographer who creates a tool for researchers or students so they can find what they're looking for quickly, and without overlooking anything important. Moreover, an exhaustive bibliography allows you to see quickly in which reading context and in which interpretative current a given article or book is situated. You get there through meta-philosophical considerations on the nature or the validity of such and such an interpretation in relation to another.

LAD: It really is the work of a monk, since you have to make an inventory of everything that's been published on Plato from around the world. How many publications are there on Plato each year?

LB: When I started, there were about three hundred per year. Now, there are around three hundred and fifty. I just completed *Plato 1990–1995*, and since 1958, I've collected about ten thousand titles (that was till 1999).[16]

LAD: I know for myself that your bibliographic work is an absolutely indispensable resource. I say this all the more willingly in that the monastic work of the bibliographer is not appreciated for its true value. I often meet academics who have a condescending, if not a contemptuous, attitude toward their colleagues who "waste time" doing bibliographies. Of course, this condescension is hypocritical, since they know full well that once these bibliographies are published, they will save them valuable time.

LB: The principal reason, I think, that specialized bibliographies are becoming more and more necessary is because, in our field, knowledge is accumulating rather than being abolished. The research dynamic in the history of philosophy is not at all that which prevails in the exact sciences, where research that is being done constantly renders obsolete results obtained a few years or even a few months prior. In the scientific realm, there's an accelerated process that constantly renders prior research obsolete. But this is not at all the case in the history of philosophy, where recent interpretations do not necessarily invalidate the exegesis proposed by a previous scholar, whether contemporary or not, and where interpretations tend to accumulate rather than replace one another. This is why it's becoming more and more difficult to explore the main interpretations of a text, and sometimes even a short passage of a text.

In an area like ours, where the corpus we deal with is closed – we will probably never discover new works by Plato or Aristotle – do you not think there are too many publications?

LAD: Far too many! We publish for two reasons. The first is for research and scientific purposes: we believe we have something new to say. The second is for professional reasons – that is, we publish with the aim of getting a position or a promotion. Nothing prevents these reasons from overlapping, but it's clear that this is not always the case!

LB: Isn't it the case that far too often we read studies that completely ignore previous work and thus repeat things that were already said or, worse again, make the same errors that have been resolved a long time ago – errors that would not be repeated if one had taken the time to read what was written before?

A bibliography like my own should enable the avoidance of this kind of waste of time and error. Contrary to Cherniss, however, I don't make any value judgments. But by reading my commentaries, one can immediately see if the work is valuable or not.

LAD: Now we come to your historical and exegetical work. You recently collaborated on a broad overview of the history of Greek philosophy.[17]

LB: Yes, I'm very happy about my work on this project. It's a collective project since Jonathan Barnes, Gregory Vlastos, Monique Canto, and Jacques Brunschwig have also contributed to the compilation of the work.

Our objective was to offer a synthesis that could replace Émile Bréhier's *History of Greek Philosophy*, the first edition of which appeared in 1926. It wasn't easy. But, I believe, the result is interesting. It constitutes a work of almost nine hundred pages, and it covers a broad span of time since it begins with Thales (the sixth century BCE) and ends with Plethon (fifteenth century AD).

LAD: What exactly was your contribution to this project?

LB: I wrote five parts: first, on the Sophists, who were opposed to Socrates; second, on the Socratics, that is, the philosophers in Socrates's circle, who set in motion a number of more or less distinct philosophical currents: the Cynics, the Cyrenaics, and Megarics; third, on Platonism, Middle Platonism, and Neoplatonism, and the primary targets of their respective philosophical positions, including Aristotle, the Stoics, and

Christian heterodoxy; fourth, on the ambiguous relation maintained between the church fathers and Greek philosophy, an attitude that alternated between conciliation and rejection; fifth, on the Byzantine world, whose faithfulness to the pagan tradition explains in large part the richness of our heritage in the area of ancient philosophy.

LAD: What inspired you to take on this immense project?

LB: Strange feelings, connected with the culmination of a work that originated thirty years before.

Since the sixth century BCE, certain thinkers in ancient Greece inquired into the nature of the physical world and of all the forms of being, including human beings, it encompasses. They asked, what could be the origin, the first cause, of the physical universe? And they refused to consider any exterior cause to account for the world's origin and development, which explains their rejection of myth and therefore of the traditional gods. Their replies were diverse, for each one identified the principle, the departure point, of the universe, man, and even society with one of the four elements – earth, air, fire, or water – or even a reality more primitive again, the undetermined (*apeiron*), which transforms by chance.

With Plato, who distinguishes levels of reality (sensible, intelligible, and soul as a kind of intermediary), everything changes. The universe, humanity, and the city-state are no longer automatically generated out of one of the four elements or the undetermined. Instead, in the *Timaeus*, they become the products of divine intention, where the divine influence persists even after the creation of the world by the Demiurge in the form of providence at the level of the world soul. In the *Timaeus*, Plato executes a very delicate and complicated synthesis that results in an unstable equilibrium between myth and reason, and between the tradition from which God emerges as a demiurge and free inquiry, which brings mathematics into the picture.

MYTH

LAD: How do you see the rôle and function of myth for Plato?

LB: I'll first note that it's Plato who gave to the Greek term *muthos* the meaning the word "myth" has today in the European languages. In the framework of Platonic philosophy, you can only speak of soul through the intermediary of myth. To illustrate what Plato understands by "myth," we can perhaps look at a contemporary example found in the movie *Titanic*, where there are several traits that characterize myth.

The movie enjoyed great popular success, because it appeals to a "large public" to which it presents, in the form of clichés, values that have been dominant during the past decades: it denounces the domination of the poor by the rich (illustrated by, respectively, the Irish and English), the domination of women by men, and the domination of nature by technology, with the former getting its revenge. The movie did make reference to a real fact, but in such a way that it's impossible to verify if the events related (which touch on the story of a particular man and woman) correspond to the reality. The hero, the only being who could corroborate the story of the old woman, is dead, and the jewel that may have belonged to Louis XVI, the only piece of evidence, has disappeared. Everything rests on the story of a very old woman. Now, following the Latin formula *testimonium unum testimonium nullum*, one person's testimony is no testimony at all.

The movie has elements that go back to Plato, who wrote about twenty-four hundred years ago. In his use of the word *muthos*, Plato accomplished two things, one descriptive and the other critical. He describes, in a manner reminiscent of an ethnologist, a certain kind of discourse, but he does so in a way that places on it a value judgment with respect to another kind of discourse he considers superior – namely, philosophy.[18]

In Plato's eyes, traditional myth is a discourse, passed down orally from one generation to the next, through which a community preserves its memory of its past (and what it considers to be its values). What does myth speak of? Of events that took place long ago and in such an indeterminate location that those relating the myth and those listening to it cannot verify them. Because the events are recounted orally, the same story never ceases to change slightly each time it's told. Writing kills the myth because it prevents it from being adapted to the expectations of its addressees, who may discover in their myths all sorts of anachronisms, improbabilities, and impossibilities.

Thus, according to Plato, myth is "produced" by the poet[19] who reorganizes a traditional narrative and gives it a particular form. When a myth is represented in theatre, the poet finds himself assisted by actors; when a myth is recited in any public forum, as during Homeric rhapsodic competitions or theatrical competitions, it's the specialists, poets or actors, who are the narrators. But in a general sense, a myth can be recounted by anyone; in this context, two traits characterize the narrator of a myth: femininity and old age (like the elderly woman in the *Titanic* movie). In a traditional society, old age allows for a kind of structure in its transmission. Usually, it's women (a mother, a nurse, a grandmother) who are the primary transmitters of myths, and the principal addressees are children. This, moreover, is what constitutes the power of myth: it's a discourse addressed to all, starting with the youngest. It's the privileged means to modify in one way or another the behaviour of all. How and with what aim? From one end to the other of the chain of communication, it's imitation that enters into the picture. The poet acts as if he were one of the characters, whether he produces or he relates a myth, and those who listen to him identify with these characters. Since this identification is pleasurable, the addressees/recipients are led to identify with the characters whose adventures they follow. We can now understand to what extent myth is a formidable means of persuasion, and why Plato feels the need to challenge its power.

On top of condemning myth on moral grounds for producing false images of the gods, demons, heroes, the dead, and even of men of the past, on an epistemological level Plato reproaches myth for two failings: myth is neither true nor false, and it's a story that has nothing to do with argumentation. These justify, in Plato's eyes, that primacy be given to philosophical discourse. However, philosophical discourse is only addressed to a few. Now, Plato has ambitions in the realm of politics. Myth thus finds its place in the *Republic* and the *Laws*. In the *Republic*, it's myth that justifies the diversified unity of the city. The three functional groups (rulers, warriors, and producers) must be persuaded of the fact that they're born from the same earth, even if they're made from different metals: gold, silver, and bronze. This is the "noble lie," the founding myth of the city.[20] In book 4 of the *Laws*, Plato explains that law must be double. It must, of course, express the spirit of the law and the list of penalties for those who violate them, but, in order for the majority to follow the laws, they must be preceded by an exhortation that introduces and illustrates the law. This exhortation is often a myth.

It's therefore understandable that Plato appeals to myth and even fabricates myths of his own. As a philosopher, he has to use this type of discourse to speak of the soul. And as a political reformer, he must rely on myth, to which everyone is accustomed from an early age, to persuade the majority, the crowd, which is not receptive to philosophical discourse, which is the preserve of the few.

LAD: In *How Philosophers Saved Myths: Allegorical Interpretation and Classical Mythology* (a German edition of which preceded the French), you return to the question of myth.

LB: I tried to show how, after Plato, philosophers wanted to make a place for myth by using allegory: a method that seems a bit surprising to us, but which was commonly practised in the Greek and Roman world and that had a significant influence up until the end of the Renaissance, including in philosophy, literature, various sciences, and the fine arts. From the time of the Stoics (or before them, in Aristotle), myths were reinterpreted with the aim of re-adapting them. Traditional materials were put to new purposes by being inserted into both philosophical and scientific discourse. In other words, allegory enabled myth to be translated into rational terms. To do this, the Stoic interpreter equates a god with either a virtue, an element (fire, air, water, earth), or a psychological function, and so on.[21]

LAD: The birth of philosophy has often been described as "the passage from myth to reason." Do you agree with this expression, which became popular at the end of the nineteenth century?

LB: Yes, but on the condition that one adds "the passage from myth to reason *and back*."

LAD: And back?

LB: Reason cannot affirm itself except in opposition to myth. But, very quickly, philosophers realized that if they stayed exclusively on the rational level, they couldn't speak of certain very important things. This is why it's necessary to find a place for myth alongside reason.

LAD: Can we say that Greek philosophy was always connected to myth?

LB: Yes, maybe, with the exception of Aristotle and his school. This is very surprising, since he was a student of Plato, and there's a very short time period between them, hardly a generation. Nonetheless, with Aristotle, we find a completely different conceptual world.

The return to myth is most evident in the Platonic reaction against Stoicism around the time of Christ. With Middle Platonism, and then later with Neoplatonism starting in the third century AD, we see a radical metamorphosis. Philosophers then have a tendency to consider philosophy itself like a theology,[22] which implies that all theologies, which are divine discourses, must agree with one another. Plato's philosophy would express fundamentally the same thing as Homer, Hesiod, and all the new religious currents that constituted Orphism in its new version, the *Rhapsodies* and the *Chaldean Oracles*, a kind of revelation composed in the second century AD that narrates the *Timaeus* in verse.[23] And all of this was to resist Christianity. The new currents were thus in opposition to Christianity, which in 529 became the state religion of the Roman Empire, a development that led to the closing of the schools of philosophy in Athens – the best products that Hellenism had created. This is a theme that is very dear to me.

LAD: But you did not simply address myth in general. You also provide an analysis of traditional myths, those of Tiresias and the different characters related to dual sexuality, especially in Orphism. That's a theme that is close to the subjects that also interested Vernant, Vidal-Naquet, and Detienne. With the issue of dual sexuality, we're pretty much at the edge of philosophy. It seems to me an issue that has more to do with anthropology than with philosophy proper.

LB: No, not at all. In my book on the myth of Tiresias,[24] my intention was to show Vernant, Vidal-Naquet, and Detienne that I could do a structural analysis of myth as well as they. I followed Lévi-Strauss very closely. I set up columns of "mythemes" and so on.[25] But very quickly, I found myself confronted with real philosophical problems.

LAD: Can you remind us of the myth of Tiresias?

LB: There are three versions of the myth. In the first version, Tiresias, while walking in the mountains, sees two snakes copulating; he strikes one, and is punished by becoming a woman.[26] Seven years later, he strikes the other and is punished again, but this time he's turned back into a man. In the second version, Zeus and Hera, the king of the gods and his wife, who are constantly quarrelling, are now arguing about whether it's a man or a woman who experiences the most pleasure during intercourse. They decide to ask Tiresias, who, having experienced both, should know. Tiresias sides with Zeus and claims that a man feels seven times less pleasure than a woman experiences during sex. Hera, who is furious with his reply, blinds Tiresias. Zeus cannot undo what has been done, but to compensate he gives Tiresias the gifts of divination, a long life,[27] and the promise of retaining his wits after death, which made him a sort of living dead.[28]

Meanwhile, according to another variation of this second version related by Callimachus, Tiresias was blinded not by Hera but by Athena, whom he surprises while she's bathing naked. His mother, a nymph who was part of her train, begged Athena to restore her son's sight. Athena instead gave Tiresias the gift of divination, a long life, a wand, and the promise he'd retain his wits after death. Dual sexuality thus disappears from this second version. But it reappears in the third version, where Tiresias changes sex six times before finally being transformed into a mouse.[29]

I wanted to show that a mediator like Tiresias, who establishes a link between gods and humans, between man and woman, between the living and the dead, between generations, must be affected by both sexes. In other words, a mediator who wants to establish a relation between opposites must participate in these opposites in his nature. This is what successive dual sexuality is all about.

During my research, I quickly noticed that there also existed in classical antiquity – and it's here that things become interesting on the philosophical level – a simultaneous dual sexuality: the same being is endowed with both sexes at the same time. The first example, and perhaps the most striking, is found in part in the androgynous myth related in Plato's *Symposium*. Ovid's' hermaphrodite is situated in a context that is a little different. Whether it's with the gods, with humans, or even with animals, the first being of a lineage or a species, which plays the role of prototype, is both male and female. We find the same idea expressed systematically and in a strong way in the well-known religious currents of Neoplatonism, that is, Orphism, the *Chaldean Oracles*, the Hermeneutic corpus, and Gnosticism. In fact, even the Phoenix that is born from the ashes is both father and mother to himself.[30]

LAD: But why would there be necessarily an original dual sexuality?

LB: The fundamental idea seems to me to be the following, and it's also found in Genesis: How to distinguish the sexes without imagining a first human who possesses both? In one of the two versions of the Creation in Genesis, Eve appears when God takes a rib from Adam. We must therefore conclude that either the primordial Adam had no sex, or that he had both, which in the case of simultaneous dual sexuality amounts to the same thing. Similarly, Ovid describes the sex of the being born from the fusion of the naiad Salmacis and the youth Hermaphroditus: *neutrum utrumque*, neither one nor the other sex, neutral, because both sexes at the same time. And in the other version in Genesis, we read that "God created men and women," which can mean, as we find in the Kabbalah, an affirmation of the dual sexuality of the original human beings.

LAD: In the very beautiful myth of the androgyne related by Aristophanes in Plato's *Symposium*, the fact of having both sexes is a guarantee of autonomy. A being who possesses both sexes is a being that is itself entirely self-sufficient. According to the description provided by Aristophanes, the androgyne is also the spherical form. Now, the circle and the sphere are the forms par excellence of this self-sufficiency so dear to Greek thought. In Parmenides, for example, the being that needs nothing is compared to a sphere. Self-sufficiency is, finally, one of the primary attributes of divinity. As long as it possesses both sexes, the androgyne is therefore protected from need, including love. The appearance of amorous feelings is, indeed, the result of a disassociation of the two sexes; once separated, they're in pursuit of their "tender half." Love and the amorous sentiment appear clearly as the expression of a lack, of a need, that the original human doesn't experience, since it possesses, reconciled within itself, both sexes.

LB: Dual sexuality or bisexuality constitutes a very important phenomenon at the mythic level. Paradoxically, every manifestation of dual sexuality was violently suppressed. In ancient Greece and Rome until the beginning of the empire, when a baby was born whose sexuality wasn't certain, and who could thus be suspected of possessing dual sexuality, it was either burned or drowned. It was destroyed because it was thought to be a baneful sign sent from the gods to show the human species that it was going to disappear because it no longer knew how to reproduce normally.[31]

In myth, on the other hand, the dual sexuality that was rejected or forced into marginality in real life played an important role, as I previously noted in both simultaneous and successive dual sexuality. From this perspective, dual sexuality is everywhere in myth. Anything that is at the origin of all things must be all-encompassing and itself imply the coincidence of opposites. In all the opposites that structure reality, it must be possible, if only in exceptional circumstances, to pass from one pole to the other.

In human life, the memory of this primordial state raises a nostalgia that is expressed with deep emotion in the myth told by Aristophanes in Plato's *Symposium*. Whatever the kind of amorous relation implied, whether heterosexuality, or male or female homosexuality, each couple, at the most intense moments of their intermittent unions, desire to realize an impossibly permanent fusion that would return them to the original state when the human couple was dual. As the desire for this permanent fusion can only lead to a failure at the level of the body, as Diotima suggests in the *Symposium* (204a–12a), and, as the supporters of the philosophical-religious currents flourishing at the end of antiquity suggest, there's the yearning to substitute a spiritual entity for a concrete individual as the object of love, a mystical élan that would enable the attainment of a true coincidence of contraries. Thus, the concern of the biological quest for immortality through sexual union prepared the ground for a quest for immortality of the soul through mystical union.[32]

LAD: Orphism is another of your research interests. What do we know about this religious current, insofar as we can reconstruct its primary features?[33]

LB: The figure of Orpheus, which so fascinated the ancients, continues to interest our contemporaries for two reasons. On the one hand, Orpheus, whose singing exerted an influence not only on humans but also on the gods, animals, and even inanimate objects, can be considered emblematic of a mysterious force and of the magic of poetry and music. This is a theme that was revived by poets, novelists, and cinematographers such as Jean Cocteau (*The Testimony of Orpheus*) and Marcel Camus (*Orfeu Negro* [Black Orpheus]).

Moreover, because of the power of his singing, Orpheus is practically the only person, in Greek myth, to descend into Hades and return. He did so to bring back his wife, Eurydice. We know the sad ending of this adventure. I published a collection of my articles on Orphism in 1995 with the title *Orphée et l'orphisme dans l'Antiquité greco-romaine*. The aim of my research on Orphism was to explore these powerful sentiments of love and the will to overcome death – that never cease to haunt the human conscience, that are associated with the adventures of the character of Orpheus to whom a theogony is also attributed, which calls into question the theogony of Hesiod.[34]

Orphism has the following two characteristics. First, it begins in ancient Greece at a relatively late date (second half of the fifth century BCE), for it's only then that we find a mythical arrangement containing a theogony, that is, an account of the origin of the gods, a cosmogony, that is, a description of the constitution of the universe, and an anthropogony, that is, an explanation of the appearance of human beings. Second, these accounts seem to follow a double movement, a back-and-forth. Whereas in Hesiod, the order among the gods and the world evolved in a linear progression and in a single direction and is established once and for all with the victory of Zeus, who becomes the king of the gods, everything in Orphism seems to challenge this because of the murder of Dionysus by the Titans, a murder that could indicate the repetition of this same process (see below). There are three versions of the theogony attributed to Orpheus, all of which I discuss in detail in *Orpheus and Orphism*. There's an older version, no longer extant, that is mentioned by Aristophanes, Plato, Aristotle, and his disciple Eudemus, and in all likelihood, discussed in the Derveni papyrus (see below). There are also two newer versions. The first is the *Sacred Discourses in Twenty-Four Rhapsodies*.[35] The second, attributed to Damascius (ca 458–550) and not without reservations to Hieronymous and Hellanikos, is only distinguished from the first by its beginning.[36]

In his comedy *The Birds* (693–702), which was created in 414 BCE, Aristophanes parodies a version of the Orphic theogony. In this, the oldest version, Aristophanes has an egg conceived by Night give birth to Eros, from which all things originate. When it comes to the generation of divine beings, we must exercise the utmost caution here, because Aristophanes makes the birds, the central characters in the comedy, appear before the gods. Also, Aristophanes is not interested in what follows this theogony and ends the narration with Ouranos (Heaven), Okeanos (Ocean), Gaia (Earth), and all the other gods. Since Plato, for his part, seems to assume that the Orphic theogony covered six generations,[37] we can also assume that, at his time, the theogony begins with Night, which seems to be confirmed by Aristotle, and ends with Dionysus. This is similar to the order found in the *Rhapsodies*. However, we don't know whether the oldest version narrates the murder and devouring of Dionysus by the Titans.

LAD: Do we have other documents that corroborate this oldest version of the Orphic theogony?

LB: Nearly fifty lines of the Orphic theogony mentioned by Aristophanes, Plato, and Aristotle have been reconstructed as a result of an archaeological find of great interest. In January 1962, during excavations at a site in Derveni, in the northwest of Salonika, Greece, a roll of papyrus was found near a tomb in which a group of six people were buried.[38] The roll in question, now known as the Derveni papyrus, was not discovered in the tomb but outside it. In all likelihood, it was intended to be burned and was not part of the paraphernalia of the deceased for the journey to the beyond. However, one end was half burned, but because it was charred, the roll did not rot or decompose. The unravelling of the remains, because of their condition, was very difficult. Yet we managed to detach the pieces with static electricity – one hundred and fifty pieces of papyrus, from which we were able to reconstruct twenty-three columns of text as well as a few fragments belonging to four other columns that preceded them. From an unofficial edition, which is now available, we know that the Derveni papyrus is, in fact, a philosophical commentary of the Orphic theogony, dating, in my estimate, from the late fourth century or early third century before Christ, and probably known to Aristophanes, Plato, Aristotle, and Eudemus.

The Derveni papyrus begins with a brief introduction in which Orpheus announces that he's going to sing, for initiates, about the deeds of Zeus and the gods born after him. His narrative begins at the moment when Zeus is about to seize royal power and asks Night's opinion. Zeus swallows Protogonos, the "firstborn." There's then a flashback evocation of the divine line into which Zeus was born: Night, Protogonos, Ouranos (Gaia),[39] Kronos (who castrates Ouranos). After swallowing Protogonos – swallowing represents total assimilation – Zeus becomes the beginning, middle, and end of everything. He then proceeds to bring about a new creation in the verses that follow. The narrative stops with Zeus's desire for his own mother, which evokes the conception and birth of Dionysus.

LAD: Does this version remain relatively fixed, or, like most myths, did it evolve?

LB: The old version seems to have undergone a major revision at the beginning of the Common Era. The result is a new, and longer, version known as the *Sacred Discourse in Twenty-Four Rhapsodies*, which I already mentioned. We can have a good idea of its narrative content, for the work is known to us through a number of important testimonies that appear primarily in the works of Neoplatonists. The title, given by later commentators, is evocative. The term "sacred discourse" is a synonym of "scripture," a genre that had a lot of success at the time. The second part of the title, "in twenty-four rhapsodies," expresses the desire to have it considered the equal of the Homeric poems, the *Iliad* and the *Odyssey*, that were divided into twenty-four songs, one for every letter of the alphabet, by editors and literary critics of the Hellenistic era. Each one of these "songs" also became a "theological" poem because of the philosophical exegesis to which they were subject, starting in the fifth century before Christ.[40] Although the *Sacred Discourse* is a valuable source of information on theological matters, we will unfortunately never know how many "rhapsodies" it contained because of its fragmentary form.

In this version of the theogony and succession myth, the primordial principle is Chronos (= Time, "who never ages"). From Chronos, Aither and Chasma (= Chaos) are born. Then, in Aither, Chronos makes (*eteukse*) a silver-plated egg[41] from which comes an extraordinary being. It was a doubled being, endowed with two pairs of eyes, and two sexual organs placed above its buttocks. In addition to wings on its back, this being is fitted with the heads of several animals, most notably those of a lion, a ram, a bull, and a snake. Just as it has multiple appearances, it also has many names. It's first called Phanes ("the one who appears," "the one who makes appear")[42] because its radiance causes all things to appear. It's also known as Eros. Sometimes, the name Phanes is accompanied by the epithet Protogonos ("Firstborn"), and sometimes Protogonos appears alone as its name. Sometimes the being is called Metis (practical intelligence). As the generator of all things, Phanes must be providential, and therefore, in the government of the universe, he must show practical intelligence. More important, since he will be swallowed by Zeus, Phanes is akin to the Metis that Hesiod's *Theogony* claims is swallowed by Zeus, thus making it possible to engender Athena.[43] Finally, it's called Erikepaios, an obscure name whose exact etymology still eludes experts.[44]

As for Night, she has complicated relations with Phanes, given his multiple appearances and names. Indeed, she's at once his mother, his wife, and his daughter. This tripling of the female primordial figure can be explained in the following way: being all things and possessing both genders (being dual-sexed), Phanes is actually in all possible kinds of relationships with his own feminine part. But it's Night, his daughter-wife, who is also his mother, to whom Phanes passes the sceptre for the second reign or succession. The third reign or succession belongs to the first true sexual couple, Ouranos and Gaia, who emerged from Night. In addition to Pontos (the Sea), who she may have engendered alone, Gaia gives birth to three groups of gods and goddesses: three Hecatonchites (hundred-handed monsters), three Cyclops, and seven Titans. These divine children are the products of the union between Gaia and Ouranos, a union considered as the first marriage, and the first generation of gods through a sexual union. They're thrown into Tartarus. One of the Titans, Kronos, advised by his mother, castrates Ouranos, his father, and liberates his brothers and sisters for the same reasons and in the same way as in Hesiod's *Theogony*. Coupled with Rhea, Kronos devours his children as they're born. To avoid the same fate as his other siblings, Rhea substitutes a stone for Zeus, which Kronos swallows. Zeus, who grows up in the cave of Night, manages to castrate his father, Kronos, just as Kronos had done to his father, Ouranos, as we find in Hesiod. Zeus then seizes power.

LAD: How is the Orphic theogony different from that of Hesiod?

LB: With Zeus, the Orphic theogony differs radically from Hesiod's and takes a new direction. It extends into a cosmogony. Indeed, after Zeus swallows Phanes, he becomes the primordial principle, and then regenerates the gods, the universe, and the actual human race.

And since Zeus now identifies himself with Phanes, as a dual-sexed being he now has with Demeter (mother of Zeus) the same relation as Phanes had with Night. As mother of Zeus, Demeter is named Rhea, and, being his wife-daughter, she's called Kore. Zeus unites with Kore to engender Dionysus, to whom he transfers sovereignty while Dionysus is still a child. Jealous, the Titans use toys to lure Dionysus into an ambush. They kill him, cut him into pieces, and then eat him, having cooked him in a manner that reverses the procedures of traditional sacrifice in Promethean style.[45] After learning of this, the Titans are punished by a very angry Zeus. Three punishments are mentioned: they're struck with lightning, enchained, and exiled to Tartarus.

Zeus gives the remains of Dionysus to Apollo to be buried on Mount Parnassus. But Athena had managed to save Dionysus's heart, which is still beating. She puts it in a chest and brings it to Zeus, who revives Dionysus once again. So, Dionysus continues to share power with Zeus as before.

Moreover, because Dionysus is called Zeus, Erikepaios, Metis, Protogonos, Eros, and Phanes, everything can recommence. Unlike Hesiod's theogony, which ends with a permanent order assured by the reign of Zeus, the Orphic theogony progresses in a double movement of dispersion and reunification that never amounts to a stable, definitive, and closed state since the end seems to coincide with the beginning.[46]

The last stage of this theogony seems to be associated with an anthropogony.[47] Proclus and Damascius suggest that humans are born from the Titans, filled with the flesh of Dionysus, and punished by Zeus. Their constitution is dual: one part comes from Dionysus, and the other from the Titans who have consumed him. From this, a sophisticated retributive doctrine seems to have developed, which involves metempsychosis – a human soul can pass into several bodies, human or animal, including even the most "vile" animals like serpents. In this sense, Dionysus ensures the ascent of the soul toward the divine, while the Titans encourage its descent into matter.

Accounts relative to this anthropogony and to its system of retribution need to be treated with caution. Because the evidence is scarce and the content obscure, any interpretation remains difficult and uncertain. The only evidence until now considered crucial is from Olympiodorus, a Neoplatonic philosopher of the sixth century AD. According to his account, humans were born from the residue of the Titans' flesh – a residue deposited by vapours that rose from the Titans when Zeus struck them with lightning after they were filled with the flesh of Dionysus. However, this might not be an Orphic doctrine as such but rather an interpretation inspired by an alchemical practice related to some Orphic verses that have since disappeared.

We may also wonder whether an already existing hymn to Dionysus was placed at the end of the *Rhapsodies* in order to complete the series, theogony, cosmogony, anthropogony. Such a hymn would have been already in use in the Dionysian Mysteries.[48]

LAD: Wasn't Plato very influenced by Orphism?

LB: It's much more complicated than it seems. Like Pythagoreanism,[49] Orphism fascinates those who are interested in classical antiquity, but the fact is we really do not know much about the true history of this religious movement. At the time of Plato, there were certainly Orphic writings in circulation, used by itinerant priests who promised healing and salvation. But it's difficult to know more.

LAD: But doesn't Plato make use of the famous wordplay *sôma sêma* (the body is the tomb of the soul), which he explicitly describes as Orphic in *Cratylus* 400c?

LB: Yes, but the problem is knowing how to interpret those words. If one wants to go further, one has to make use of texts written several centuries later, during the Christian era. At that time Pythagoreanism exerted a considerable influence on Platonism.[50] In this context, a new version of the Orphic theogony was composed that inserted Platonic doctrines from a Middle Platonic perspective everywhere.

When Neoplatonists read this new version several centuries later, they were amazed to find so much of the Platonic doctrine in it. But their interpretation was grounded in a vicious hermeneutic and epistemological circle. The Neoplatonists found a version of Orphism in the writings of Plato that was probably inspired by Plato himself. I identified this as a problem in most of my articles on Orphism after reviewing virtually all the evidence, including all the Orphic citations found in Proclus, Damascius, and Olympiodorus. It must be said that these Neoplatonists were highly credulous. They put their faith in the truth of a myth – one that Iamblichus presented in the fourth century AD in his *Life of Pythagoras*, a work that Alain Segonds and I translated for the first time into French.

Here, in a few words, is the foundational myth that the Neoplatonists blindly believed. In Libethres, in Thrace, the homeland of Orpheus, someone named Aglaophamos, literally "he whose reputation extends far," initiated Pythagoras into Orphic mysteries. Orpheus's mother was Calliope, the muse who was first in line after Zeus,[51] which shows how close Orpheus was to the divine. When Plato travelled to southern Italy, the Pythagoreans initiated him into Orphism. Through the mediation of Pythagoras first, and more distantly Orpheus, Plato experienced the words of the gods themselves being revealed to him. Plato's philosophy thus derives from, and embodies, revelation. This way of conceiving Platonic philosophy, which was the official interpretation of the Neoplatonists of the fifth and sixth centuries, and which was transmitted to western Europe through the Byzantines, continued into the Renaissance. For example, Marsilio Ficino, who died in 1499, was persuaded that this story was true.

PHILOSOPHY AND COSMOLOGY

LAD: What connection do you make between your research on myth and the books on reason that you co-authored with Walter Meyerstein?

LB: Before answering that question, I want to recall my meeting with this extraordinary person. One day, at the end of the 1980s, I receive a telephone call from a person I did not know, who had a heavy German accent. We were to meet at the bottom of the stairway that leads to the library of the Sorbonne. It was then that I met Walter Meyerstein. Born in Germany in 1929 to a Jewish family, Meyerstein's father was a doctor and the head of a pediatric clinic in Berlin who had to leave Germany in 1938 (the year of the Munich Agreement) even though he had lost the use of one of his legs from an injury sustained while serving in the Kaiser's army at Verdun in 1916. The family first went to the Netherlands, and then to Chile, where Walter Meyerstein pursued his studies in physics and became an engineer and director of a company. He remained there until things began to go wrong for Salvador Allende. As the political unrest worsened, bad memories of the past returned. Since he had no family there and was single, he sold everything he owned and settled in Europe, and, more precisely, in Barcelona, a city very open to all kinds of influences. He became a scientific adviser to the Autonomous University of Barcelona. Being responsible for the preparation of meetings and symposia, he invited people to give lectures in all fields of science. At the time he became interested in the big bang theory, and, after reading my book, he found a number of similarities with the cosmological model that Plato offers in the *Timaeus*. He then wanted to meet with me to pursue the topic. Since one of his friends, Josep Montserrat, knew that I worked at the CNRS in Paris, Walter Meyerstein then contacted me to set up a meeting. This unexpected encounter is still one of the most moving experiences of my life. One writes a book like one throws a bottle with a message into the sea, and fifteen years later someone gets in contact with you because they found your message.

Writing each of the three books that we co-authored, and in which we examined all the details, was a challenging but also very fruitful experience. Both of us were concerned about the constraints imposed on reason considered as a deductive activity, which takes as its starting point a small number of axioms and follows rules accepted by all. We attempted to describe these limits, first in the context of science and then in works of ethics. The relation is obvious, since our goal was to show the limits of reason when it takes as its object the universe or values, and, more precisely, how in these two realms, reason is forced in a way to return to myth.

LAD: Is philosophy, therefore, unable to transcend myth?

LB: That all depends on what we mean by "myth." Modern philosophy casts aside the traditional stories – the ones "everyone knows" – that form the cart that carries a religion. But philosophy is impotent to describe its own starting points. It finds its starting points in the past – these are unverifiable discourses that everyone accepts as necessary. This is the broad sense that Plato attributes to "myth." Let me give you an example. The idea that the human subject reconstructs the object via the forms of sensibility and the categories of understanding[52] is not based on any foundation and is not corroborated by anything verifiable. It can, therefore, be considered a "myth," an unverifiable discourse. The return to the poets lauded by a philosopher like Heidegger is symptomatic of a consciousness of this.

LAD: The book the two of you wrote, *Inventing the Universe: Plato's Timaeus, the Big Bang, and the Problem of Scientific Knowledge* (1991), draws on older preoccupations of yours, for your analysis of the *Timaeus* plays a determining role in it.

LB: We wanted to show that the *Timaeus* and the standard model of the big bang are founded on very similar axioms, and that only experimental verification would enable one to make a distinction between various cosmological models. But when you examine the issue more closely, one sees that the standard big bang model is bolstered by three – and only three – experimental verifications. On the other hand, it's subject to very serious difficulties that allow its close connection to myth to shine through. The book concludes with the limits that reason quickly encounters even in domains where it seems to rule, that of numbers. Here are a few specifics.

In the *Timaeus*, Plato proposes a cosmology, that is to say, a coherent and rigorous representation of the physical universe founded on a limited number of presupposed axioms, of which the properties of the universe appear as logically deductive consequences. Though traditional in its aim, the *Timaeus* is nonetheless very innovative in the nature of the explication that it proposes, and it does this in three ways. First of all, for the first time in history, Plato poses the problem of scientific knowledge: a scientific explanation must present characteristics of necessity and ideality that cannot, in an immediate way, be provided by sensory perception. Next, to resolve this problem, Plato provides the steps in what will later become the method utilized in all scientific research – and this is the case, even if the axioms that constitute his system are set down a posteriori, even if the rules allowing the deduction of axioms from the theorems are only implicit, and even if observation and experimental verification are possible only very rarely. Lastly, and most importantly, for the first time in the history of science, Plato makes mathematics the instrument that permits him to express certain consequences that follow from the axioms that he proposes. Although since Aristotle the extent of scientific method has been recognized, that is, the hypothetico-deductive model, the formal tool to which cosmology has almost always appealed to the time of the Renaissance was ordinary or everyday language. These are three points that make a possible agreement, from a scientific viewpoint, between the cosmological model proposed by the *Timaeus* and the model proposed by the standard big bang theory.

LAD: How can we explain Plato's interest in cosmology?

LB: For Plato, cosmology must answer one decisive question: Under what conditions can the sensible world become the object of knowledge and discourse? There are two conditions under which this is possible. There must exist somewhere entities that genuinely exist that do not change and therefore can be the objects of knowledge and real discourse. These entities are distinct from sensible things – indeed, they're radically separated. They're the intelligible forms. And to be knowable, the sensible world, that is to say the physical universe, must present something that does not change amid all that does. This stability in the sensible world, which makes it similar to the intelligible world, is found essentially in its symmetry, and it's mathematical relations that assure this symmetry. And this could only be the case if sensible things and the intelligible forms have a relation that Plato likens to the relation between a copy and its original.

And so, the question becomes the following: How can the sensible world be fabricated in such a way that it can be considered a copy of its intelligible form? An answer to this new question can be provided by considering the notion of an image. An image resembles its model, but it must remain different or else it can no longer be an image. In the *Timaeus*, it's the figure of the Demiurge that explains how the image resembles its model, and it's the notion of *chôra*[53] that explains that the image remains irredeemably different. The *chôra*, which has existed from eternity and is independent of the intelligible forms and the Demiurge, is the "material" on which the Demiurge works, the "that from which" sensible things are made and the "that in which" they're found. Moreover, insofar as the loss of its primordial indeterminacy causes in the *chôra* purely mechanical sequences, the *chôra* is presented as a principle that offers resistance and that fixes and limits the actions available to the Demiurge. In the part of the universe where the Demiurge is able to introduce order and measure, it creates the soul and the body of the world. In the world soul, which presides over all movements, and notably those of celestial bodies, the only things taken into consideration are the circle and three kinds of proportional means: geometrical, arithmetical, and harmonic. The body of the world is made of the four fundamental elements (fire, air, water, and earth), which are likened to the regular polyhedra: tetrahedron, octahedron, icosahedron, and dodecahedron. We therefore see that the limits of Greek mathematics in Plato's time also determine the mathematics employed in the cosmology of the *Timaeus*.

We can now see why Plato understands his own work as a kind of *eikôs muthos*, a likely myth, following the usual translation. In fact, we can also see that the *Timaeus* is a work that concerns copies, that is, sensible things that are only copies of the intelligible forms. In the *Timaeus*, Plato's description of the creation is itself a copy, and it therefore does not attain to the truth. And he recounts this creation as if it were a story, where the Demiurge is the protagonist who behaves, thinks, and deliberates like a human being, and even has the same emotions as a human being. This story focuses on the origin of the universe, a time of which no one can provide direct testimony, and that concerns the unity of all the sets of sensible realities, an object that therefore far surpasses anything we can experience. Lastly, and most importantly, Plato refuses any attempts at experimental verification under the pretext that it would be foolish to attempt to reproduce the action of the Demiurge, who created the universe.

LAD: Unlike Plato, don't contemporary astrophysicists claim to be able to obtain experimental verification of the model they propose?

LB: It's precisely on this point, in fact, that support is found among those who reject the idea that the standard big bang theory can, like the *Timaeus*, be more or less interpreted as a myth. In this respect, the following three experimental verifications are put forth: Hubble's law, the cosmic background radiation at 3 kelvin, and the relative abundance of light elements. But the major questions have not been answered. They concern the horizon, the flat character of the universe, and dark matter.

When we measure the radiation that comes from two regions of deep space 180 degrees apart, what is it that we're measuring exactly? Following the standard big bang theory, this radiation was emitted when the universe was only one hundred thousand years old. Since this radiation only reaches us today, we "see" clearly regions that have not yet reached each other's horizons. These two regions have, therefore, never entered into causal contact. And yet, the observations show that their temperatures are the same. How can regions that have never causally been in contact come to possess the same temperature? Just like its geometry, the development of the universe depends on its density. If it surpasses its critical density, the universe's expansion will one day end; the pull of gravity will reverse the direction of the movement and lead to a big crunch (the crunch would cause the universe to collapse into itself). If the density is weaker than the critical density, the universe will see its expansion continue indefinitely, until it surpasses the attraction exerted by the gravitation and breaks up in the weakest densities. Now, the data provided by observational astronomy presents a strangely precise adjustment that borders on a critical density representing a quantity of matter weaker yet than the vacuums that we can actually achieve in laboratories, which allows us to suppose that the universe is perfectly flat and that its expansion will continue for eternity. Finally, we have known for some time that the galaxies contain more matter than what is represented by luminescent matter. We can, in effect, measure the speed of the rotation of galaxies (both spiral and elliptical) that have been in existence for a billion years. How, then, is it possible to explain that a rotating system, which should break up because of its kinetic energy, can have such a long life?

Only gravity can account for this phenomenon. Now, for this to be the case, one has to suppose that the halo of the galaxies contains enormous quantities of "dark matter." This missing matter is characterized as "dark" precisely because up to now, no electromagnetic interaction has been detected. To assure the physical coherence of the standard big bang theory within the framework of physics, we must take for granted that we still haven't observed between 80 and 99 per cent of all the matter in the universe that reacts but very weakly, so weakly that it escapes all detection up to now. We can add to this list, of course, many more problems that make the conclusions of the three spectacular experimental verifications mentioned above fragile at best. This leads to the tendency to drive the standard big bang model to the side of the *Timaeus*, and thus to the side of myth, understood as a discourse whose status remains problematic in relation to the reality on which it's supposed to focus, and that consequently falls short of true and false.

The standard big bang theory is presented, moreover, as a story even though it introduces chemical and physical processes rather than anthropomorphic characters. The causal chain of events that the theory outlines could have gone in several different directions depending on decisions taken during a given time.[54] This explains the plurality of scenarios that are taken for granted – which is far from being certain – that the laws of physics and chemistry that we know are then applied to.

The big bang constitutes a "singularity" that must be situated outside the "space-time continuum" that the universe represents, an origin on which by definition nothing can be said directly, for any discourse on this origin must be confirmed by retrospective observations, and we have seen that they're far from being coherent and satisfactory. In other words, the hypothesis of the existence of an enormous quantity of undetectable matter constitutes a formidable restriction to an attempt to run the film of the events backwards.

Lastly, and this is an old argument that applies not only to the standard big bang theory but to any cosmological account, the ambition to explain the origin and the evolution of all sensible realities – that is, of the universe – constitutes a project that certainly fascinates human reason but that transcends human reason because of the extent of its object, and because of limits that are present in the algorithmic theory of information, limits that come when the privileged instrument is mathematics.

The algorithmic theory of information can be considered an extension of Gödel's theorem, formulated as follows: "In a formal system, if a theorem contains more information than is contained in the axioms of its system, then the theorem in question cannot be deduced from those axioms." In fact, the algorithmic theory of information permits the calculation – whence the adjective "algorithmic" – of the content of information of an object X (a system of axioms, for example), and to determine to what point knowing X helps to generate Y (a theory formulated by a series of propositions, for example).

These considerations bring us, then, to wonder whether there can exist a discourse of everything, on the universe, its origin, and its evolution, that is not a myth. Highlighting the mythical aspects of the standard big bang model helps us to remember the limits of reason – while we must, nonetheless, admire reason's power when trying to describe the region of the universe we inhabit.

LAD: We find again the idea that reason cannot account for ultimate principles. Does reason realize that it must transcend itself? What is the connection between this book and the subsequent work you co-authored with Meyerstein, *Power and the Limits of Reason*? The problem of values?

LB: In *Inventing the Universe*, we tried to offer a kind of critique of pure reason. With *Power and the Limits of Reason*,[55] we tried to offer a critique of practical reason.

Defining the human being as a rational being, and considering a human as but a rational being, was first attempted in Greece, around the sixth century before our era, by some individuals to whom we afterwards gave the name philosophers. By appealing to reason alone, that is, independent of any sensible experience, it seemed possible, by imitating geometers, to arrive at certain conclusions by means of axioms deemed complete and self-evident.

This definition involved a way of life founded on liberty understood as autocracy and autonomy. By means of reason, and reason alone, people could accept, to govern their actions, laws that were not imposed externally by brute force or even by traditions passed on by poets or priests; in short, by utilizing their reason, human beings could escape all external constraints. Only reason was admitted, since it did not violate liberty conceived of as autonomy – internal constraints give rise to rational conclusions valid for all in all circumstances. Just as the demonstration of a theorem should cause a feeling of certainty in a rational being, a certain number of values founded on reason should naturally impose themselves on all rational human beings.

Two convictions were behind this rash program: the heavens could be described using mathematical formulas to predict the movements of the stars within it; and a human being could attain an intuition of the good that, because truth and goodness coincide, was able to automatically guide human action.

Whoever subscribed to these convictions became free, free in relation to events, but also, and especially, in relation to others. Ideally, in fact, it should be possible to organize a society where a group or an individual could only compel themselves and others by reason, a society where any form of physical or moral constraint is definitively abolished, not by decree, but because human beings could not act otherwise. Socrates, who tried to offer this program, experienced how difficult it could be to realize it. After he was ignored and mocked, his fellow citizens condemned him to death.

LAD: Socrates' project, did it not remain, in spite of everything, a Western philosophy?

LB: Despite the fate of Socrates, the "philosophers" gave themselves the goal, over twenty-five centuries, of making that program realizable, by providing indisputable foundations. The other two examples invoked in the book, that of Kant and Heidegger, bring with them evidence of a final failure of the enterprise.[56] A failure that was always recognized, but the real cause escaped those who repeated it. However, the cause of this failure is complexity – that is to say, the gigantic quantity of information in the sequence of symbols describing a phenomenon, whatever the phenomenon.

Complexity fixes the limits of reason itself in the sense that reason demands that the complexity of any conclusion cannot surpass that of the postulated axioms. The possibility of finding self-evident axioms, on which complex conclusions are founded, diminishes and in fact disappears. Additionally, because they were not able to translate into a symbolic language, giving rise to number and measure, the ideas and concepts they used without a nearly total loss of information, philosophers could never evaluate the complexity of the axioms they postulated and the conclusions at which they arrived. They stumbled around in the darkness since they were not in any position to determine whether or not their deductions were valid.

That leaves science. There remained hope that science, which has had such a considerable ascent in this century, would be in a position to provide the answers that are sought. But in this domain as well, complexity fixes radical limits. Science is founded on numbers and measurement. It thus has nothing to fear regarding the translation of numbers and measurements into symbols. But as the sequences become longer, their complexity grows exponentially. However, complexity resists any effort of reason. And if the world and man are complex in the sense intended by the algorithmic information theory, then reason can never assure the rational ideal of liberty that was that of the philosophers.

The failure of philosophy is not only a literary question, a subject for historians of philosophy. This failure, made essential and definitive by the issue of complexity, opens a new chapter in the history of mankind, or rather brings us back to a previous situation – the one that a Socrates and a Plato knew. Indeed, it appears irresponsible and even dangerous to maintain that a theory like the big bang could explain the universe in its entirety, that neuroscience, by developing ever more powerful drugs, provide solutions for all of an individual's problems, or that a utilitarian pragmatism could come to propose for the entire planet, for all societies, a model of organization that guarantees a real freedom for its members.

In *Power and the Limits of Reason*, Walter Meyerstein and I show where the limits of reason are situated. But is it possible to show that, in spite of these limits, reason remains powerful enough to guarantee to humans an autonomy that permits them to determine their actions for themselves – that is, without bringing fear into the equation, whether fear incited by the use of various kinds of force or fear incited by diverse kinds of moral pressures? Maybe not, but one thing is clear: only the exercise of reason, promoted to the forefront by philosophers for twenty-five centuries, has until now fostered and continues to foster the ability to become conscious of the unjustified and unjustifiable character of a certain number of propositions advanced by religion, by science, and by mass media, which make it their goal to modify the behaviour of a human being.

LAD: In this context, what can be the goal of philosophy?

LB: Instead of considering philosophy as the purveyor of a system that is accountable for everything, we must conceive of it as a questioning of axioms; that is, a questioning of the main principles, the assumptions that direct all life – a task that Aristotle himself assigns to philosophy in his *Metaphysics*.

Part Three

GLOBAL CITIZEN

LOUIS-ANDRÉ DORION: It has been thirty years that you've lived in France, where you've married, had children, and where you work. At the beginning, however, you planned to return to Quebec.

LUC BRISSON: After my doctoral defence, I didn't find a position in any North American university. In Quebec, in particular, the positions left vacant by the collapse of the church were quickly filled. Also, I needed funds to prepare the publication of my dissertation. Vianney Décarie, therefore, applied on my behalf for a Government of Quebec scholarship. And, to obtain that scholarship, I had to leave France. I then found myself at Oxford.

M. Décarie knew very well Alan Montefiore, who had previously taught courses at the University of Montreal. For the 1971–72 school year, Montefiore invited me to be a post-doctoral student at Balliol College, where he was a fellow. I arrived in Oxford in September 1971, just in time for the ceremonies during which entering students, dressed in cap and gown, swear an oath of allegiance to their college and to the university.

LAD: You explored England?

LB: I really only saw a lot of Oxford, which is not at all England, but a world in itself. At the time, the situation was tense. For example, on the street where I lived, on one side, there were Pakistani Muslims, and on the other, Indian Hindus.

LAD: Where did you spend your time?

LB: At Balliol, my tutor was Malcolm Schofield. He had written on Anaxagoras and had prepared the new edition of *The Presocratic Philosophers* in 1983.[1] Afterwards, he became president of St John's College at Cambridge. His tutorials were very much like training exercises. He asked me to read a given text; with him, I translated the text, made comments, and asked questions.

I also attended lectures where big name philosophers spoke on various subjects. At the time, one of the most celebrated was Peter Strawson, who propounded a Kantian metaphysics without the transcendentalism. He had already published *Individuals*, *Introduction to Logical Theory*, and *The Bounds of Sense*. In his classes, he presented what would become the substance of *Subject and Predicate in Logic and Grammar*. His courses were at once very descriptive, clear, and subtle. However, he needed to rely on his good sense of humour to keep his audience from falling asleep.

Richard Hare was a strange personality, tormented from his experience in Japanese camps after he was taken prisoner after the fall of Singapore in 1942, and absorbed with his role as municipal councillor at Oxford. His ethical positions, formulated in *Freedom and Reason*, continued to have much influence.

Alfred J. Ayer was an exuberant personality. In 1966, he published an interesting collection of articles titled *Metaphysics and Common Sense*. In the courses he gave between 1971 and 1972, he touched on ideas that he would go on to develop in *The Central Questions of Philosophy*. He professed a logical empiricism very much influenced by Hume. Ayer, dressed in cap and gown, would literally give theatrical performances, changing the intonation of his voice and making ebullient gestures. On the first day of class he would pose the question, "Is a dog in water soluble?" The answer he gave in his last class was, "Yes, just as long as the dog is never put in water." For an empiricist, it's the only possible answer, since until the moment that we have verified whether or not dogs are soluble in water, we can think as we please. I have fond memories of his courses. They were truly marvellous. Alfred J. Ayer was a small man with very bright grey hair. He spoke impressive English and sometimes, for a quarter of an hour or so, he would express himself in impeccable French. I was told that he was a British officer who was sent to support the Resistance in the South of France.

In ancient philosophy, I attended John Ackrill's seminar on Aristotle's *Categories*. Present at this seminar were the best of the Anglo-Saxon world specializing in this domain, including Jonathan Barnes, the brother of writer Julian Barnes. John Ackrill invited me for tea from time to time. Between sips of excellent tea prepared by his secretary, we would discuss, with a biscuit in hand, some words from Plato's *Protagoras* or an expression from the *Categories*. These conversations took place at the end of the day, when the light began to dim. I retain from these melancholy discussions with Ackrill a memory of his considerable affability and great intellectual acuity.

Gwilym Owen, who came to give a few lectures, could never fulfil his engagements; his alcoholism made him far too ill. It's too bad, for even though I never agreed with him, he had an intellectual power and a persuasive force comparable to no other.

LAD: And how do you situate yourself with regards to analytic philosophy? Do you have an affinity for the philosophy practised in the Anglo-Saxon world?

LB: I always had a lot of trouble getting into this context. Nonetheless, I could understand how the Oxford scholars worked. I always admired their efforts to distinguish the exposition of a fact from the interpretation of a fact. This distinction prevents rhetoric from introducing unacceptable distortions. That being said, I was far too interested in the historical contexts of works to pay attention to only the strict analysis of argumentation. Argumentation is always situated in a historical context, whether we like to admit it or not. You can't read the *Timaeus* as if it were the front page of *The Times*.

I don't really have any affinity for that kind of philosophy, except for what touches on moral philosophy. English moral philosophy is based on consensus. A group of relatively violent animals, human beings, are forced to live together. How can this be made possible? Very simply, by saying, "You have such and such a conviction, faith, principle, postulate; put all of this together and let's try to create a system, as fragile as it might be, that forms the smallest common denominator, and let's try to live in accordance with this system."

LAD: Whether this system is a religion or an ideology.

LB: In fact, this resembles what Aristotle recommended. I admire two things about Aristotle: his tolerance and his acceptance of common sense in many areas, whether in rhetoric, in politics, or in ethics. It's in this sense that Anglo-Saxons are Aristotelians and not Platonists.

LAD: I'm also convinced of this. Paradoxically, this is what explains Aristotle's modernism. On the other hand, with Plato, we see a bit of Descartes. We make a blank slate, we erase everything, and then we start over.

LB: Yes, Plato, the Plato of the *Republic* and even the Plato of the *Laws*, can be considered a revolutionary compared to Aristotle. The certainty of attaining truth, an unheard truth and one even in conflict with tradition, led to the promotion of a new form of social organization. However, the return to tradition, ever-changing and even contradictory, leads to a more flexible and more nuanced position. The modern revolutions (in France, the Soviet Union, and China) wanted to break brutally with the past by creating a blank slate by erasing tradition, while liberal democracies (England, the United States) allowed compromise as the foundation of social and political negotiations. We see, then, how Anglo-Saxons are more Aristotelians than Platonists.

LAD: What other things did you learn during your stay in England?

LB: The year I spent in England, 1972, was a difficult history lesson for me. There was a major strike by the coal miners. In the house my friends and I had rented, there was no central heating. We had to use electric bars that only worked once you inserted a coin that triggered a timer. That same year, because of the miners' strike, electricity was cut eight out of twenty-four hours, from four in the morning until noon or from noon to eight in the evening, depending on the neighbourhood and the day. It was very annoying, especially when we woke in the morning and there would be no electricity before noon. I remember all of it very well. I'd jump up from bed and immediately go to the centre of Oxford, to a large and popular restaurant where all the lost souls would get together. The kitchen and the lighting were gas-operated. In a stinking half-lit room, we were served coffee, sausages, etc. It was terrible since we were without electricity for almost the entire winter.

Also, the entire society seemed to stop functioning on account of cascading strikes. An example: at the Bodleian Library, the catalogue consisted of large, bound books, with cards glued to the pages. In the corner of the library where the catalogues were located, the electricity had broken down. An entire section could not be lighted and required repairs. To do the repairs, an electrician was obviously needed, but the electrician wouldn't come if there were no carpenter available to unplug the wires, which were inside a plinth, and the carpenter would not come if there was not another aide available to remove the old plinth and replace it with a new one. You can imagine what happened. The three types of tradesmen were never available at the same time, and so the library was without electricity for an entire year. English society was in such disarray that I was not surprised by the eighteen years of Conservative rule that followed.

LAD: Were you able to travel to see much of the country?

LB: No, not at all. I went to London almost every week, usually to go to the cinema. At Oxford, there were only three theatres, one that played Westerns exclusively (Oh yes!). I really like London despite its ugliness. As Simone de Beauvoir remarked, it's a city entirely constructed by engineers, but it's such a lovely city to live in, and in general, the people were – compared to the Parisians of that day – incredibly friendly.

LAD: For a number of Québécois, a stay in England is an occasion to understand all that we should about the morals and customs of the English. For example, it's without a doubt the English, and not the French, who gave us the civility and courtesy that make common urban life in large cities more tolerable. Our common language with the French can obliterate, to a certain point, the values that we have in fact inherited from the English.

LB: Culturally, my point of reference is Paris. But in terms of everyday life, I feel much more comfortable in England.

LAD: For the university year of 1972–73, Vianney Décarie was able to arrange for you to teach some courses at the University of Montreal. In the meantime, you also took another important trip, this time to Turkey.

LB: I wanted to take a last trip at Easter before returning to Canada, where I was convinced that I'd find a position. I wanted to go to Turkey to see the vestiges of Byzantine civilization, which, in my mind, is often neglected. I also wanted to get an idea of the might that destroyed Greek civilization. Moreover, I wanted to see the Ionian coast, where what we today call "Greek philosophy" was born. It was during this trip that I met Catherine, who would become my wife. I returned to Oxford for the last term. In June, I returned to Paris to be with Catherine. With the goal of making a bit of money, I had to leave at the end of August to teach in Montreal. I did not want to live off of someone I loved. M. Décarie only taught one course out of three, and I taught the other two, an introduction to research in philosophy and a more general course on Greek philosophy from the Presocratics to the Stoics.

LAD: Did this first experience of teaching please you?

LB: Very much so! I especially enjoyed the introduction to research course because I got to show students how to work. The Quebec students were certainly less "bright," in the sense of being less "brilliant" in their ways with words than the French students, but they were more excited about learning even though less calculating. In general, they were not interested in "getting rid" of their neighbours to get ahead, and from the outset, they seemed not to think of their professor as "someone" who preferred to be elsewhere. In France, on the other hand, everything came down to the same problem – the national competitions and exams. In the logic of competitiveness, each student is in perpetual rivalry with the others, each of whom is a potential enemy. At the same time, the students have, with the teachers and examiners, a very strange relationship that combines submission with an unfathomable distrust.

LAD: When the courses ended, you returned to France. You didn't find a position in Quebec, and so you decided to present your candidacy to the CNRS.

LB: I would never have tried my luck at the CNRS if I had found a steady job in Quebec. Jean Pépin, whom I met in Montreal, seemed very interested in my becoming part of his team at the CNRS. This team was still in the midst of being established. After May 1968, the

Greek Philosophy Department at the Sorbonne, under the leadership of Pierre-Maxime Schuhl, was split into two groups for political reasons. In 1969, Pierre Aubenque, who had just come to be nominated to Paris-IV, took charge of the conservative portion, where the focus of study went from the Presocratics to the Stoics. At the same time, Jean Pépin left to found a group proper to the CNRS that was more leftist, and that would focus on the period from the end of antiquity to the early Middle Ages. Recruitment was far more difficult for him since Paris-IV was in the spotlight, while the CNRS remained mostly in the shadows.

During the year 1973, I made corrections to the first proofs of my book. It was at this time that I met Alain Segonds, who, though he had never met me, insisted, after a brief meeting with Jean Pépin's group that I was attending, on rereading and correcting the proofs of my book on the *Timaeus*. These revisions, done by a student of Festugière, who knew philosophical Greek like no other scholar in the world, was for me, publishing my first book in France, an invaluable resource. This was also the beginning of a friendship that would last forever. Just as Pierre Vidal-Naquet said about *demiourgos* (a Greek term usually translated as "artisan") that he was "the secret hero of Greek history," under Segonds's instigation, research on Neoplatonism and the history of astronomy increased considerably. We might say that Alain Segonds is "the secret hero of classical studies in France." His inexhaustible work as the publisher of Les Belles Lettres explains, to a large extent, the quality and vitality of Greek and Latin studies in France. In 1973, I was also preparing my state doctoral thesis, for which I had enrolled in Nanterre in 1971 under the supervision of Clémence Ramnoux. This work was important, for it constituted the framework of the research proposal that I was to present to the CNRS. This proposal of a few dozen pages had to be submitted on 15 December 1973 at the latest. Moreover, I also had to meet the most influential members of the committee that was going to decide my fate: Pierre Hadot, Pierre Aubenque, and Édouard Jeauneau.

LAD: In autumn 1973, you returned to Quebec to teach again at the University of Montreal and the University of Quebec at Montreal. These were limited-term appointments that would not lead to any longer-term appointments. However, if you had been offered a position, would you have accepted?

LB: Yes, once again. When it became evident that I'd enter the CNRS and that I'd remain in France, we decided, Catherine and myself, to have a child and to marry. It was no problem to have a child. But to marry was very difficult. I had to provide a birth certificate, and to do that I had to ask for one from the Government of Quebec, since all I had was a baptismal certificate. I had to undergo a medical examination and obtain a new residence permit. All of this slowed down the process, and so we were not married until June 1974, and our eldest daughter, Anne, was then born in December 1974. Everything was like a bad soap opera, a couple forced to marry by an untimely pregnancy!

LAD: When did you get elected to the CNRS?

LB: The official and definitive announcement was made in October 1974. However, the decision was made earlier. The commission met in May or June. It's for that reason that my file had to be completed and submitted by 15 December 1973. I have to say that the CNRS administration was very tolerant because at the time I was elected, I still didn't have all the necessary papers.

LAD: Did you know at that time that you would, without a doubt, spend your life in France?

LB: Yes, I burned all the bridges, and I hardly felt any guilt. I couldn't stand unstable work, and I wanted to have children.

LAD: When you joined Jean Pépin's group, what were they working on?

LB: We worked on the translation of *Enneads* VI 6, Plotinus's treatise *On Numbers*. I learned a lot working as part of Jean Pépin's team because it was the only one where we all worked in concert. We met once a month for a whole day. The remaining time was devoted entirely to personal projects. The CNRS, founded by the Front populaire in 1936, was roughly similar to the science academies that flourished in the Soviet world (though with no ideological constraints, of course!). At the time of its foundation, it was concerned only with "hard" sciences, but it expanded to include many other disciplines, including philosophy. The structure has changed over the years, which makes it difficult to sum it up in any general fashion. The CNRS is composed of thirty-five sections (from mathematics to philosophy) grouped into research teams by field. Each section is directed by a committee, a third of whose members are elected by the researchers at the CNRS, a third by university faculty, and a third by the minister of research. The commission decides on issues related to the formation and the direction of the teams, the engagements and career advancement of its researchers, as well as the allocation of credits and subsidies for publishing. It meets at least twice a year. A researcher, at least a researcher in the human sciences, has quite a lot of freedom. They can do pretty much as they wish. That being said, we have no official office or study location and, in principle, we're given no resources for individual projects.[2] One's career moves less quickly than in the universities. Ultimately, a position at the CNRS is the equivalent of what was called an "office" under royalty: the inspector of waters and forests for the fabulist Jean de La Fontaine, for example. One receives a salary and works on what one pleases. It has to be said that the majority of researchers work quite a lot, not out of imposed constraints but just for the pleasure of it. I was able to do all that I have because I was at the CNRS. I had plenty of time and was surrounded by outstanding specialists. This is why I am so grateful to Jean Pépin.

LAD: Since 1974, you've had about the same routine, that of a researcher, punctuated by the birth of two children, and quite serious health problems.

LB: Yes, I had very serious health problems in 1984. I had surgery for the removal of an acoustic neuroma. This is a non-cancerous tumour affecting the auditory nerve, at the place where it enters the brain and an area in close proximity to other nerves. Following the operation, I lost the use of my left ear and facial paralysis set in, which is why I do not produce tears in my left eye. At first, I was very nervous about teaching, since I couldn't tell where sounds were coming from and I couldn't follow discussions involving many people. I also had very serious difficulties with balance. I had to relearn all the ordinary movements of life: how to stand, to walk, how not to fall out of bed. My sense of direction – ahead, behind, above, below, left, right – became confused, disappeared. I really had the impression that reality was relative, like good and bad habits. It seemed to consist of nothing more than an interaction between the brain and sense impressions.

Moreover, as a result of this operation, fat was cut from my stomach to fill the hole in my skull. During the night after the surgery, lesions in the fatty tissue caused very serious bleeding. As a result of all this, I almost died. The experience was strange. I had the impression that death was just any other natural act. It was not a drama, not a battle like the etymology of the word "agony" leads us to believe. It's easier to die than one imagines.

After this, I became much more of a fatalist. I really feel that each day is just another day of avoiding death. It's maybe for this reason that I began to publish what I was thinking as fast as possible. Since 1987, I have had five operations on my eyes: twice because of detached retinas, two cataract surgeries, and reconstructive surgery to my face to ensure a suitable opening for my left eye. Thanks to the cataract surgery in 1993, I no longer have to wear the thick glasses that disfigured me and gave me tunnel vision. When my lenses were replaced by two bits of corrective plastic, my whole life was turned upside down. A few millimetres of plastic and your perception of your place in the group changes: your appearance has changed, and thus the eyes of others focused on you have also changed. How, under these conditions, can one not be a Platonist and consider all of the sensible world appearing to our nervous system as but an illusion? How can one not understand that in our sensible universe, the highest intellectual activity depends on the proper functioning of a very small piece of human flesh?

LAD: That's a reflection one would expect from an Aristotelian rather than a Platonist. Plato argues, indeed, that to exercise thought fully and freely, the mind must free itself from relations with the body and utilize but itself.

LB: In a certain sense you're right. But to say, as Aristotle did at the time and as biologists do today, that the forms of energy (light rays, sound waves, etc.) have to be processed by the perceptual and nervous systems of biological organisms only postpones the problem. In fact, Plato draws our attention to an insurmountable gap between the intelligible and the sensible, on which intelligence depends in order to function. This explains why the essential message of Plato might be summarized by saying that "the true reality is elsewhere." This still fascinates even those who, like me, are wary of any belief in an afterlife. Since we cannot understand how the intelligible might depend on the sensible, we reverse the relation, making the sensible dependent on the intelligible. How else do we explain, for example, that a mathematical theory developed as a mind game can explain the sensible world and even act on it? At first, this reversal seems inadmissible. But the opposite reversal remains mysterious. How can the spiritual be derived from the sensible? Justice cannot be deduced from just acts! How can intelligence be dependent on a secretion of the gland that is the brain? This is the question. In fact, Plato and the Platonists were intrigued by the fact that the sensible is up to a certain point intelligible – that is, orderly enough that we can talk about it, think about it, and act on it. This is the same for human beings, who consist of far more than the motions of their bodies.

To respond, Plato proposes a reversal of all of the points of reference, making the sensible dependent on the intelligible in ontology, the body on the soul in anthropology, the good on knowledge in ethics, and power on knowledge in politics. Even if this seems counterintuitive, this reversal allows us to understand at what points the world that surrounds us is strange and paradoxical.

LAD: To go back a bit, what was life like for Quebec students in Paris in the sixties?

LB: It was overwhelmingly separatist and leftist. From time to time, I went to gatherings that were held by the General Delegation of Quebec on rue Pergolèse.[3] But I had no particular interest in separatist theses or Marxist propaganda. At the time, it was better not to say this too loudly. It was impossible to adopt a critical position, even a moderate position, with respect to either independence or Marxism. I never believed that we could create a better society by radically changing institutions, as if by magic. A society is steeped in its own history, making its changes slow and hesitant. This is why I rejected the idea of revolutionary change. I'd add that this Québécois affiliation with Marxism involved an allegiance, if only intellectual, with the French revolutionary movements, which were themselves following an international context in which the Soviet Union and China were the driving forces. This Marxist orientation sterilized Québécois thinking as surely as the Catholic Church had previously done in Quebec, which required an alliance with Rome. Bad habits are not easily lost.

LAD: Let me point out once again that you're much more of an Aristotelian than a Platonist!

LB: Yes, in this respect. I *never* believed, contrary to Plato, that the radical and brutal transformation of a society in terms of religious or metaphysical values was an acceptable solution. And this first example will really show the failure and limits of this method. In the *Republic*, making a clean break from all the traditional values transmitted by the poets, Plato proposes a political organization where power is in the hands of those who possess knowledge of the intelligible forms, of the true reality of which sensible things are but copies. The famous "myth of the cave" illustrates this very well. Our human condition resembles that of men chained in a cave, with the cave corresponding to our universe. The only thing the cave dwellers know or understand of reality are the shadows cast on one of the walls of the cave by the true realities that are found outside the cave and that are also the source of the faint light of a fire within the cave. The philosopher is the one who escapes from the cave and who, "being forced to return," attempts to help his less fortunate fellows escape as well. It's interesting to note that in the *Republic*, it's at precisely this stage that Plato encounters problems. As I have just said, the philosophers are forced to return to the cave. To assure the unity of a city-state composed of different functional groups, a myth of autochthony is recounted to citizens – all are children of the earth on which they live. Here, the limits of the Platonic program become apparent. But, myth, considered as a "noble lie," solves the contradiction of how a city made of three distinct groups can be united.[4] The critiques formulated by Karl Popper, which I don't have the time to enumerate, are largely anachronistic since they identify Plato's program with that of modern totalitarianisms. Nazism and Communism utilized violence to coerce individuals with weak/attenuated ties to society, at least compared to the ties that existed in the ancient city-state.[5] In the time of Plato, citizens were not isolated individuals; they belonged to families, tribes, and demes, and the systematic use of violence in politics was, with the exception of tyranny, rejected in favour of the rule of law, written or unwritten.

Whatever the case, I do not accept any idea that advocates the reorganization of society by breaking with its past and attempting to recommence with a tabula rasa that tries to impose a rational model that fails to take into account material interests that have piled up in layers over the ages. Violence then always becomes inescapable, and most of the time the society remains largely unchanged after the massacre.

LAD: Concerning the milieu of Québécois students in Paris, it has to be said that this was a fairly artificial situation and not particularly representative of Quebec society. Its "leftism" and its nationalism at all costs is indubitably explained, at least in part, by the fact that many pursued studies in sociology, in political science – in short, in areas that were very politicalized.

LB: Maybe, but it was the environment in which I lived. And this environment imposed unbearable constraints on expression and behaviour. In one way, this pressure was even stronger than that exerted by the Catholic Church, for the prolonged exercise of power had weakened it: as time passed, a sense of a bad conscience weighed more heavily on it. In the environment in which I found myself, we were in the midst of a pervasive, triumphant ideology that saw no boundaries.

LAD: In October 1970, Quebec experienced a political crisis. The Liberal Party headed by Robert Bourassa won the election with more than 70 per cent of the seats in the National Assembly. In Montreal the FLQ kidnapped the British commercial attaché, James Cross, and the labour minister, Pierre Laporte, who, as the "fixer" of the Liberal Party, did not have the reputation of being an irreproachable political figure. Prime Minister Pierre Elliot Trudeau invoked the *War Measures Act*. Certain civil liberties were suspended, and arrests were made. The body of the assassinated Pierre Laporte was discovered. You were in Paris at the time. How did you experience this?

LB: In Paris, the repercussions of this crisis for the students were very serious. I was personally implicated in one of the incredible events of this affair. I had a friend who was a former student of the University of Montreal. He lived in the USA House (La Maison des États-Unis) at the Cité internationale universitaire de Paris but came to have breakfast with us in Canada House.[6] This friend had come to Paris to complete his doctorate on Descartes, which he had begun at Oxford under the direction of Gilbert Ryle, who wrote *The Concept of Mind*, a famous book that is a critique of Descartes.

LAD: Ryle also wrote on Plato.

LB: Yes, he published *Plato's Progress* in 1966, but it didn't impress me. When one reads Gilbert Ryle, one has the impression that he met

Plato the evening before at dinner. But let's return to the Québécois student. He was in the process of quietly completing his thesis when he was brought to the police station, put in detention for several hours, and then released but kept under surveillance at his residence. Twice a day, he had to report to the police station in the fourteenth arrondissement near the Porte d'Orléans subway station. What crime did he commit? None. But his name was Paul Rose, the same name that belonged to the individual who the police were looking for and who was suspected of having participated in Pierre Laporte's assassination.[7] We went with him when he would go to sign the register. And I must honestly say that the police officers were well-behaved and even friendly, as they did not believe for a moment that the Québécois student had something to do with a dangerous terrorist. In any case, when Laporte was kidnapped and killed, this Paul Rose was with us in Paris, several thousand kilometres from the crime scene. Nonetheless, he was asked to come to the police department twice a day to sign a register.

I don't know what Aristotle, always sensitive to the irreducible homonymy that affects language, would've thought of all of this. Paul Rose sent a letter to *Le Devoir* entitled "Victim of Homonymy." I'm not sure if this letter was ever published. I never found it. In any case, one day when we accompanied Paul Rose to the police station, we said to a police officer, "You must understand that none of this makes any sense. It's all purely administrative and absurd. Why are you continuing on with all of this?" The officer looked at us and said in a very sententious and calm tone, "Gentlemen, remember that the French government is never wrong." I found this an extraordinary response. Later, I had the painful experience of realizing that he was not the only civil servant of this opinion.

That said, the situation created by the October Crisis was really very dramatic. As soon as he learned of Pierre Laporte's death, Pierre Vidal-Naquet called me with considerable emotion to ask what was happening in Quebec. He supported the separatists, but never would've thought things would go the way they did.

LAD: What did you think of the crisis itself?

LB: I have a lot of difficulty expressing myself on this subject, for I never experienced the trauma of those who saw the intervention of the army, who were arrested, who were infuriated with the suspension, quite temporary, we must admit, of certain individual liberties.

LAD: In the sixties, you saw the FLQ's acts of terrorism. Did these events surprise you?

LB: No. They seemed to follow the order of things. The outcome was the logical result of a series of speeches and actions. You have to put it all in the context of the times. Marxism was not an old, tacky fad, as is the case now. Almost half of humanity was more or less driven by the revolutionary ideology in which violence played a determining role, one that revealed the nature of a people, of the value of the revolutionary elites who thought they deserved power. There was also this old dream of the purification of a rotten and corrupt society by fire and blood. The war in Vietnam was in full force. Laos and Cambodia were caught up in it. Latin America was in full swing. Fidel Castro was looking to export his revolution and Salvador Allende had just come into power. Many African "democracies" were feeling the heat. Europe also witnessed daily violence – the Red Brigades in Italy, the Baader-Meinhof Gang in Germany. You had to live a day in this atmosphere to understand. In the world in general, and Europe in particular, revolutionary violence permeated everyday life. It was frightening.

LAD: Apart from the crisis of the early seventies, did you follow the political debates in Quebec and Canada: the election of a separatist party in Quebec City, the "patriation" of the Constitution, the first referendum on Quebec independence?

LB: Quite honestly, I do not have any lasting memories of most of these events. Of course, when René Lévesque and the Parti Québécois came to power in 1976, this seemed very important. I was not a separatist, but I was interested in this victory. I was curious to see what consequences it would bring. But I didn't believe in the imminence of radical change. That being said, I have a lot of esteem for René Lévesque, but I always thought that his entourage, those with whom he shared power, were not up to the task; their rather pathetic disappearance, due in large part to infighting, has shown the vacuity of their project.

I was interested in what was happening in Quebec, both the events that you mentioned and others, but I tend to place myself in the context of a broader history and to pay attention to events and trends beyond those of the people who live in Quebec today and who are preoccupied with daily needs. I remember, for example, the death of Salvador Allende in Chile during the coup d'état that overthrew him, and the moment when Vietnam, Laos, and Cambodia fell to the Communists in 1975. This defeat, which I had always regarded as the inevitable conclusion of an absurd war from any perspective, seems to me, more than twenty years later, to be the beginning of the end of the illusions of liberation by violence in the Third World under the aegis of world communism. The horror of the fallen discourages any hope.

I followed the 1980 referendum from afar. But the removal and assassination of Aldo Moro by the Red Brigades in Italy in 1978, the fall of Pol Pot in Cambodia, that of Idi Amin Dada in Uganda, and that of Somoza in Nicaragua in 1979 are for me much more significant events. Europe was still shaken by terrorism, and at the end of the year the shah was overthrown and the Islamic Republic was established in Iran. Though confused, we all felt that something serious had happened. Religion took over the political struggle. The Soviet Union would undergo a painful experience with the election of Karol Wojtyła to the papacy.

As for the "patriation" of the Constitution in 1982, I think it was a purely technical move that did not change daily reality. It was an inevitable political move, nothing more.

REFLECTIONS ON LANGUAGE AND CULTURE

LAD: This is not the opinion of most Québécois, or their governments, who all refused to sign their names to this Constitution, which is to say it would not be recognized, even if it applied to the rest of Canada. Moreover, the introduction in the Constitution of a *Charter of Human Rights and Freedoms* had the effect of limiting the sovereignty of the provinces in areas under its jurisdiction. Pierre Elliott Trudeau knew very well that the reasons, completely legitimate, for which certain provinces had opposed the inclusion of a bill of rights would not be understood by most Canadians. Indeed, how can we oppose a bill of rights without, by extension, seeming to support a kind of fascism?

LB: Yes, human rights, which promote universality, accommodate the idea of national identity very poorly, for the objective of the latter is the cohesion and the creation of particular and exclusive communities. The problem of Indigenous peoples is also related to this. The Quebec that I knew based its identity on religion and language. The Québécois population, francophone and Catholic, knew where to find their identity and knew who was an enemy. All organization and propaganda implemented by the clergy was designed to define and maintain the cohesion of the community with the help of three instruments: isolation, a high birth rate, and in particular, a church-run education.

The first instrument used was isolation – isolation from Europe, from the United States, and from the rest of Canada. The maintenance of a rigid Catholic morality and an avoidance of all other languages contributed, along with poverty, to this isolation. The important participation of French-speaking Quebecers in the Second World War constituted the beginning of the end of this isolation. In my town, it would've been unthinkable, or worse, for a Catholic to marry someone of another faith. Marrying allophones was almost as bad, but really!

The second instrument was the birth rate. In the villages, priests directly intervened in families, encouraging them to have many children. The story of my mother shows that this was typically the case in the fifties. The sharp decline in birth rates followed the loss of power by the church and explains the push toward separatism. An a posteriori proof of this hypothesis is Jacques Parizeau's statements that the last referendum was lost, in large part, because of the ethnic vote. The fact that people stopped having large families is just part of reality and is irreversible. The only way a population can thus increase in the following generation is through immigration.

The third instrument is education. The stranglehold of the Catholic Church on education as a whole enabled it to shape children's behaviour beginning at the "age of reason." The seminary also allowed the church to choose the brightest individuals among the commoners to become the leaders of tomorrow. I already addressed this issue.

Now, the election of the Liberal government on 22 June 1960 marked the beginning of the Quiet Revolution. The power of the church crumbled rapidly and then collapsed. There followed a hemorrhaging of the religious vocations. The Québécois community found itself within a few years deprived of its traditional managers, the members of the clergy. With its isolation broken, the society looked abroad, to Europe, to the United States, and to a lesser extent to the rest of Canada. People stopped having large families. And the education system, heavily affected, resumed slowly, but to train managers of a new kind: civil servants or entrepreneurs.

One of the pillars of national identity, the Catholic religion, had just collapsed. More numerous, more surprising, and even delusional sects would come to fill, in part, the void that was created, but without reconstituting the lost cohesion. But on the contrary! In the intellectual community, Marxism attempted to replace Catholicism. I was surprised to find that some of the most convinced Marxists were those who had been particularly virulent priests: a secular faith replaced clerical faith. The fact that the incredible influence of Marxism was prolonged all the way into the eighties is, for me, somewhat of an enigma. It was probably that the French intellectuals chose to mimic Marxism in its Soviet and Chinese versions to assert their identity against Anglo-Saxon culture. Their lack of clarity regarding this dishonesty leaves me dumbfounded. One must reread the articles appearing in *Le Monde* concerning the polemics a group from the review *Tel Quel* spouted on their return from China to understand the abyss of credulity some French intellectuals fell into. Their aggressiveness was quite disturbing. The articles by Sollers and Barthes constitute, for me, testaments to the stupidity of the human spirit. That said, in the middle of the seventies, in the midst of Mao's power, I saw things that were absolutely incredible – students who waved around Mao's "Little Red Book" in front of the University of Quebec at Montreal, screaming, "Students, read this little red book and nothing else!"

LAD: In short, the two traditional pillars of Québécois identity are no more. All that is left is the French language, since religion is no longer a factor in social cohesion. In the sixties and seventies, it seemed as though everything that was previously invested in religion was reinvested in language. This is evidenced by all these laws that have made French the language of work and culture, and finally the official language of Quebec. Obviously, making the French language the principal pillar of Quebec identity brings conflict since there are more than a million Quebecers whose first language is not French. It's clear that nowadays, French-speakers feel increasingly uncomfortable, and even seem to have somewhat of a guilty conscience with respect to the constraints, restrictions, and enforcement actions that Law 101 imposes in terms of commercial signage and education for anglophones and immigrants. This equally brings difficulties for nationalist intellectuals, who must redefine the project of sovereignty. Just as the nationalist revamping can no longer rely on religion as it once did, it can no longer rely on the French language. Rather, it attempts to rejuvenate itself in light of a "civic nationalism," that is to say a collective project of sovereignty that addresses itself to all citizens of Quebec, regardless of their origin, their religion, or their mother tongue. But we see now more than ever that the francophone population is divided on exactly what, if any, role anglophones and immigrants can play in this nationalist project, "civic" or not. Doesn't Canada offer, on a larger scale, a similar project in its proclaimed respect for diversity and minorities? The two pillars of traditional Quebec identity did not have the same destiny. Religion is in decline and is confined to the private sphere, and the French language, which remains the distinctive trait of the majority of the population, still plays, despite the conflicts it engenders and the bad conscience that exists regarding the laws that protect it, its role as –

LB: The principal unifier. Yes, I remain very attached to this culture, to this language in which I grew up, and which I try modestly to promote. But once more, one must be clear and honest. French, despite being a national language, has regressed in the world over the last thirty years, especially in light of the irresistible expansion of English. English has become the "common" language, the equivalent of *koinê* for the ancient world.[8] This kind of English, raised to the status of an international language, is not wholly the same as the English spoken in the anglophone countries. Certainly, the supremacy of English became unavoidable once India made it one of their working languages and once the Japanese decided to sell their products in English. In any case, in international meetings, being unable to speak English certainly constitutes a practical handicap – the room will empty. Also, even in countries where language does represent an element of unification – for example, in Sweden, Norway, and Denmark – English is taught to children beginning in primary school, which also explains how and why, in the universities, most of the theses and works are written directly in English. Given our conflicting relations with the English, I don't think the francophones of Quebec would appreciate this solution.

Finally, the French language as spoken in Quebec seems very poor when compared to the French spoken in France. But it must be recognized that even in France, the quality of spoken and written French is steadily and increasingly declining. The collapse of traditional education in Quebec and the dissemination of minimalist slogans – "The spelling is not important, provided that we understand" – has taken its toll. Newspapers are full of errors. I refused student essays at the University of Montreal because I could not understand a single paragraph – it was almost a different language. How can a student be admitted into a university with such language skills?[9] The teaching of ancient languages always forced one who translated a text of Plato, Cicero, or Caesar to write well. I don't want to go back in time, and I think this is evident to everyone, but this kind of exercise has completely disappeared.[10]

LAD: What advantage comes, or can come, from knowing Greek and Latin?[11]

LB: Learning Greek and Latin allows students to understand the history of the French language. But I think that knowledge of these two ancient languages is much more important at another level, that of translation. Translation happens in two steps. In the first, one tries to understand the text at hand, and in the second, one attempts to communicate what one has come to understand to one's contemporaries. The transposition of ideas expressed in Ancient Greek or Latin into modern language presents an even greater challenge than attempting to write in one's own mother tongue. It's like a compulsory figure in a figure skating competition. One can neither cheat nor cut corners with the translated ancient language or with one's mother tongue. Working with Greek and Latin is a very educational exercise in itself, helping one to learn to use French with relative ease and with a kind of virtuosity. But translation also has a social and political function. Translation allows us to know the past, and thus to uncover to what degree the way of life and values it offers can be different from our own. So it's possible to avoid being stuck in the present, as it's now the case with most of our contemporaries. We're only in one moment of history, and in realizing this we can confront the future. In the case of Plato and Aristotle, it's clear. They presented the problems, which are, for the most part, still our own. While the solutions they advocated, at least in politics, cannot be reused, their efforts in how to deal with the problems, at least in ethics, are still worthy of interest.[12] In sum, to know the past enables preparation for the future.

LAD: I most certainly agree, and I'd even go one step further. We must, of course, communicate the ideas of texts, but also, and perhaps more importantly, we must reconstruct those translated texts. It's precisely this reconstruction that constitutes, from the perspective of language itself, a kind of exercise that has no equivalent when we write directly in French. We can always rework a text to have correct but poor syntax by simply employing the same sentence construction as the original. However, the translator, confronted with the classical texts and their rich and complicated language, must make sense of this richness and complexity, not only by conveying the meaning of the original but also by providing a sense of its structure without simply replicating its word order. To me, this seems to be a very formative exercise with no equivalent when working directly with the French language – that is, such as it's sadly and poorly taught today. The pathetic news clips from tabloids have replaced the models previously provided by great authors. It's no wonder that our students do not know how to write.

LB: Yes, but the problem of language is even deeper than that. It's not that one must return to the formulas of the classical colleges or that one is obliged to study Greek and Latin. But, we should be honest and to the point. A language is a technique of communication, and to learn a technique one must work, do exercises, that is to say one must accomplish a number of mechanical tasks in order to acquire a certain ability and even virtuosity. One can't remain at this stage, however, without falling into pure rhetoric, that is, in being only aware of its verbal effects. But we can't think that language abilities are merely acquired by intuition either.

There's another problem in North America – that of cultural impregnation. How can one acquire and excel in a language like French when, for the most part, our ears are attuned to songs in English and our eyes are fixed on a screen where the actors express themselves in English? This problem is becoming more and more acute in Europe as well.

LAD: In the case of Quebec, it's clear that French, in the North American context, is a threatened minority language. Even France, a unilingual country with a population of sixty-five million, felt the need to resort to legislation in order to defend its language.

LB: When I left Quebec, I had the impression that I'd arrive in an impregnable citadel. With the years, I realized to what extent French was threatened all over the world, but particularly in Europe. There was a time when, in Spain, in Italy, in the Netherlands, in the countries of northern Europe, and in Greece as well, intellectuals and cultivated persons spoke French on top of their national language. Today, it's not French that they speak but English. France itself feels both its language and its culture threatened by the rest of the world.

LAD: The threat that the French feel concerns not so much issues internal to France itself, but rather the influence their country exerts abroad. They have even more difficulty accepting their country's loss of influence and prestige in that French was once a universal language. I don't believe, for example, that the Danish or even the Germans are as pained as the French are about the fact that the world is ruled, without sharing, by English.

LB: Yes, France has a lot of difficulty accepting that it's no longer the model for the world it once was in the seventeenth and even the eighteenth centuries. The French have a tendency to universalize their rhetoric, but circumstances force them to realize the gap between the rhetoric and reality. However, to the extent that Quebec depends on France, at least culturally, we perceive this gap more clearly, and this poses a real identity problem.

LAD: The problem is probably worse in Quebec because of two additional threats facing French. First, our birth rate is one of the lowest in the West. If we're not willing to have more children and to survive, if we're committing what looks like a slow but inexorable mass suicide, what is the good of defending French? Is it not paradoxical or even contradictory that we impose French on the children of immigrants while we hesitate to have children of our own who could transmit the language?

LB: There's no longer a priest in each village to remind women to have many children, more and more children. The practice was in itself ridiculous, especially from someone who had taken a vow of chastity. But in terms of political and social consequences, the plan was rational. The will to forge an individual destiny, and more importantly, a social destiny, cannot be reconciled with the exclusive choice of individual values such as comfort, leisure, and enjoyment. In our culture that gives first priority to individuals, these are the values most commonly accepted. It's not a question here of giving a speech on civic morality, talking like a priest from my village. But it's important to remember that the maintenance of the French language and the maintenance of a reasonable birth rate (which does not imply, obviously, a return to the "large families" of yesteryear) are the only two instruments that can ensure that French survives in North America.[13] How can one supposedly be in favour of maintaining the cultural identity of Quebec by refusing stubbornly to address these issues under the pretext that they were the same propagandistic themes advanced by the clergy? Real problems have no timeline or political allegiances.

LAD: Secondly, French is threatened by the pitiful quality in which it's so often spoken and written. Quebecers are very attached to their language, but on the condition that they're allowed to speak and write as they please. They don't understand, or they don't want to understand, that they cannot continue to commit abuse with impunity. Not only do they feel no pride and no pleasure in speaking well, but anyone who uses refined language seems to them immediately suspect. Also, we can't expect immigrants to respect the French language if francophones themselves won't. If we want immigrants to adopt the French language, French must exert a kind of force of attraction over them.

LB: This social and political dimension was absent when I spoke earlier of the quality of written and spoken French. In any case, it's evident, unfortunately, that a non-French-speaking immigrant who comes to North America will always prefer to learn English. If they don't want to go to Montreal, they can go to Toronto. If they don't like Toronto, they can leave for Vancouver or Los Angeles. This is why I don't feel uncomfortable in the broader context of a truly federal Canada, notwithstanding my wanting to preserve a particular culture in Quebec founded principally on the French language, which I practise, love, and try to promote in my books and articles. That being said, it must be admitted that the Canadian government utilizes the issue of human rights in a perverse way, to oppose Quebec independence. But how, in your view, can we explain the resurgence in the determination to pursue independence?

LAD: "Determination" is too strong a word, since it presupposes a resolve that is lacking in the majority of Quebecers. It would perhaps be better to talk of a "hint" of this determination. In any case, the issue of independence will exert its attraction as long as francophones in Quebec, who form a people and a distinct nation in Canada, have the feeling that their threatened specificity is neither recognized nor protected. As long as the federal government and the other provinces are not disposed to recognize this distinctness, other than in a purely symbolic way, the desire for independence will remain alive. Moreover, independence always plays the role of a mirage: we present it like a panacea, as a definite guarantee of economic prosperity, as assuring the survival of the French language and culture. It's evidently a lure, but it's cleverly maintained.

LB: There's the problem. Ever since the sixties, Quebec has expended a considerable amount of energy attempting to realize this project of political independence without asking itself where this desire came from and without asking itself whether it was the best way to assure the cultural independence that I think, as I said before, all francophones in Quebec, myself included, are strongly attached to.[14] Since the sixties, the world has changed radically. Europe constructs itself in a painful but inescapable fashion. It's a Europe where countries, for better or worse, are necessarily interconnected, a Europe where the English language is often the connection between those who speak different languages, a Europe whose only serious interlocutor is American power. What interest is there in creating a New France in North America? And is the weight of the federal power so heavy? Can one, without being ready to laugh, denounce its "violence"?

LAD: But independence also serves as a vanishing point, which Régis Debray has shown is necessary for the cohesion of any political community. In one of his books, *Praise Be Our Lords* (*Loués soient nos seigneurs*, 1996), Debray explains that the "vanishing point" is necessitated by what he calls, echoing Gödel's theorem, the "incompleteness" of any human society. Under this incompleteness, "the foundation of a community cannot be internal to the community," so that "each is in search of something other than what it is." The vanishing point of Quebec society, the quest for a foundation or an external ideal to ensure cohesion, constitutes the very idea of independence. If we removed the idea or the hope of independence from Quebec society, it's a safe bet that the tensions and political conflicts internal to Quebec society would be much more serious than they are now. But, since the "national question" will probably not receive a definite answer one way or the other for some time, independence understood as "a vanishing point" has a bright future.

LB: Yes, that's where the problem is. But the issue is knowing what kind of action will bring us closer to this "vanishing point." A useful action that advances things, or defeatist behaviour, repetitive and sterile? In reality, things are not so simple. The future is nowhere written yet. Individuals and the societies in which they live are not impregnated with reason, far from it. Feelings, resentments, fantasies, and even the most disreputable interests play obscure but crucial roles. That's why I don't want to give any lessons. I only ask that all the cards be put on the table and that all questions be asked.

LAD: Certainly.

LB: Because in fact, and I'd like to repeat this, whatever the political position of the Québécois, everyone wants to maintain their culture, the distinctness of their culture, their cultural identity.[15] Despite differences between individuals, awareness of who we are as a people is the way to achieve this goal, and there's no need to hide it. In Quebec, we're in the presence of two hegemonic cultures. French culture dominated in the seventeenth and eighteenth centuries, and now it's the turn of Anglo-Saxon culture with all the reservations that I listed above. France is still dealing with being ousted from North America and with its loss of pre-eminence in the world. The French-speaking Québécois suffer doubly – on the national and international scenes. One can't forget that the United States was at one time a collection of English colonies in America.

LAD: Yes, but Canada is a country without mythology. It doesn't have a founding myth capable of bringing these two communities together. History, language, and politics do more to set them in opposition than bring them closer together. Even the Americans have their mythology: the Revolutionary War, the conquest of the West, the American dream, the American way of life – these all qualify as myths. Hollywood movies feed off of these myths, which they maintain, revise when needed, and propagate in other parts of the planet. But coming back to you, if I may – and I think I understand this better thanks to this interview – I have the impression that you're in certain respects a bit stateless.

LB: I am indeed. But I've felt this painful sense of not belonging since the age of eleven and a half. In entering the seminary, I was torn from my family and my community. It's important to understand what this means, for a child from Saint-Esprit, the son of a baker and the grandson of a homeless man, to do Greek and Latin, to read the French classics, to translate Tacitus, Horace, Plato, to love Plato! When one has thick glasses, when one doesn't like the taste of beer, when one isn't interested in sports, when one doesn't have a driver's licence, and when one prefers the city (whatever the size) to the countryside, this irremediably puts you outside of Québécois culture.

LAD: You've lived in France for almost fifty years,[16] and have French citizenship, but you don't feel French, and neither do you feel like a "French intellectual of Québécois origin," as you've been described in *Le Devoir*.

LB: In an old country like France, a first-generation immigrant cannot feel fully French. Even the family group to which you're supposed to belong doesn't really consider you as such.

LAD: But, on the other hand, do you miss Quebec? Are you never homesick?

LB: I was happy to return to Quebec, but I don't suffer when I'm away either. Like my paternal grandfather, I am a kind of nomad. But my nomadic feeling is tempered by a very strong sentiment of belonging to French culture and, through it, to this history that begins in India, which, after transiting Europe by way of the cultures of ancient Greece and Rome,[17] comes here to North America. This is why I have a tendency to go back in time toward the past, and to navigate in space toward the East. The piece of earth on which I breathe makes no difference to me. And, insofar as I've been successful in achieving results that I'm satisfied with in my life and work, I'm happy. I hope, moreover, that the people around me are mostly able to say the same thing.

Happiness is the feeling of having lived the best life that one thinks should be lived. From this perspective happiness doesn't need to derive its reality, contrary to Plato, from the idea of the good. Happiness accompanies a life that adapts to everyday reality in spite of the transient and uncertain nature of its events.

For almost fifty years I have devoted myself to the study of religion and philosophy in antiquity, and I must admit that until very recently there's never been a more profound and sincere interest in Greek philosophy among people I've been speaking to. How can I explain this? The question is too big for a simple answer, but I can risk the following, partial hypothesis: The general movement of disaffection in the most advanced countries vis-à-vis institutional religion, and especially the dissolution of Marxism in the troubled waters of history, have left those who question the meaning of life adrift when it comes to reference points that could provide answers. By the force of things, we therefore have to go back to the beginning, to Plato's accounts of Socrates's conversations on the streets of Athens, in which he directed his companions to seek out virtue – that is, human excellence – the possession of which gives access to happiness, and, finally, happiness itself, this sentiment of plenitude that accompanies the consciousness of having attained the objective one has been seeking.

It's in the same vein, in recent years, that Pierre Hadot explains how those who came after Plato, including the Stoics, the Epicureans, and the Platonists, continued in the same direction by considering philosophy not as an acquisition of information or knowledge but as a spiritual exercise designed to transform the life of the individual. To attain happiness, the Stoics advocated detachment from the passions, the Epicureans advocated detachment from the fear of death, and the Platonists advocated access to true reality and becoming as like God as possible.[18] Considered from this point of view, and not only from a historical point of view, the past becomes present. This is to say that Greek philosophy rediscovers its actuality and constitutes for our contemporaries a powerful tool for transformation.

Even though I am under no illusions about the fickleness of human nature, and even though I do not share the positions of Socrates and Plato, according to which virtue is inseparable from knowledge, I remain firmly convinced that devoting time to questioning, along with the philosophers of antiquity, the beautiful, the good, virtue, and happiness can only make one a better human being by making one realize that the practical necessities of life as well as competition cannot constitute the horizon of existence, and especially that to live in community with others, human beings must admit that the various principles that guide their existence and to which they must remain faithful on pain of falling into insignificance also calls for respect of the principles that guide the existence of other humans. In reality, it isn't easy to reconcile these demands.

As Socrates says in the *Apology*, an unexamined life is not worth living. It's to this examination that Greek philosophy invites us, and this call, to judge by the reply of several of our contemporaries, has lost nothing of its pertinence and actuality.

Part Four

WORK SINCE 1999

GERARD NADDAF: Much has happened since your autobiographical interviews with Louis-André Dorion in 1999. At the time, he noted your enormous intellectual output; yet since 1999, you have published more than ever. Indeed, since your "retirement" in 2012, you have, if anything, accelerated the pace. Let me provide some statistics, if I may, from your CV. Since 1999, when the original version of these conversations was published, your CV lists 4 single-authored books, 18 co-authored books, over 200 published articles, over 350 talks, to say nothing of book reviews, prefaces, radio interviews, editorial boards, and the famous Platonic bibliography (14 volumes). Moreover, you've also supervised the theses and been involved in the examination committees of nearly 150 students, many of whom were not French nationals. I'd like to return to this later for other reasons. For the moment, could you tell me about the driving force behind your incredible intellectual productivity since 1999, and how you were able to achieve so much. Indeed, I'll note in passing that you also had, and continue to have, a rich family life, including raising three children, and are now quite active with your wife, Catherine, in enjoying life with your several grandchildren.

LUC BRISSON: There are many reasons why I'm productive. Firstly, it's a consequence of my life in the seminary. My everyday life is very well-organized. I always work several hours a day except on Sundays. I don't work long hours, but when I do work it's with considerable intensity. Secondly, since 1995 I've been working with Jean-François

Pradeau and a group of young scholars who are very active because they have to be successful in the university. In ten years, we were able to translate and publish all the *Enneads* by Plotinus in nine volumes,[1] and we also published the periodical *Études platoniciennes*.[2] I've always been helped by a talented team of young scholars.

Moreover, in the CNRS I don't have to teach, and my talks and publications are a result of my ongoing research. When you're translating Plotinus, for example, there were lots of problems that are not solved immediately, so you had to find answers. Moreover, my team in the CNRS worked on Porphyry, on the *Sententiae*,[3] for example, and now we're translating the *Elements of Theology* of Proclus. As there are always problems to be solved, I have to prepare myself accordingly. For the thesis supervisions, let me say that when one is teaching in a university in Paris, it's much more rewarding to supervise students coming from the École Normale Supérieure than foreigners because these students are well trained and going to easily find positions in universities in France; it's a way of imposing your power on other French universities. That is why French professors are not interested in working with foreign students. Moreover, I was interested in foreigners because it was for me a means of understanding other traditions, interpretations, and cultures. In any event, I had no power in the French university system.

GN: Seminars aside, the intellectual work of most philosophers and/or historians of philosophy is of a solitary nature, and I know you excel at this kind of research. But I also know that you've been involved on collaborative projects. Indeed, many of your publications since 1999 are collaborative, and you mentioned earlier that you find working in this way most rewarding. Could you tell me why this is the case, and maybe provide a few examples?

LB: Yes, I think I'm not that interesting as an individual. I don't believe in individuality because of my upbringing. I was born in Saint-Esprit in a family of six children, and, as I mentioned before, we were integrated with the family of an aunt and uncle that had eleven children. In all there were seventeen of us. We were raised not as individuals but as a group, a large family, and as a group we worked together. I was the oldest in my family, and along with a female cousin who was the oldest in the other family, we were like a mother and father for the others. I always thought in terms of a group, and I think it's the same when working as an intellectual. I always worked in a team. Since 1974 when I started my career with my CNRS team, we translated Plotinus, then Porphyry, and now Proclus.[4] We were always working as a group, and I learned a lot from working this way, even when it wasn't always easy and the discussions were animated. It's very different when there are several competing interpretations.[5] I don't like interpretations that proclaim that they're unique. In order to understand the work of a writer or a philosopher, you need different points of view because a written work is in itself always ambiguous, always open to different interpretations.[6]

GN: Well, what about writing your doctoral dissertation? Wasn't it a solitary endeavour?

LB: No, that's not really the case. I worked with Professor Clémence Ramnoux, and we met and discussed my work often with her. Moreover, I met often with Jean-Pierre Vernant and Pierre Vidal-Naquet to discuss certain themes, such as the notions of the Demiurge and "necessity," and my research moved in a different direction as a result. My chapter on the Demiurge in the *Timaeus* takes a sociological approach because of them. It was also at this time that I met Alain Segonds at the Bibliothèque nationale, and we regularly engaged in discussions. So, I never really worked alone.

GN: I think the convention once again is to see philosophy as a solitary pursuit. We think of Kant as the epitome of this. He pursued his philosophical quests like a kind of hermit. We thus get the impression he wasn't sharing. On the other hand, if philosophers didn't engage with one another then there would be no progress. Philosophy is its history. One philosopher is always replying to another, and this was the case since the advent of philosophy in ancient Greece.

LB: That's why I've been working on bibliographies. I want to show that there are different people in different cultures working on Plato, and not only in English. The idea is that it's impossible to be absolutely original; originality is always dependent on history. And for me, it's impossible to work alone. Not because I want to be helped by others, but because, as I said, a work is ambiguous and to understand it you need many points of view.

GN: So, originality is a kind of *trompe l'oeil*?

LB: I don't believe that originality exists. There may be different interpretations. Someone working alone in a shack in the forest would still not be original. On the contrary, originality would entail working with a group in, say, an urban area with a lot of people.

GN: What about the example of, say, Einstein, whose originality is seen as a kind of paradigm? Are you saying that Einstein isn't a counter-example?

LB: Einstein emerged within a group of scientists. He was original insofar as he could give an answer to the questions others in the field were raising. But the questions were not his! It was a group question. He emerged in a community of German scientists who were the best in the world. My point is not to criticize Einstein, but if he's original, it's because he belonged to a group. They were also people who were opposed to him, but that's part of the quest.

GN: To follow up on what you're saying, when we talk about having our eureka moment, when suddenly we have a flash of brilliance that may lead to a great discovery or work of art, are you saying that it's still the result of mulling over the ideas of others?

LB: Yes, I'm not saying that there isn't a eureka moment, but that this moment is prepared by initial discussions, criticisms, and so on. And Einstein is a very good example because he would never have been able to propose his theory if he were working alone.

GN: What about Shakespeare? I note this because in the English-speaking world we often say that there are very few geniuses of the calibre of, say, Shakespeare, Newton, or Darwin.

LB: Shakespeare is a strange example because we really know so little about him. Actually, it's not certain that Shakespeare was an individual. I think that Shakespeare, as was Molière, was working in a group. His plays were made by a group. They were not only his but also those of his actors and so on. They worked together, in my opinion, on a play as a group. We know that this was the case with Molière, and I have little doubt that Shakespeare worked the same way. Molière had an idea and then the actors enacted it, and the play changed as they tried to reach a consensus. His plays probably changed many times due to the contributions of the actors. For me, in any event, Molière and Shakespeare worked in collaboration with others, with their troupe. It's obvious! I don't believe in absolute individuality. It would be limiting and restrictive. You and I are individuals, but 80 per cent of our personalities are dependent on our families, work, being a Canadian in your case.

GN: So life in general is a kind of collaborative project!

LB: Yes, life in general is a kind of collaborative project. And absolute originality is a kind of mythical concept![7]

GN: Your translations of Plato's dialogues have sold hundreds of thousands of copies. Plato's *Apology* or *Defence of Socrates*, the *Phaedrus*, and the *Symposium* are bestsellers. This must constitute some kind of record for "scholarly" books in French, given the size of the French or francophone market, which is at least ten times smaller than the equivalent anglophone market.[8] How do you account for this success?

LB: This success isn't surprising as such, since it's a consequence of what I wanted to do. When I was asked by Flammarion to make a new translation of Plato's works, I stipulated several conditions that GF accepted. First, I wanted to be able to do a new translation that fell between the scholarly editions we find in the Belles Lettres collection and popular translations such as the Penguin editions.[9] My idea was that Plato's works should be accessible to a wider audience and not only to scholars. This required a language that was very clear and not technical, and with up-to-date information. Second, I wanted to make the translations readable to everyone even if they didn't know the Greek language. Thus, I added a transliteration of some terms which shows how the Greek language was linked with modern languages. Last, I insisted that there would be a lot of endnotes, not to show that I was a great scholar, but because I think that most contemporary readers should be aware of the cultural context of ancient Greece. I wanted to make everything as accessible as possible. I wanted to show Plato as a contemporary. Not because Plato has provided answers to all our contemporary problems, but because he raised almost every important question that concerns us now. This explains why Plato is more popular now than ever before. Until now the questions Plato raised were answered by religion or political movements such as Marxism. These political movements, at least in France, have since sort of disappeared and religions are now less important. Well, maybe there's an exception with Islam, but that's another topic.

GN: Well, I'd like to discuss religions in context later.

LB: Let me say that if the *Apology* is so popular now, it's not only because the young in France are reading it in high school, but because the *Apology* addresses the main problems in our society. Socrates meets people and asks them to explain the meaning of their lives, of what they're doing in society; if what they're doing can be justified, and if what they're doing is true or if it's just a lie. I believe that only in the *Apology* do we find something so important. Is it possible to live our life without inquiring about its meaning? In a way, it's the same thing in the *Phaedrus*. Why are we talking and writing? Is it to pursue the truth, or to be successful in politics, in worldly affairs, etc.? In the *Symposium* we see a similar phenomenon again: How and by what means are we seducing other people?

But let me add a few words about my translation and edition of the *Symposium* because it represents a number of firsts. If I am so fond of Plato, it's because of the *Symposium*.[10] In my course on classics at the Terrebonne seminary I had to translate Alcibiades's speech at the end of the dialogue with all sexual connotations censored. But I think that with my translation of the *Symposium* for Flammarion (1998), I was one of the first to make it clear that in ancient Greece, *paederastia* was a well-known form of education for the rich or important citizens; these citizens make it easier for the young males with whom they're having sexual relations for a specific period of time to integrate into society. Plato tries to show there was another approach to education besides what we find in *paederastia*. I make it very clear that the *Symposium* is a celebration organized by Agathon, who had a permanent living relation with his lover Pausanias,[11] and that's why it's mocked by Aristophanes in his comedy *Women at the Thesmophoria*.

I also make it clear that in opposition to this type of masculine model of education, Socrates, speaking for Diotima, a woman, offers a feminine one.[12] I was, therefore, the first in France to discuss the *Symposium* in this way, when homosexuality in France was becoming a very important subject, thanks to Foucault and others. For Socrates tries to explain to Alcibiades that knowledge was not something you should pay for (with money or sexual intercourse) because you already have everything in yourself (the feminine or procreation model),[13] and you have to make yourself conscious of this.

GN: I'd like to return to the great number of supervisions, doctoral examinations, and university habilitations you've been part of. These consume, as we all know, enormous amounts of time and energy. When Pierre Hadot was my doctoral supervisor, he introduced me to you as a sort of co-supervisor, and you spent considerable time reading over my work and providing the guidance that one would normally expect from a supervisor. I was most fortunate to have both of you. But as your wife, Catherine, pointed out recently with some displeasure, you've never been compensated for your supervisions, contrary to other university professors in France, and in most other countries too. This is the case, I'm told, because of your position with the CNRS. And yet you supervised over forty theses, and you were the examiner and/or co-supervisor in over one hundred and fifty others. Some of these files can take a couple of weeks to appraise, and doctoral supervisions considerably more time. Nonetheless, you continue in your retirement to supervise many students and also serve as a member of numerous examination committees. I know your former students now have academic positions, including professorships in countries around the globe, which thus gives your own work a considerable sphere of influence. At the moment, you're also giving lectures at the prestigious École Normale Supérieure and organizing lecture series there and elsewhere. And again, you're receiving no compensation. Is this fair? I know you have a passion for your work, but would you care to comment on this rather anomalous situation. I couldn't imagine it in another Western country.

LB: I don't think in terms of fairness. It's my choice. Many of my colleagues in the CNRS systematically refuse to supervise the young. But for me it's stupid to think this way. I have time to do so, and I did not want more money. There's a proverb in Quebec saying that in your funeral procession no one will see your safe behind your tomb. For me, money is for freedom. You should have enough money to get along, and that's it. When I was young, we were poor, always looking to even satisfy our basic needs. You're free when you don't have to find money, but you're free, too, when you don't have too much money. There are lots of people who live for money. I just want enough to maintain my freedom, and that's it.

GN: So in the final analysis, it's consistent with the way you were raised, but also with Plato's philosophy.

LB: Yes, in a way! But I think you need to live well but not in pursuit of more and more money. I know that in some American universities professors make a lot of money, because you can negotiate your salary, but I don't think I'd be happy there. I think one's attitude toward money is a question of character. I like to talk to people and make them understand. It's about an intellectual commitment. I'm not the kind of person who likes parties and so on. In sum, there's the intellectual commitment and the public commitment. It's the same with family. I tried to live by changing the Latin proverb *Liberi aut libri* (either children or books), to *liberi et libri* (children *and* books).

GN: There's arguably more published on Plato ever year than on any other philosopher, ancient or modern. In fact, in the recent Platonic bibliography that lists works published between 1950 and 2017, the list includes over fifteen thousand publications (see part 2, note 16). Why do you feel this is the case, and do you feel that there have been any "breakthroughs" in the interpretation of Plato? Better still, what would constitute a breakthrough in your opinion?

LB: First, you should make a clear distinction between articles and books. Most are connected with academic publishing. By this I mean that they're connected with the publish-or-perish phenomenon in academic circles. From this perspective, I'd say that 85 per cent fall into this category, and only 5 per cent are really significant, 10 per cent being not so bad. Nonetheless, I think it's important to collect everything in order to show that there are many people in many countries publishing on Plato, and how these publications reflect what's happening in their countries. Otherwise, everything would be published in English, and we'd not see the same wealth of ideas.

I don't think there could be a breakthrough in interpretations, but there can be, and are, trends in interpretation. The first one is, according to me, historical interpretation. Greek philosophy is dependent on tradition, and it should be explained in terms of its social and political contexts. There have been very interesting novel interpretations in this regard under the influence of Marxism and structuralism. The second trend is the esotericist interpretation that comes from Germany. It's interesting in the sense that it's influenced by German philosophy, and in particular Leibniz. For him, philosophy should be a system, and so in Plato there must be a system. But since we don't find any system in Plato's dialogues, the systemization is found in what is supposed to be Plato's teaching in the academy. The esotericists explain Plato through the lenses of Aristotle, the Academy, the Middle Platonists, and the Neoplatonists. This is interesting, but it's not Plato at all. Plato is not systematic. For me, this lack of systemization makes Plato all the more interesting. He's first and foremost a writer, and as a writer he becomes more and more interested in what are now called "philosophical" problems.

The most important current approach to interpretation is the analytic. It started at the beginning of the twentieth century with Russell and Whitehead. English and American philosophy were interested in logical empiricism, and that's why the interpretation of Plato evolved in this way. Following a critical reading of the first part of the Plato's *Parmenides*, the doctrine of ideas disappears and is replaced by concepts analyzed logically in a theory of predication. Also, with the analytic tradition, one had to get rid of the notion of the soul, which was something religious. This is the main theme of interpretation since the Second World War. But since the death of the great scholar Gregory Vlastos, it seems that there's an evolution in the United States and Great Britain. Many scholars there are now less interested in the content of the dialogues than in their form. Argumentation becomes less important. That's why there can be no breakthrough in interpretations of Plato. Everything changes according to the philosophical context, and trends change as well.

GN: As a follow-up, when you hear some students talk about Plato who haven't taken classes in ancient philosophy or from a Platonist, they're often influenced by Leo Strauss. Sometimes, I'm fascinated that there are so many Straussians. It's as if they never read Plato except through the lenses of Strauss.[14] What do you make of this?

LB: I forgot about Strauss, and thanks for reminding me of him. In France, you rarely hear of Strauss, and in England too. But in the United States, and Chicago in particular, he's very important, and in Quebec as well. As to why he's influential, I think you must remember that he was Jewish and left Germany, where he was initially interested and trained in Jewish philosophy. I find Leo Strauss, whose works are now translated into French, interesting from the perspective of the social and political context on which I worked with Jean-Pierre Vernant and Pierre Vidal-Naquet, but I think that his interpretation has much more to do with the Jewish and Islamic context than with the Greek. In the Islamic context, there was no place for philosophy because theology was everything. Philosophers under the caliph were only tolerated, as they were under the emperor of the Byzantine Empire. After a while, many were killed. Not because they were philosophers, but because they were a threat to the ruler's power. Thus, the philosophers had to disguise what they were doing. That's why Leo Strauss taught that philosophy was a kind of art of lying and dissimulation. He thus read the Platonic dialogues differently. Take, for example, Plato's *Republic*. It's supposed to be a dialogue on justice. For the Straussian, it's a dialogue on war. It's the same for the *Symposium* and the *Phaedrus*. That's the first thing. Another reason why Leo Strauss is so influential is that, according to Jewish and Islamic philosophy, the most important thing isn't the experience of existence, but nature, and in particular the immutable laws of nature. Many Americans and Canadians, contrary to Europeans, cannot stand relativism.[15] They want to get back to the laws of nature. Let me give you an example. In the early 2000s I was in Quebec to promote my translation of Plato in the Garnier Flammarion series, and I gave a lecture at a CEGEP. Everyone was angry and critical of me because I seemed to be supporting relativism. They were opposed to relativism concerning sex and drugs and so on. The right wing in Canada and in the United States found in Leo Strauss and his interpretation of the laws of nature a weapon against relativism.

I think when you work on Plato you work on your society. It's hard to read Plato without taking a stand on certain political issues, in contrast to doing work on many other philosophers. Plato incites a wide range of different interpretations. He can be read as a historicist, an esotericist, an analytic, a Straussian ...

GN: I try to keep an open mind because students have interesting things to say.

LB: I learned much from the CEGEP encounter. But to understand Leo Strauss, you also have to understand Jewish and Islamic philosophy.

The Greeks just didn't think of philosophy and politics as incompatible. Socrates was tried because Alcibiades, Critias, and Charmides were in his entourage.[16] And Plato, who was so critical of myths, and who makes sacrifices impossible with his doctrine of reincarnation, had no problem with the politicians. In the Jewish, Christian (not so long ago), and Islamic traditions, on the other hand, philosophy was always in confrontation with theology.

GN: I have a follow-up question on Strauss, but first, what do you mean when you say that Plato's doctrine of reincarnation makes sacrifices impossible? The notion of sacrifice is very important for Plato. It's omnipresent in the *Laws*. In fact, at one point he claims that there should be religious festivals and corresponding sacrifices three hundred and sixty-five days of the year (828a).[17]

LB: My reference was first and foremost to animal sacrifice. If men could be born again into animals, it means that animals are men but without the full use of their reason. So, if you kill an animal, you kill a human being; and if you eat an animal, you eat a human being. Plutarch and Porphyry are very clear on that point. The conclusion is that human beings should eat only plants, as it's clear in Plato's *Timaeus* (76e–77c) and in the writings of the Platonists. Plotinus and the Neoplatonists were vegetarians. It seems to me very strange that today's vegetarians do not refer to these thinkers, who have written very interesting treatises on these topics.[18] And you should take into account a very important consequence. The civic cult in Athens and other city-states was based on animal sacrifice and the shedding of blood.[19] Bulls, goats, and pigs were killed, and their flesh consumed by the citizens. So, Plato and the Platonists were refusing to join this most important religious rite, and there's no record of them being charged with impiety for refusing to participate. But no one seemed to have been accused of doing so. That being said, isn't it beautiful to think that humans and animals have kindred souls?

GN: I'd like to return to Strauss and his contention that revelation and philosophy are irreconcilable. This is what he calls the irreconcilability between Jerusalem and Athens, or between the Bible and Greek philosophy. But for Plato, philosophy and revelation are hardly incompatible. In the *Symposium*, for example, if the initiate has beheld beautiful things in the right order and correctly, then he will suddenly (*exaiphnês*) catch sight of the Form of the Beautiful (210e). And this seems to be the case with the apprehension of the Form of the Good (*to agathon*) in the *Republic* (517b–c). Finally, in the *Laws*, Plato claims that laws (*nomoi*) are dispensations of divine reason (714a) and that the law code of Magnesia, the ideal city, is akin to a divinely inspired (*tinos epipnoias theôn*) poem (811c), and thus a kind of divine revelation. Is the difference between Strauss and Plato the fact that for Plato divine revelation is always based on *nous* or *logos* – that is, reason or intellect – whereas for Strauss divine revelation is based on blind faith?

LB: The difference is clear. The God that Strauss is talking about is an individual, who thinks and behaves like an almighty human being, while reason or intellect (*nous*) is an impersonal power attached to the soul of the world and of man, where it provides the opportunity to know. This power doesn't reveal anything; it makes you able to understand the truth wherever you are looking for it. No one is going to tell you what to think or do. And you will have to make an effort to find the truth.[20] Let's remember that revelation within the framework of a monotheistic religion is an act by which God, an all-powerful being, manifests Himself to humans and indicates to them the rules to follow to assure their salvation. The church is the depository of the revealed gift, and it's in charge of conserving and transmitting it.[21] For Plato, on the other hand, the most important divinity is the intellect that controls the world soul, and this intellect is also found in each of us. In sum, it's the same impersonal entity that controls nature (notably, the movement of the heavenly bodies) as the one that should enable human beings to make laws that allow them to live in a city-state, which has as much regularity and permanence as the world in which they live (see *Laws* 6, 737e–747e). As a result, the law is not external to nature, but internal. It's not the result of a divinity superior to humans, but of one or more human legislators exercising their intellect in an appropriate way.[22]

GN: You're implying that humans are just part of the world furniture and happen to be endowed with reason. But doesn't Plato imply that the universe was crafted by the Demiurge as a model for humans to follow? That the key to happiness is to make the motions of our soul conform to those of the universe?

LB: Exactly. Human beings must try to conform the motions of their souls and bodies to those of the universe, which is but an image of the intelligible. And this is the key to happiness (*eudaimonia*). That said, "happiness" for Plato doesn't only mean "well-being," as is the case today. For Plato, happiness refers to *eu-daimon*, which means "having a good daimon." This daimon is our intellect or our reason. It's impossible to think of happiness in terms of the individual. It's the disposition of human beings imitating the world in which they're living. Consequently, knowing oneself is not introspection; rather, it's having a real knowledge of the universe one is living in, and hopefully of its model. Self-knowledge is merging with the universal.

GN: What insights has your most recent work led you to that you may have overlooked prior to 1999? Perhaps you could also comment on why you chose some of the specific projects you did and the correlation between them? Indeed, your previous projects reflected a kind of general world view in which making sense of myth played a dominant role. Has this continued?

LB: There are two topics in particular that are very important for me. The first is the question of teleology. In the *Timaeus*, the forms are the models of sensible particulars, which are copies or images of the forms. Since any images must be at the same time similar and dissimilar to the model, the *chôra*[23] explains why the sensible particulars are different from the model, and the Demiurge explains why they're similar to the model. Aristotle rejected the idea of a demiurge for two reasons. It was impossible for a god to be a worker and not an aristocrat. Also, a worker begins and ends his work, and this means for Aristotle that if the world had a beginning in time, it would also have an end. So, Aristotle changed completely his mind about the world having a beginning and an end, and in order to explain why this is the case, he introduced a prime mover, constantly taking care of the world.[24] If you follow Aristotle's solution, you cannot explain why there are so many mishaps in the world. On the other hand, even though Plato's Demiurge is a god, this god is trying to do the best it possibly can.[25] But there's always a part of the world that is not ruled by reason, which is a fact.

The second topic is related to soul. I'm an agnostic and I don't believe in soul or that my soul will go to a special place after death.

But what's interesting in the hypothesis of the soul (a shunned word for many people nowadays) is that it changes a lot of things. If you define a human being not only by his or her body but also by their soul, that implies a big change in society, especially for women. It has been a common and long-standing prejudice that, because of her body, a woman is supposed to bear children, raise them, stay at home, cooking and working, and not engaging in politics. But if you say a human being is defined by the soul, there's a place for women in society – namely, in education, and even in politics. Furthermore, in Plato, soul is connected with the idea of reincarnation or metempsychosis. Because the soul remains constant, whether incarnated in a human being or an animal, ensouled beings should not be killed or eaten. I'm not a vegetarian, but the world of animals appears very differently if you believe in reincarnation. So, the soul in Plato is on the side of feminists. Moreover, I just can't understand why environmentalists are not drawing on arguments from Plato. He was already an ecologist and a feminist![26]

GN: Plato consciously makes his myths, and they play a crucial role in most every dialogue. But it's in his political dialogues in particular in which they play the most important role. For Plato, every means must be used to make the citizens as virtuous as possible, even if that involves not telling the truth. Plato, moreover, sees a correlation between the order the universe exhibits and how we should behave. This, too, of course, is presented in the form of a myth. Humans, for Plato, are not only part of the world furniture but also exist for a reason.[27] Could you comment on how this constitutes an innovation on the part of Plato with respect to the cosmogonical myths and cosmological accounts of his predecessors?

LB: I think this question is linked to that of the soul. A human being is defined by her or his soul, and politics and ethics are linked to the destiny of the soul. That's why Plato is obliged to invent myths linking ethics and politics. In relation to ethics, there's a short myth[28] in the *Republic*, the ring of Gyges (2:359a–2:360d), the famous ring that would make one invisible and thus capable of doing whatever one wants without fear of punishment.[29] If you think that a person has only this one life, it's possible for that person to escape punishment through the successful exercise of extortion, violence, or deception.

The only way to avoid the problem for Plato is to introduce a notion of rewards and punishments in the form of a myth of the survival of the soul after death. In conjunction, it's also interesting that in the *Republic* and the *Laws*, the societies espoused there are based on a critique of the family, or *oikos*.

GN: Just so I'm clear on family in the Republic, do you mean the philosophers and guardians being in a family?

LB: In the *Republic* and *Laws*, Plato wants to establish a conflict-free society. According to Plato, the cause of conflicts is the *oikos*, the large family with women, children, slaves, etc. The large families want to become richer, trigging civil war and even foreign wars to enlarge their territories. So, he proposes to abolish the *oikos* and to install all the citizens in a large family, the city. In the *Republic*, it's thus clear that the philosophers and guardians[30] cannot have families.[31]

GN: Before we move to the *Laws*, I want another clarification on the *Republic*. The soul is immortal in the *Republic* and cannot escape its fate, as in the Myth of Er (10.614–21). But the problem there is that if you look at the *Republic*, the focus is on justice in the city-state. In the here and now! The question is, how can we create a just state in the present? For Plato, as I understand him, if everyone performs the function that nature meant them to perform, a just state would be the result. So, you're going to provide everyone with educations tailored to their specific functions. Therefore, it doesn't matter, so it seems, if the soul is immortal or not.

LB: That brings me back to the family. In the *Laws*, a citizen can have a family, and he can transfer the *kleros*, or inheritance, to his son, but that's it. He can't own land.[32] The children are to be raised by the city after the age of three. In both cases the problem is how to create unity in the city. In both dialogues, it's the myth – the "noble lie" – of autochthony (people are born from the earth) that serves this purpose. This myth is thus very important, for it shows how society can be united. You're right to point out that for Plato the idea was to make all the citizens as good as possible. But even in an excellent city, there will always be people who violate the social norms, as we see in books 8 and 9 of the *Republic* and in book 10 of the *Laws*, because they think they can escape what should be the consequences. As we see in the myths concerning the destiny of the soul after death, it's impossible to escape punishment.

GN: But one problem as far as myths are concerned is that you're always going to have individuals in society who do not believe the myths.

LB: Plato is very conscious of this in the *Republic*, and that's why he claims (or suggests) that everyone should be compelled to believe in the myths. And recall that book 10 of the *Laws* is, in fact, the preamble to a law against atheism.[33]

GN: So when you say that the guardians should obeys the myths, you're referring to the passage at the end of *Republic* 3, where he claims that the guardians are to be tested to be sure they're subscribing to the social norms or laws.

LB: Yes, that's a good example!

MYTH AND SOCIETY

GN: As you noted before, myths are about social control, but they're also essential to the survival of the social group. They are, in fact, a socio-biological phenomenon, the origin of which seems to be lost in time. Now, people in an oral or preliterate society who narrate a myth (usually a cosmological one), and who live according to it, never question (or never seem to consciously question) why they live the way they do. The myth does that for them! Lévi-Strauss has, in fact, argued that myths are a subconscious phenomenon. Yet, when the circumstances warrant it, new myths are introduced. These introductions could be due to a number of factors, including conquest or changes to the environment in which the people reside. But one factor in particular that has played a determinant, albeit ambiguous, role in the analysis and evolution of myth is writing. Indeed, it has often been argued that writing kills myth, for it fosters a critical approach to myth that had hitherto not existed. And yet writing existed for over two millennia before it took hold in ancient Greece. So why in Greece? We know that the Greeks were the first to create an explicit category of nature, or *phusis*, and to identify "natural" phenomena in contrast to those that are "supernatural" or "cultural." They were also the first to innovate with the axiomatic deductive demonstration. Is this part of the answer?

LB: It's even more difficult. In an "oral" society, the last version of a myth is the good one, and so there's no criticism of myth because there's no point of reference. When writing appears, and when writing and reading come within the scope of many people, as was the case in Greece, it becomes possible to make a comparison, as we see in Herodotus. So, with writing appears a new way of behaving: criticism, which is essential in philosophy and science.[34] With myth in a non-literate society, the transmission not only of values but also of knowledge changes slowly. With writing, changes become more rapid. But the problem is that with criticism, you have relativism.[35] And this is a problem, because the most important thing in a human life is the fear of death, confronting death, knowing why one has to die, and this is not something that critical reasoning can address. Only religion and myth provide answers to this question.[36]

GN: Getting back to the point that writing kills myth, what about ancient Mesopotamia, where writing had already existed for such a long time?

LB: In the societies of Mesopotamia, writing was restricted to a small group of professional scribes, while in Greece writing was quite widespread (democratized so to speak). So, this class of scribes could maintain the myths in their original state for a very long time.

GN: As we see in ancient Greece, and indeed throughout history, philosophical and scientific concepts tend to be the preserve of the elite. But with the advent of Christianity, individual salvation (or the threat of damnation) was offered to all. The key to happiness is not knowledge but faith. Why did so many philosophers and scientists become enthralled with Christianity, and live as if it were the only way of life possible? Recall that even Darwin delayed the publication of his theory of human evolution because he didn't want to offend many of his Christian colleagues. Is it purely because of social control?

LB: It's a question of social control, but it's more complicated. I gave a lecture once on *pistis*, and I used the example of Porphyry, a disciple of Plotinus (see above). He used the formula *alogos pistis* in the *Letter to Marcella*, who was a widow he married. You find *pistis* in Plato linked to *doxa* – that is, opinion or belief – which is something very different from the certainty connected with science (*episteme*). Pagan philosophers were not rejecting belief as much as trying to attach it to reason. If you take the message of Christ, there's nothing else but belief. To be a Christian you only need the faith (*pistis*) that Christ has risen from the dead, which is really incredible. And that's why Porphyry used *alogos pistis* as irrational opinion or faith. Porphyry wanted to show that this faith was not linked to reason in any way. For Platonists like Porphyry, belief was possible because the objects of belief, the sensible particulars, were linked to the soul, to the intellect, and even to the One. But this practice was the privilege of philosophers, an intellectual elite. Reason was only accessible to a small number of individuals while belief was accessible to everyone. That's why Abrahamic religions are so appealing. And that explains why Porphyry wrote his important book *Against the Christians*.

GN: In conjunction, how would you characterize the primary difference between the Greek gods and the God of the Abrahamic religions?

LB: Every human community we know of seems to have retained relations in one form or another with what we call "religion," a set of myths and rituals whose primary actors and recipients are gods. This observation implies that human beings have always felt a need that couldn't have been fulfilled otherwise: to recognize an order in the universe, in society, and in the individual, and the survival, in one way or the other, of one's existence in the beyond. It seems to me that there are two inseparable things that distinguish the Abrahamic religions from others: the unicity of God, and the fact that this God is all-powerful. Let's take the Greek gods as an example. The gods are numerous, and it's possible to play one off against another. Moreover, they're not all-powerful. They're able to establish a kind of order in the universe, but they do not create the universe. Indeed, the universe restricts what they can do. This is the same for society and individuals. A god can try to take his vengeance out on a society or on an individual because of their arrogance or hubris. But this vengeance is limited and can be attenuated by the intervention of another god. In the context of the Abrahamic religions, there's only one God who is all-powerful. This God creates by decree the universe from nothing, or for the most part, as I'm also aware that in Genesis a primordial substance is coeval with God. Meanwhile, He's the only shepherd of his people. He demands absolute submission from all humans. In this context, a human being is required to obey the established laws of this God under the pain of punishment, and without discussion or any recourse to another power. Worse again, this punishment is for a sin that carries an eternal punishment,[37] which in my opinion makes no sense. We can understand the horrors that can be committed against the infidels by religions of this kind that pretend to a kind of universality.[38] History is full of these horrors.

GN: As should be clear from the above, humans have always had a propensity to create myths as a form of social control, but also to explain the world around them. But how do we determine who is wrong? I think you'd agree that our point of view isn't the only one, and thus that there must be tolerance.

LB: A myth, according to the definition given by Plato, is a story that is neither true nor false. There's no experimental verification giving the opportunity to choose between myths. But this isn't as problematic as it seems. You and I, and it's true for everyone, live largely in a world of fantasy. We're dependent on our psychology, on our social origins, on our political milieu, and, if we're believers, on our religious creed. Where's our true self? It's impossible to say. This explains why we're always dependent on myth. As for tolerance, we now live in an open society (or aspire to). Groups and individuals are demanding the right to be different, and that's great. In such a society, there can be no uniformity; its very existence requires mutual tolerance.[39]

GN: Sometimes we're highly critical of myths, in particular those expounded in preliterate societies, because they come across as being absurd, and yet we still have philosophical and scientific colleagues who take, say, transubstantiation (see the appendix in part 1) as it's taught by the Catholic Church quite literally? Why is this the case?

LB: If one thinks that a myth is neither true nor false, and that its only justification is fulfilling a need, it's impossible to be highly critical of myths. Myths analyzed by Lévi-Strauss may seem unbelievable,[40] but how believable are the myths told by the Catholic Church? For example, the belief that there's one God but in three persons, that the father created the world in six days and relaxed on the seventh, that in paradise Adam and Eve commit the original sin, that the father sent his own son to save humanity, that this God was also a man, the son of the Virgin Mary, that he was killed like a thief, that he was raised from the dead, that he went back to his father, that the Holy Spirit inspired the apostles, that the Virgin Mary was preserved from the original sin transmitted by the sperm of men and returned to God with her own body, that there will be a final judgment and men are going to be saved or damned for eternity, that in order for a Christian to go to paradise, they should attend Mass and believe that during this rite a piece of bread and some wine are transubstantiated and become the body and blood of Christ?[41] Christians believe in these stories because they were raised within the Christian faith, and because they want to live eternally in paradise after their death. These people are not mad, and they're good citizens, good scientists, good parents. But they just don't want to die. Moreover, these stories provide them with a certain way of life and an explanation for why there's evil in the world.

GN: At some point in the evolution of human culture many societies began to use gods as reference points in their myths to explain where we stand as humans (in the preliterate Amazonian societies, beasts were used; they were thought to eat, drink, sleep, and dress like humans). The problem with gods (or God) is the insistence that our gods/God alone are real, and this belief can destroy human solidarity. Indeed, many of the wars that have ravaged the planet have had a religious nature – that is, were conducted in the name of God/gods. They were thus seen as enforcing the will of the creator.[42] This brings me to multiculturalism and religious tolerance, which have never been more debated in the West, I believe, than they are now. There's little doubt that we can learn how to make better-informed political and moral judgments, and thus to get to know ourselves better, when we study the beliefs and ways of living of others. Logic isn't always the common currency to comprehend the complex myths or cosmologies of others. Tolerance is a *sine qua non* of Western democracies, but for many citizens there are breaking points. The Western democracies have undergone dramatic demographic change in the past generation. In Toronto, the largest city in Canada, almost half the population is foreign-born, and the vast majority of these are from non-European nations. Now Canada has always been a country of immigrants, and so there has always been a plethora of contrasting and competing religious identities and corresponding myths.[43] Indeed, I vividly recall when Protestants and Catholics rarely mixed. That sounds laughable now. I'm thus optimistic that a similar acceptance is forthcoming vis-à-vis other religious and cultural groups, but it must run in both directions. Often "visible minorities" tend to live in their own communities, which causes some problems for integration. On the other hand, it seems to me that many, if not most, Canadians, in particular those of European origin, are no longer interested in organized religion. This is happening just as waves of new Canadian immigrants feel that it's first and foremost their religion that defines who they are. They identify with their religion first and what it means to be Canadian second. Could you comment on the situation in Europe in general, and France in particular? One major difference, of course, is that many of these immigrants have come from former colonies where religion and its myths defined first and foremost who they are, whereas France likes to see itself as a secular nation where religion should be a private matter and not a public one.

LB: This is a complex question. I'll note in passing that I've always been interested in the Amazonian myths and their relation to different creatures in that environment. I've never criticized the myths, because I can understand why the people living in a hostile environment need them to survive and define their identity as members of a social group. The problem with myth and religion now is that you have to take both into consideration. I don't think that myth and religion are dangerous in themselves. The problem is that wars begin when myths and religions are used as political instruments, and this begins with monotheism. With the Greek and Romans, or those I'm most familiar with, there are no wars in the names of the gods. For example, there's no war in the name of Poseidon, Zeus, or Jupiter. The Greeks and the Romans organized sacrifices in order to make their cities successful, but they didn't fight in the name of, say, Jupiter or Athena.

The problem with monotheistic religions is that these religions (Judaism, Islam, and Christianity) are in essence dictatorial because there's one and only one almighty chief. And if your identity is defined by this dictator, then those who don't follow this dictator are enemies and must be destroyed. Moreover, Catholicism (in Greek *katholikon* means "universal") and Islam aim to convert everybody; they're proselytizing religions and want to convert all of humanity. This is clear from the religious wars in Europe. But a cruel example of what I'm talking about is the wars that took place between the Catholics and Protestants in Europe in general, and in France in particular. In this case, it's the same monotheistic God. The number of people killed in the name of religion between the Catholics and Protestants was horrible. It was not very clear in Quebec, but you felt it. When a Protestant ate at our house, my grandmother would wash the dishes twice, even if he was a nice guy. It's ludicrous, but true.

GN: You could also mention the conflicts between Pharisees and Sadducees in antiquity, or again between Orthodox and non-Orthodox Jews in contemporary Israel.

LB: Yes, you're right, but these conflicts are not global, and very few people are involved. Humanity is not at stake.

I just don't understand how someone who identifies with a single God should be unhappy with people who don't believe in this God. And a few decades ago, it was the same thing with politics – Marxism, for instance. The problem will disappear when, as you said, we cease to believe in instrumentalized religion. If you believe that religion isn't the basis of your identity, or you can believe in God without feeling that people who believe differently are your enemies, then there's no problem.

But let me return to Europe and the war between Protestants and Catholics in France. The Saint Bartholomew's Day Massacre of the Huguenots in 1572 is an example of fanaticism.[44] You can still see the place near the Louvre where de Coligny was beheaded and castrated because he was Protestant. Pregnant women were gutted and the fetuses discarded. Thousands of Protestants were massacred and their bodies thrown into the Seine. The rue de Rivoli, in the middle of Paris, was a scene of countless murders. In the French nobility, some were on the side of the Catholics and some on the side of the Protestants. Religion was highly politicized. It was not a question of religion as such but of using of religion to settle scores.

And it was the same thing with the Crusades. If you believe that your God is an almighty God, and that the son of that God was born in Bethlehem, it's impossible for you to accept that this land was in the hands of infidels, thus Muslims for the case at hand. So that's why some Christian extremists initiated the Crusades.[45] But if you look closely at the Crusades, you'll see that most of the victims were Greek Christians, and most of the wealth that was stolen was from Greek Christians from the Byzantine Empire. They were wealthier than the Muslims. The same thing always seems to happen. This time it was a way for the king of France to rid himself of most of the nobility, and for the nobility to bring wealth back to their fiefdoms. It's something the Muslims don't understand, and some of them use it to make war on the Christians. Europe is now much more conscious that religion should not be used as an instrument of political power.[46] This explains the political harmony in Europe. And this explains probably why Europe is a victim of terrorism.

France is now a secular country. Before the revolution, royal power was based on Catholicism, and that was the real problem. It wasn't possible to get rid of the royal power without getting rid of Catholicism. When I say that Catholicism was the foundation of royal power, it's not only because the cardinals were in the king's court fighting against the royal power of England, as we see with Richelieu and Mazarin, but the power of the king was dependent on religion. Thus, in France, if you wanted to destroy royalty, you had to destroy Catholicism. And why? Well, not only because cardinals were in the court of the king (wielding enormous amounts of power), but because priests were taking care of education. This is the problem of myth and religion. Religion made identity through education. If you want to get rid of a political system, you must change the educational system. In England, on the other hand, it was possible to get rid of the political system without a revolution. In Europe, the problem is no longer the opposition between Catholics and Protestants, but – or at least it seems – with the immigration of Muslims.

GN: A reader of this book will come away with the impression that you look favourably upon myth – that in the *Republic* the mythic "noble lie" provides the basis for social cohesion in, and indeed for, the very existence of the polis; that you believe "it's necessary to find a place for myth alongside reason"; that philosophy is itself grounded in myth, since it "is impotent to describe its own starting points."[47] However, you are also critical of the "myth" of monotheism that is the basis of Judaism, Christianity, and Islam. You mention the Saint Bartholomew's Day Massacre and the Crusades – just two of the many instances of people murdering countless others in the name of their religion. There are many others.

What about "myth" in the modern world? There are stories, myths, that, in some places and times, "everyone knows": to take a primary example, that "the Jews" conspire to destroy us. These are lies, and there's nothing "noble" about them. Given all that Europe, and the world, has gone through since 1914, have not secular, political, or quasi-religious "myths" been responsible for tremendous suffering, and led to the deaths of millions? In our world, why should a person trust any mythmaking, or mythmaker, at all? What comes to mind is Goya's famous etching *The Sleep of Reason Produces Monsters*.

LB: This is the human dilemma. Myths are essential for showing us our place in the world, for defining our identity as belonging to a people. And yes, the sleep of reason does breed monsters. In our time, certain myths have led to the deaths of millions. We live with this tension: myths are inescapable – and we must escape them. The only way to make them inoffensive is to refuse to consider them as a political instrument. If myths are dangerous, it's because many people have no other references with which they identify, and in which they believe. If one doesn't believe in the same myths, one is not a member of a group, and thus becomes an enemy to suppress. However, with education, a multiculturalism is possible, and even necessary.

GN: This means we must maintain a critical approach to myth, one that recognizes both its value and its danger. What does a critical approach require?

LB: We must begin by seeing myth for what it is, and that means differentiating it from rumour. Marcel Detienne and I were supposed to write a book together on myth, but because of our radically different views on the subject, it didn't work out. According to Marcel Detienne, a myth is no more than a rumour, a rumour accepted by a community and considered as true because it's known by everyone.[48] I did not agree with his definition. In fact, the example you cited, that "the Jews conspire to destroy us," is a good example of a rumour, a ridiculous and sad rumour, and is thus not a myth, as I understand it.

Let me add a few words about myth, and these can serve as a supplement to some of my previous comments. First, myth is an instrument of communication that uses language as a medium. It's a narration that's composed of a number of sentences. As such, these sentences are in a sense neither true nor false. A myth can be a story of extraordinary events – for example, the creation of the world, the origin of mankind, etc. It can also be a narrative of historical events that once took place, but for which there are no living witnesses. This historical past can be that of an individual, but it's first and foremost the past of the group to which the individual belongs. Finally, it can be a story that's recognized as fictive, but that's accepted for its pragmatic value. This is the case, for example, with Rousseau's tale of the social contract. Second, the myth shapes the identity of the group. It deals especially with the events that define what the group knows about itself and values. As such, it's a socio-political instrument with a considerable power, for it conditions each member of the group by getting them freely or by constraint to buy into the rules the group recognizes. Myth is thus highly important for every one of us. As individuals, we're each the product of a narration of our own past, whether this past is real or fictive. The stories we tell enable us to understand and govern our present lives. But I also think that our identities as individuals are inseparably bound up with the identities of the groups to which we belong – that is, with the myths that define the group's identity.

GN: In other words, a myth is a story that is resistant to disruption, and one that contributes to a sense of self-identity. The resistance to disruption depends on the type of narrative. A story of gods and heroes set in *illo tempore*, "once upon a time," "in the beginning," is beyond verification or falsification. As such, it's, as you say, neither true nor false. None of our kind was ever there to witness it. In contrast, a historical event can be resistant to disruption because of its profound significance to the people who commemorate it. In this sense, for Serbs, the Battle of Kosovo has a fixed, timeless meaning, as does the death of Husayn at Karbala for Shia Muslims. No matter what revisionist historians find out about what really happened, the meaning of the event remains constant. And finally, even a fiction like Rousseau's story of the social contract can have a mythic quality, as long as it serves a lasting purpose.

LB: A myth can change over time, in some cases losing its potency as its usefulness diminishes, but it will not ever collapse as rapidly as will a rumour. A living myth is something that changes through generations and becomes polished like a stone of the sea.

Take the example, once again, of the myths of autochthony and of the three different kinds of humans in the *Republic*. This is the key to the political system in the *Republic* because if you have the partition of society, with the producers completely separate from the warriors and the philosophers, how are you going to discover the unity in the city? The only way is to tell this myth, which is obviously false because Plato and his contemporaries know how to make children; that is, he knew very well that children were not born from the earth. So, in a way it's a lie, but it's a noble lie. I don't like the word "noble" because the Greek expression is *gennaion pseudos*, and *gennaios* means "related to generations of birth." So, it's a myth related to birth.[49] As for our contemporary society, you find something similar in the fundamental secular myth of democracy: Rousseau's social contract, which I previously mentioned is a perfect example of this.[50] No one gets together in, say, a café discussing with others and saying that, "even if we're free, we have to accept the rules of others in order to avoid fighting with one another." This is a myth! It's not true. There's no social contract. It's the same thing with the notion of voluntary servitude of La Boétie (1530–1563).[51] No one meets another man and says, "In order not to be killed by you, I'm going to be your slave. You, too, will be the slave to the law!" And it's the same thing with Hobbes and so on. These are secular myths. Our democracies are founded on such myths.[52] It's impossible to prove rationally that democracy is the best political solution. It's the best in the sense that it avoids war – that is, civil war, and thus killing ourselves. So, you first have to make a distinction between rumour and myth. And second, you have to remember that everything in ethics, politics, and even cosmology is based on presuppositions. But these presuppositions, as I noted earlier, are neither true nor false. So, our democracy is founded on myths, on fictions.

I became interested in myth because I quickly realized that the truth value of speech wasn't as clear-cut as one imagined. The narration of the past of which myth consists already transmits information of considerable value, and the specialized discourses that we consider true are rooted in what we call "myth." In sum, between *muthos* and *logos*, there's no clear divide, but a continuity that must be constantly examined to understand to what degree the discourses in question are true. The individual myth enables the structure of a personality, whereas the communal myth enables the control of the individual within the group insofar as the structure of each individual follows the rules admitted by the group. Moreover, in the case of myth, I believe that this performative power is much more important than the value of truth or falsity. In brief, myth is the instrument to restore order and peace in a given community. But this is dangerous because when myth is exploited within the group by one party or another, the result can be atrocious civil wars. Moreover, myth can be used as a pretext to launch an exterior war, as in the case of the Crusades, which I mentioned earlier.

GN: When discussing myth a moment ago, you used the example of myth as a noble lie. But these were myths developed by Plato. If you go back further in time, myth has more of a socio-biological origin.

LB: Yes, and one realizes this especially in reading the works of Lévi-Strauss on the myths of Amazonian peoples.

GN: With a myth, the further back in time you go, the more unconscious the myth becomes, as in the case of myth having a socio-biological origin. Humans are by nature cultural animals. So, nature and culture are inseparable as far as humans are concerned. It's as if biology adapts to the complexities and diversities of human culture through myths. From this perspective, myths tell us something about our flexibility and imagination, and, indeed, our credulity. But again, without myths humans may not have been able to survive as a species. That's what I mean by myths as a sort of socio-biological survival mechanism.

Actually, case languages such as Sanskrit, Greek, Latin, and other Indo-European languages are a good example of what I mean. The cases are a natural part of the language, but for someone learning them as a second language, they come across as consciously contrived, as with, say, Esperanto. Or again, we know of no societies that didn't practise some form of divination. It's like there's a natural impulse to do so. But at some point, some claimed that it was nonsense. But this was, historically speaking, quite late!

It's a stretch to think that a critical approach to myth begins with, say, Xenophanes or with the advent of philosophy in ancient Greece. That it's somehow connected with the famous Greek expression *logon didonai*: to justify an action, theory, or policy, which is inseparable from the birth of philosophy. Or maybe you see the first chapter of Genesis and other cosmological myths as conscious attempts to manipulate a human group. Clearly, that's not the case with the Amazonian myths, to cite but those. Do you have some inclination as to when a critical approach to myth begins?

LB: To have a *critical* approach to myth you have to have a certain distance from it; most people lived in the myths and by the myths. Myths are stories told to explain the origin of everything and to control society. In Greece, this distance begins with writing, as I mentioned before, which enables the possibility to compare different myths and different versions of a myth. Then the *phusiologoi*, or natural philosophers, wrote different stories on the origin of universe, man, and society in rapid succession. The question for the philosophers, from Plato on, was to decide what to do with myths; that is, whether to criticize them or to use them. Plato did both, because as you said nature and culture cannot be separated. Reason can do a good job, but it has its limits. And when referring to the beyond, only myths can be used. More generally, you have to tell a story to give meaning to your life, and this is the same with the history of society, and even of the universe we're living in.

GN: It's fair to say that your research on myth and its applications has been your greatest achievement in ancient philosophy. Indeed, you have shown the degree to which it's relevant to contemporary thought, including science and ethics. This is somewhat analogous to Pierre Hadot's discovery, so to speak, that ancient philosophy is first and foremost about a way of life, and this is how philosophy should be practised today. He has had tremendous influence, and not just in ancient philosophy. I have, for example, members of my own department who have no background, strictly speaking, in ancient philosophy, but who teach Hadot on some level, including in their courses in the philosophy of psychology and psychiatry. How would you like to see your research applied?

LB: My work on myth is both historical and critical. I have always tried to show that myth was linked with identity: first, the identity of a community, but later with the rise of religion, it became connected with individual identity. The aim of my research is to show that in order to have an identity, you have to accept a story. For example, a story of the universe (a story about the origin of humanity in the universe), a story about the society you were raised in, and even a story about your existence – and I think that myth is that kind of story. But a philosopher must be critical of that identity. It's important not be exclusive and not to take others as enemies. I'd like people to be interested in mythology in order to see how it builds one's identity, but also to use rationality to be critical toward this ideology and become aware that it's not the only one.

So, in a sense, it's similar to Hadot's contention that philosophy is about a way of life, about becoming conscious of who you are, and having a model to follow, which, in the case of the Platonists, to use but one example, was perfection associated with the figure of God. But in the case of myth, it's a little more complicated. To understand who you are it's not just a question of individuality. Your individuality is something built and not something given. It's built with myths, and it's difficult to understand who we are without understanding the context. And I also want to show that when you use your reason, you are dependent on something deeper than reason. It's the story told by the community you live in, and I think this is true for everyone in philosophy. How, for example, can you understand Kant without knowing that he was a Pietist?[53] So I think it's very important, as Walter Meyerstein and I tried to show in our book *Puissance et limites de la raison*, that what makes a difference between us in the West and other cultures was the power of reason in science and technology. In order to avoid the dark side of reason, we have to understand that reason can often engender evil. If you try to rely only on reason, there will be catastrophes.

Afterword

OUR *HOMO* ANCESTORS[1]

Anyone following human evolution can only be fascinated by the extraordinary progress in our understanding of the story, although there's still much fluidity due to the continuing discovery of new fossils, the development of novel technologies, and the contribution of the science of genetics. There's a consensus that the genus *Homo* originated in East Africa between 2 and 4 million years ago. Around 2 million years ago hominins and their innovations (especially in stone tool making) spread around the world. There's evidence that *Homo erectus*, the first species to possess modern, human-like body proportions, and with an average brain size of 950 cubic centimetres (and some as large as 1,200 cubic centimetres; for comparison, the average modern brain size is 1,350 cubic centimetres), emerged in Africa around 1.9 million years ago and then spread around the world.[2] While there were a number of other species of *Homo* – somewhere in the range of a dozen over the 2-million-year history of our genus, by some accounts – *Homo erectus*, with whom we associate the Acheulean culture, or stone tool industry,[3] is used to describe most all populations of archaic humans from about 1.8 million years ago till around 500,000 years ago, when, as a result of a number of pressures (environmental, in a large sense),[4] *Homo erectus* underwent evolutionary transitions that gave rise to later forms of *Homo* with larger average brain sizes.[5] These are the ancestors of *Homo heidelbergensis*, who, in turn, serves as the link between Neanderthals, Denisovans (from about 500,000 to 40,000 years ago),[6] and *Homo sapiens* – that is, us.[7]

The most recent archeological and genetic evidence indicates that anatomically modern humans (AMH) – or at least *Homo sapiens* looking like us – began to emerge in Africa around 300,000 years ago.[8] These more primitive *Homo sapiens* were followed by others around 200,000 years ago that were again closer to AMH,[9] but it was only around 100,000 years ago that we find *Homo sapiens* with braincases that are essentially modern, similar in size and shape to ours.[10]

It's around this period, many specialists claim, that behaviourally modern humans (BMH) appeared.[11] This dating also corresponds to about 80,000 years ago, the last time *Homo sapiens* migrated out of Africa.[12] Much of the controversy, of course, is on what counts as behaviourally modern.[13] Some specialists argue that we only have true BMH with the creation of highly complex tools or advanced technology, the production of representational art, and evidence of widespread trade systems.[14]

Nothing, however, can be more important to human evolution than the emergence of spoken language. But, as I noted in the introduction to this book, the scientific evidence suggests that language and speech capabilities began to emerge between 500,000 and 300,000 years ago, based on skeletal remains and, most notably, the evidence of structures related to speech production such as the position of the vocal tract and the organization of the brain.[15]

The reason for this digression is to draw attention to how long ago the seeds of storytelling and mythmaking first began to germinate. Just as language is in our genes (we're born with the capacity for speech), there's a powerful claim that humans are also hard-wired for storytelling. In this regard, gaining the capacity for language changed us profoundly, both cognitively and emotionally. This is captured by Daniel Dor and Eva Jablonka's formula, alluded to earlier: "First we invented language. Then language changed us" (2015, 4).[16]

One culture I'd like to highlight as it concerns the role of myth in anthropogeny is that of the Ju/'hoansi hunter-gatherers of southern Africa, which I mentioned in passing on several occasions. The Ju/'hoansi are part of the San hunter-gatherer tribes, which began to split off from other *Homo sapiens* groups around 200,000 years ago and which were completely isolated around 100,000 years ago (Reich 2018, 17).[17] Their genomes imply that, contrary to other *Homo sapiens* groups (or AMH), and, most notably, the out-of-Africa migration of modern humans who began to disperse around

80,000 years ago[18] and who ended up in the Middle East, Europe, Asia, and most other locations around the globe, the San have few shared ancestors over the last 100,000 or more years.[19] They have, in fact, the oldest modern human lineage. Despite their isolation, the San hunter-gatherers created a sophisticated culture alongside what appeared to be an unchanging Stone Age culture, which attests to a creative spark that has been a driving force in human evolution. The first human abstract representation dating to 73,000 years ago is attributed to them, as are spectacular rock paintings around 5,000 years ago (Henshilwood et al. 2018).[20] Moreover, the oldest extant ornamental beads, dating to 75,000 years ago, are also credited to them (Henshilwood 2004). To this we can add evidence of the oldest bows and arrows (poisoned too), the ultimate innovation in hunting and warfare, dating to around 64,000 years ago (Backwell et al. 2018).

The Ju/'hoansi example confirms that all *Homo sapiens* groups prior to the dispersion contained the seeds of BMH.[21] Moreover, the evidence also suggests that the Ju/'hoansi (and other San tribes) would have been practising storytelling and mythmaking in an isolated setting for tens of thousands of years – if not long before they became isolated from other *Homo sapiens*. As noted earlier, storytelling and mythmaking may be as old as language itself; they're a socio-biological phenomenon and an intricate part of what it means to be human. Despite certain innovations, the Ju/'hoansi of southern Africa remained hunter-gatherers whose Stone Age culture changed very little over countless generations.[22] There is, of course, an intricate relation between myth and identity that is almost impossible to escape, and even less so in a Stone Age culture.

I don't wish to imply that human psychology as it concerns the Ju/'hoansi (or any other culture) is static and fixed rather than dynamic. Human psychology is by nature dynamic under certain cultural conditions, and I'll have some important observations to make on this in the context of human evolution and mythmaking later on. But I'd like to draw attention to the claim grounded in the latest anthropological research: that it is in human nature, and thus in our genes, to learn from each other "unconsciously."[23] If this is the case – and I'm convinced that it is – at what point does consciousness awaken, and specifically "conscious reflexivity"?

HOMO PHILOSOPHICUS AND THE EMERGENCE OF REFLECTIVE SELF-CONSCIOUSNESS

Just as the myths proper to a society change over time, so also has the individual qua self within the community.[24]

From an evolutionary perspective, the self has changed, first slowly and then, eventually, dramatically, but in this case, the change was connected with new degrees of consciousness in the sense of self-reflection.[25] The most recent instance of this was the self that gave birth to philosophy and science in Greece during the sixth century BCE. It was here that a new form of reflexivity, reflective self-consciousness,[26] emerged, one that is generally ignored by specialists outside of the area of Greek philosophy,[27] and more precisely the origins of philosophy.

Starting with the Milesians, with whom this revolution is traditionally said to begin, the Greeks adopted a critical approach not unlike what we find in contemporary science: we should never be bound to uncritical acceptance of a particular explanation. This explains the plethora of new and competing ontologies about nature, or *phusis*,[28] that arose with them, an intellectual revolution that had not been seen till then.[29]

This phenomenon isn't addressed, strictly speaking, in the context of these conversations with Luc Brisson. Yet it's fundamental in the sense that it's at this time in ancient Greece that *logos* as reason awakens and becomes conscious of itself. It's also at this time that new masters of truth emerged to *consciously* contest the traditional masters and traditional myths.[30] As I have argued on a number of occasions, with the advent of philosophy we find a radical new self, just as there's a radical new society unlike anything that had hitherto existed before in human history. This new kind of self consisted of a reflective self-consciousness (some may call it the Western self or subject), without which philosophy and Western science would not have seen the light of day. In some respects, as I hope to show, this was so radical a transformation that we can talk about a new kind of subspecies of *Homo*, the *Homo philosophicus*.

I'd like to provide a detailed sketch of what happened in history from an evolutionary perspective in order to lay the groundwork for this new phenomenon, as it comprises a developmental background to Brisson's perceptive thesis on myth, which in turn is fundamental to any understanding of who we are as individuals and the future of humankind.

As I noted above, there's a correlation between myth and the evolution of the self; they're interrelated socio-biological phenomena. Both are also inseparable from the evolution of consciousness. My hope is that the following short digression on consciousness will help the general reader put this fundamental correlation between myth and the self into some perspective.

CONSCIOUSNESS, MYTHMAKING, AND THE EVOLUTION OF THE SELF

The Latin word *conscientia*, from which we derive our word "conscience," means "to know together," "knowledge within oneself," or "to know within one's own mind" (as per the *Oxford English Dictionary*). The etymology, as Agnes Heller notes (2003, 1029), indicates that the role played by knowledge in the construction of this feeling is intimately connected to the activity of a reflective self-consciousness. But how did we get there? Theories of consciousness abound. Indeed, there's no consensus on what it is or how it originated. Some argue that the phenomenon of consciousness is what distinguishes humans from other living things, but most scientists and philosophers understand consciousness as a phenomenon that predates humans.[31] Despite the different scientific and philosophical positions on the origin and meaning of consciousness, most agree that the human species in its present form evolved over time and that consciousness, or rather a certain kind of consciousness, very much defines who we are as a species.

The neurobiologist Gerald Edelman captures the importance, and ambiguity, of consciousness for philosophers, scientists, and religious leaders alike when he claims that "consciousness is the guarantor of all we hold human and precious. Its permanent loss is considered equivalent to death, even if the body persists in its vital signs" (2004, xi). At the end of his recent book *The Origin of Creativity*, the biologist E.O. Wilson claims that the grail to be sought in philosophy and science "is the nature of consciousness and how it originated," for these are inseparable from understanding the meaning of humanity (2017, 197). The neuroscientist and neurologist Antonio Damasio captures the same spirit when he defines consciousness as the mind endowed with subjectivity, without which we'd have no way of knowing that we exist, let alone who we are and what we think (2010, 4, 18).[32] For Brisson's general thesis on the correlation between the self and myth, and my own considerations here, Damasio's *The Self Comes to Mind* (2010) is of particular significance and applicability.

Damasio provides a detailed evolutionary analysis of how the brain constructs the mind and makes that mind conscious.[33] He's quite explicit that humanity would never have developed without consciousness, and so it must have come into existence because it has biological value (2010, 5). Damasio sees the conscious self as having evolved through a series of stages over millions of years, from what he calls the "protoself" (primordial feelings that originate at the level of the brain stem) (11, 22–3),[34] to core self (action-driven, so that it can modify primordial feelings and thus the protoself) (11, 24, 183), and finally to autobiographical self, which has several stages.[35] The latter is also described in terms of a reflexive self, a robust self, and a rebellious self, and it's Damasio's description of these that suggests we have now arrived at a purely human dimension of the self and the emergence of consciousness (305–11).[36] It's here that the relation between biology and culture become intertwined, which echoes (if not supports) several of the points I made above about the intimate relationship between the self and myth.

Until the so-called cultural revolution, it was biological homeostasis that was the driving force behind evolution, including the origin of the proto- and core self. Homeostasis is a dynamic process of life regulation that begins with unicellular living creatures (Damasio 2010, 27). It's an *unconscious* guide, operative until the advent of the autobiographical self, that somehow generated the biological revolution called *culture* – that is, the human capacity to classify and represent experiences through symbols (306).[37]

The catalyst behind culture is another kind of homeostasis that Damasio calls "socio-cultural homeostasis" (28). The two kinds of homeostasis, biological and socio-cultural, are separated by billions of years of evolution, but they promote the same goal: the survival of living organisms. Yet in the case of the socio-cultural, there's *deliberate* seeking of well-being (28–9, 310–11).

There's obviously no exact date for when "full-fledged human consciousness" developed – that is, a mind with an autobiographical self "capable of guiding reflective deliberation and gathering knowledge" (309). But Damasio seems to connect it with when humans discovered the drama of existence (309), and rebellious selves came of age and questioned their status in the universe, including their origin and destiny, and adopted norms of behaviour and consequences for those who break the rules. This is when "myths" are developed; they're a way of making everything stick, of encoding the wisdom and making it comprehensible (311). Storytelling or mythmaking, as Damasio correctly notes, is something that the brain does "naturally and implicitly."[38] Such storytelling or mythmaking is the method by which the self is created, and it "pervades the entire fabric of human societies and cultures" (311). However, Damasio understands storytelling as a much later phenomenon than recent research and our own analysis (see above) suggests. Indeed, he connects it with a certain kind of autobiographical self – a phenomenon to which I'll return.

As I noted above, the anthropological evidence suggests that mythmaking is an integral part of preliterate hunter-gatherer societies, such as the Ju/'hoansi of southern Africa, who may have had the same egalitarian social structure and storytelling technique for 100,000 or more years.[39] Anthropological studies, meanwhile, tend to downplay concepts of the self and its evolution. But, as in the case of Damasio, they do suggest that mythmaking or storytelling performs an adaptive or biological function. Such studies can in some respects also illuminate the evolution of mythmaking. That is, as societies change, so, too, do the myths that account for these changes. While the myths of preliterate hunter-gatherers may have remained essentially unchanged for countless generations, as human societies expanded and became more complex with the advent of agriculture, storytelling/mythmaking became more complex, with appeals to all-knowing and punitive high gods as a way of maintaining order and social structure (see Smith et al. 2017; Purzycki et al. 2016).

I have used Damasio's work to provide a historical or evolutionary background to Brisson's correlation between myth and the creation of the self, as well as to draw some attention to the correlation between culture and biology. But there's another important dimension that is noteworthy for my own thesis. Damasio insists that there are stages to the development of the autobiographical self, culminating in the establishment of autobiographical memories that are also reflective. Damasio suggests that the autobiographical self that we connect with "reflective consciousness," and thus contemporary humans, emerged late (2010, 307). He claims this may be due to an altered structure of the autobiographical self resulting from persistent reflection on humans and the universe. Damasio argues that such an autobiographical self – one "capable of guiding deliberative action and gathering knowledge" – appeared "only after full-fledged human consciousness developed" (309).[40] Interestingly, Damasio believes this alteration may have occurred as late as 800 BCE, or the period *between* Homer's *Iliad* and his *Odyssey*, a contention that reflects two radically different notions of the self.[41] He understands the final stage as connected with the development of writing, or more precisely, a particular kind of writing, the alphabetic script (306).[42]

I'd like to draw the reader's attention to another phenomenon that specialists in most fields ignore, and that's the correlation between the advent of philosophy in ancient Greece and a new way of thinking, a new kind of reflective self that helped usher in philosophy and science. This phenomenon is totally absent from Damasio's account, and also, I might add, from the accounts of specialists working in interrelated fields, including cultural anthropology, evolutionary biology, cognitive science, philosophy of mind, and so on.[43] Indeed, shortly after the emergence of this new kind of consciousness, we find, as noted above, a critical approach not unlike what we encounter in contemporary science: the conviction that we should never be bound to uncritical acceptance of a particular explanation.[44] This is a phenomenon, a conscious phenomenon, that was absent in any other culture or civilization until then. It's the world of competing *logoi* or arguments and the freedom to do so (discussed above).[45]

This is important for Brisson's theory of myth insofar as it introduces the second crucial element into his equation: the invention or discovery of reason, or *logos*, myth's nemesis but also its indispensable partner. Given the significance of this iconoclastic shift, I'd like to provide for the general reader some background on the origins of ancient philosophy and the enormous psychological, social, political, religious, and scientific changes that accompanied the movement to this new mindset over a short amount of time. During this period, the Greek world witnessed several important changes as regards attitudes toward myth (as understood here), reason, and what it means to be a reflective self or person that were in some respects similar to those that emerged with the seventeenth-century European Enlightenment. Indeed, many philosophers and scholars see the concept of the individual in Western thought as beginning with Descartes (1596–1650) and via Locke (1632–1704) generating the notion that we're all born free and equal, an idea that culminated in the American Constitution and the capitalist notion of ownership.[46] But, as I hope to show, the individual, including the individual of today, is never divorced from society; in other words, the individual must, as a means of survival, remain socio-centric.[47]

THE HOMERIC ORAL MINDSET AND THE PRE-REFLECTIVE SELF

I'll begin with the Homeric period to give some idea of the mindset (and notion of the self) *before* the birth of philosophy. In the Homeric poems, as Gregory Nagy correctly notes, "The narrative structure of epic, as in the case with myth and mythopoeic thinking in general, frames a value system that sustains and in fact educates a given society" (1982, 43). These poems appear shortly after the advent of writing in ancient Greece (ca 750 BCE). Because Homeric society was an oral society,[48] we can see what changes occurred with writing, or rather a new form of writing, the form we still use today.

The first poets in Greece – first and foremost Homer and Hesiod – were known as "singers" (*aoidoi*) rather than "poets" or "makers" (*poiêtai*). And their songs were considered sacred.[49] Indeed, they were thought to be "divinely inspired." Homer and Hesiod both make this claim (Hesiod, *Theogony* 31; Homer, *Odyssey* 8.539, 22.347–8). Moreover, because of their privileged relation with the Muses, the daughters of Zeus and Memory (*Theogony* 52–3, 915–18), who know all things, Homer and Hesiod claimed to have knowledge of all things past, present, and future (Homer, *Iliad* 1.70, 2.484–92; *Odyssey* 12.191; Hesiod, *Theogony* 38).[50] From this perspective, the poems of Homer and Hesiod became the closest things the Greeks had to sacred texts. There's no doubt that these "oral" compositions were the first literary masterpieces to be committed to writing when the alphabet took Greece by storm in the eighth century.

Let me turn to Homer in the context of the thesis I'm arguing for: the emergence of a new kind of mindset, a new kind of self, and with it, a new kind of subspecies of *Homo*: *Homo philosophicus*. The Homeric poems, and the characters they portray, do not draw a distinction between the literal and the figurative. This distinction occurs for the first time with the advent of philosophy. Related to this is the fact that Homeric man does not have a sense of a unitary self or a comprehensive consciousness, or what will emerge as a self-conscious intellectual self.[51] I'm assuming that this was the case for *all* people before the revolutionary change that began in seventh-century Greece.[52]

In the case of the confusion of the literal and the figurative, I'll restrict myself to the notion of inspiration. For the Homeric Greeks, the word "inspiration," as in English, is synonymous with "breath,"[53] and the most common verbs and corresponding nouns in Homer (and early Greek poetry) to convey this notion are derived from the root **pnu-* (breathe).[54] The early Greeks understood that physical life would be impossible without breathing. This, of course, is a physical fact, but in Homer there's no clear distinction between the physical and the figurative meanings in the context of "inspiration."

A few examples. Homer frequently speaks of a god or goddess "breathing *menos*" – that is, might, spirit, or battle rage – into a hero as air into the lungs prior to an important endeavour (e.g., *menea pneiontes*, *Iliad* 2.536, 3.8, 10.482, 11.508; see also Hesiod, *Theogony* 31, and the *Liddell, Scott and Jones Greek–English Lexicon*). A deep breath of air endows the hero not only with might, but with a type of madness as well. Thus, at *Iliad* 10.482, Athena breathes strength (*menos*) into (*empneuse*) Diomedes as he begins to slaughter his opponents. In sum, the hero with *menos* breathes it in, and the god or goddess who gives it "inspires" or "breathes" it into him and places it in his soul (*thumos*) or heart (*phrenes*). This is also the case with feelings, emotions, and even thoughts. Thus, Penelope notes that some god breathed into (*enepneuse*) her heart (*phrenes*) a ploy that she should set up a great loom and weave a robe (*Odyssey* 19.139).[55]

The language is no less clear when Homer and Hesiod refer to the *aoidos*, or poet-singer. The bards have a privileged relation with the Muses and/or gods (*Odyssey* 8.45, 63; *Theogony* 94–5). Hesiod states that the Muses breathed a divine voice into him (*enepneusan de moi audên thespin*, 31) in order to celebrate past, present, and future events (32, 38). Neither Homer nor Hesiod are contemporaries of the events of which they sing, but as bards under the inspiration of the Muses who know all things (*iste te panta*, *Iliad* 2.485; *Odyssey* 12.191; *Theogony* 27–8), they have access to divine truths. Via the Muses, they enjoy access to Zeus, who knows all. What all this strongly suggests is not only that the physical and figurative notions of "inspiration" in Homer and Hesiod are not *consciously* distinguished for the poets, but that poetry itself for Homer and Hesiod must have been understood as a divinely inspired gift. Indeed, it's the will of Zeus that the Muses (and thus the minstrels) sing of his power and glory. This would bode well with Bruno Snell's highly influential, but controversial, thesis in *The Discovery of Mind* (1953) that Homeric man has no organ of comprehensive consciousness, no sense of the self (or the whole personality), and was thus incapable of making decisions. External forces – in particular, the gods – are behind all choices, and thus for Snell, the Homeric hero never sees himself as responsible for his actions.[56] At this stage, the body in Homer *always* has precedence over the soul. The body *is* the person, or, more precisely, the bodily part that is designated as such. Indeed, in Homer there are various words for organs of thought or emotion (notably *thumos*, *phrenes*, *kardiê*, *noos*) that are also connected with parts of the body and located, for the most part, in the chest.[57] The inner self is imagined in terms of bodily parts. There simply is no word for inner self or comprehensive consciousness that corresponds to our notion of soul or mind; instead, there is a kind of psycho-physical fusion made up of psychic organs.[58] It's what some anthropologists call the "dividual" self.[59] After Homer, these bodily parts will slowly fall out of use or be subordinated to parts of the *psuchê*, or soul. In Homer, the word *psuchê* signifies "life"; it's the life force or power by which we breathe. It's the "breath soul" because *psuchein* means "to breathe, to blow." It gives life to all bodies. It's only when the *psuchê* leaves the body that the body dies. The *psuchê*, meanwhile, is also what persists *after* death without any *consciousness* in the house of Hades, where it's identified with the *eidolon*, the visible but intangible semblance of the once living person (*Odyssey* 11.220–4). In this case, the *psuchê* is often characterized as the "ghost soul" as opposed to the "breath soul" when it's living. *Psuchê* will in time stand for the psychic unity of the person, that is, the person qua self-conscious psychological subject.[60] This will emerge when both the reflexive[61] and *psuchê*/soul refer to the new concept of the person, and it'll occur with astonishing speed (Jeremiah 2012, 52).[62]

THE ADVENT OF REFLEXIVITY IN LANGUAGE AND THOUGHT

A radical new notion of the individual developed during the Archaic period in ancient Greece (ca 776–480) and culminated with an entirely new notion of the self.[63] This is a fact that is overlooked by those working in fields connected with consciousness and notions of the self.[64] Shortly after the advent of the alphabet around 750 BCE – which is itself a stroke of genius, something to which I'll return below – we find literate personalities who exhibit their self-conscious egos, including opinions and feelings, in their poetic works. One of the very first is the literate mercenary/gentleman soldier and poet Archilochus of Paros (ca 680–640). In one renowned poem, Archilochus reports, without regret, discarding his shield in battle: "I saved *myself* (*auton*). What do I (*moi*) care about my shield? The hell with it! I'll acquire another just as good" (Archilochus frag. 6 Edmonds).[65]

In the second half of the seventh century the reflexive (e.g., "myself") appears for *the first time* in Greek to designate the new notion of the individual and the self.[66] Here are a few examples. The lyric poet Mimnermus of Colophon (ca 660–600) uses the complex reflexive (not found in Homer) with the accent on the cultivation of the self or inner conscience: "Please (*terpe*) *your own* mind (*tên sautou phrena*). Citizens are cruelly capricious, and one will no doubt speak badly of you, another more highly" (Mimnermus frag. 12 Edmonds = frag. 7 West).[67] We find here a shift from the other-centred system in Homer to a self-centred system (Jeremiah 2012, 74). One's first moral obligation is to oneself and not to what others will think.[68] The lyric poet Alcaeus of Mytilene (ca 625–560) uses the reflexive to connect *nous/noos*, or mind, with one's conscious reflective self: "He heartens (*aerrei*) *his own* mind (*noon de Fautô*) completely" (Alcaeus frag. 378 LP = frag. 137A Edmonds). Theogonis of Megara (ca 620–550) uses the simple reflexive when he claims that innate intelligence (*gnômê*) is a man's best possession, and there's no reference here to an external supernatural force: "A man has nothing better *in himself* (*autos en autôi*) than intelligence (*gnômê*), Cyrus, nor more painful than lack of intelligence" (Theogonis frag. 895–6 West = frag. 1171–2 Edmonds). What we have here is a thinking man whose *gnome*, or intelligence, is his best property. We also have a unified sense of personhood with the accent on the self-conscious reflective self. This is a long way from the Homeric notion of the self.

Perhaps the best examples of reflexivization in the post-Homeric period, and the ones that best reflect my own thesis here, are the uses of the verb *sunoida*, which are first found in Solon (ca 640–560) and Sappho (ca 630–550). The verb *sunoida* expresses a knowledge of facts, as in knowing something about a person, but its etymology (see below) is also connected with one of the key words of the Greek Enlightenment: *historia*, which denotes a self-conscious intellectual activity (see above).[69]

Let's begin with Sappho's use of the reflexivization of *sunoida*: "I know this within *myself* (*em' autai tout'egôn*) / am conscious of this (*sunoida*)" (Sappho frag. 16.11–12 LP = frag.15 Edmonds). There's a unified notion of the self here, unlike what we find in Homer. Consciousness becomes her own judge! What we have is an act of introspection, as the *Oxford English Dictionary* defines it: "the action (or ability) of looking into one's own mind; or examination or observation of one's own thoughts, feelings, or mental state."[70]

It's Sappho's older contemporary, the celebrated Athenian law-giver Solon (ca 640–560), who provides us with the first occurrence of *sunoida*, assuming, of course, Solon composed his verse before Sappho's. Before citing Solon's occurrence in context, it's worth noting that Solon is often cited as the originator of the Delphic maxim "know *thyself*" (*gnothi sauton*). A word that often appears in Solon's fragments, in a context radically different from what we find in Homer, is *nous* (mind/soul). We have eight occurrences, and they attest to a subjective conscious mind. Indeed, the notion of moral responsibility is developing. It's not the gods, Solon notes, who are responsible for unrest in a society, but the unrighteous minds (*akikos nous*) of its leaders (frag. 4.7 Edmonds). Excess, he says, is due to an unsound mind (*mê nous artios*, frag. 6 Edmonds). Deceitful citizens are said to have a porous *nous* (frag. 10 Edmonds). Of course, good government (*eunomia*) is a question of looking into our souls and doing what is *dikê*, or right; reasonable compromise among social groups and an intolerance of crooked human judgments are necessary conditions for a peaceful and prosperous society (frag. 4.30–40 Edmonds).

Solon's use of *sunoida* also expresses a knowledge of facts, and it's related to the previous context in which he's taking to task the greedy and crooked nobles responsible for the civil strife of the period: "[Justice] is silently conscious (*sigôma sunoide*) [for mortals] of present and past occurrences" (frag. 4.14 Edmonds). Solon is outraged at the manner in which the Athenian nobles abuse their power for their own self-interest; only those with an unrighteous mind or soul (*nous*) would perform such wicked deeds. They're responsible for their own actions, not the gods.[71] Indeed, Justice (Dikê), who has been silent until now, will exact revenge for past and present unjust actions. Justice sees and knows all, including in one's own mind! And her revenge will be nothing less than civil war or psychological torment! Good government (*eunomia*, frag. 4.33 Edmonds) and the prosperity that follows it can only be achieved if the nobles self-regulate their minds. Solon is indeed an intellectual maverick, a strong practitioner and advocate of the positive results of self-conscious deliberation. And *nous*/mind is the seat or space in which the deliberation takes place.[72]

The relation between consciousness and the autonomous self as expressed in the verb *sunoida* and other complex reflexives culminates, so to speak, shortly thereafter with the advent of self-conscious guilt as expressed by the philosopher Democritus of Abdera (460–370): "The cheerful man (*ho euthumos*) is compelled to just and lawful acts, and so to rejoice both in waking life and in sleep, and is strong and without worry. But whoever takes no account of justice and doesn't do what's right, all such things cause him displeasure when he remembers them, and he fears and torments *himself* (<u>*heôuton*</u>)" (DK68B174).[73] The orator Isocrates (436–338) expresses the conscious autonomous self in an even more uncompromising way: "Never expect that your commission of any shameful act will pass without notice. For even if you escape the notice of others, you will be conscious of it with *yourself* (<u>*seautôi suneidêseis*</u>)" (Isocrates 1.16). There's no room for the gods or any other-directed constraints! These examples reflect a polis in which the rule of law is the order of the day. Of course, this idea was by then around for several generations (see below), though rarely expressed in such a forceful way.

I note these two later examples before I return to the sixth century again in order to show the degree to which the notion of consciousness had changed.[74] What we have is evidence of autonomous reflective minds for the first time in human evolution,[75] and the consequences for the evolution of human culture would be just as astonishing, for a whole new way of thinking about the world and humanity's place in it would subsequently emerge. It's the beginning of Western philosophy and science and the practice of marshalling arguments (*logoi*) to support one's claims (see above).[76]

HISTORIA AND *PHUSIS* AS CATCHWORDS OF THE IONIAN ENLIGHTENMENT

Few concepts reflect the spirit of the new age in Greece better than *historia* and *phusis*. Both were the catchwords of the Ionian Enlightenment. *Historia* (*historiê*)[77] is an action noun related to the agent noun *histôr*, which means "one who knows because he has *seen*" – whence the meanings of "judge," "witness," or "expert." *Histôr* itself is derived from the root **wid*, meaning "see," which also provides the verb *oida*, "I know" – whence the correlation between "knowing" and "seeing." *Sunoida*, which expresses a knowledge of facts, as in knowing something about a person or oneself (see above), is also derived from the same root and verb. *Historia* is also associated with the verb *historeô*, "inquire into," "examine," "investigate." This explains why *historia* is often translated as "inquiry," "investigation," and, of course, "history." In the final analysis, *historia* denotes both a self-conscious intellectual activity and the learning via "investigation" of many interrelated things with the aim of becoming *sophos*, or wise. This is corroborated in a fragment from Heraclitus of Ephesus (ca 540–480) in which he draws a close connection between philosophy and *historia*: "Men who love wisdom (*philosophous andras*) must be good inquirers into many things (*eu mala pollôn historas*)" (DK22B35, trans. Kahn).[78]

As for the word *phusis*, it captures an entirely new ontological category that had no equivalent until then.[79] It enabled the Ionians to present a new conception of the world in which natural causes replaced mythical or supernatural ones. The universe is wholly natural, beyond the control of human "actions" (prayers, sacrifices) and the supernatural forces such actions presuppose. The entire universe is now explained in terms of the "predictable" properties of its basic components themselves.[80] Moreover, what characterizes "investigations," in addition to the predictability of the basic components, are economy and symmetry – all of which are intellectually and empirically justified. We also find in the Greeks the advent of conscious methodologies and rigorous proofs – an unprecedented development in human history.[81]

UNIQUE FACTORS BEHIND THE INTELLECTUAL REVOLUTION

Starting with the Milesians, with whom this revolution traditionally begins, we find this new self-conscious critical approach to inquiry. It's this entirely original mindset that I connect with *Homo philosophicus*. Without this new *Homo*, civilization as we now understand it may never have developed. But how did it happen? What were the unique factors behind this intellectual revolution? I'd now like to address these, or some of these, briefly. There's no one particular factor behind the "original" Enlightenment, but some appear more indispensable than others, notably the alphabet and the advent of the polis. I'll limit myself to these two.[82]

Writing, or, more precisely, the alphabetic writing system, was a necessary factor behind the *historia* phenomenon. The Greeks borrowed the Phoenician consonantal alphabet, and some genius adapted it to the Greek language by adding the five vowels that were accorded equal status with the consonants. Eric Havelock has argued that by simply adding vowels to the consonant symbols, the Greeks discharged a surge of psychic energy that radically and permanently transformed human consciousness (1982, 82).[83] This is quite a contention, and I have no time to address it here.[84] What is certain is that shortly after the introduction of the alphabet (ca 750 BCE), individuals expressed their personal thoughts in writing, reflexivity in the Greek language and thought emerged for the first time, the codification of "secular" law began (ca 675), the iconic poems of Homer and Hesiod were recorded (ca 650–600), and the first critical and "secular" prose treaties appeared (ca 575).

Writing enables comparing and questioning, which can lead to skepticism and alternative explanations of what can be known (Goody and Watt 1963). The examples of this in sixth-century Greece are numerous. But this raises a question: Why didn't this happen in other literate societies? Some would argue that the Greek writing system, the paradigm for our own, was much easier to learn. To some degree this is true, but unlike other civilizations, the Greeks were not dominated by a religious scribal class at the service of a monarch (or his powerful priestly cohort) who was understood as God incarnate or, at the least, as God's representative on earth. This may explain why writing in ancient Greece was never an esoteric craft. Greek religion, meanwhile, was a kind of religion without priests; that is, there was no caste of priests with affixed tradition, education, initiation, and hierarchy along the lines in most other civilizations. And even in cults that were well-established in Greek city-states, there was no class of priests; instead, anyone who followed the usage of the community could become one. As Burkert notes, "In Greece the priesthood is not a way of life, but a part-time and honorary office" (1985, 97).

None of the factors mentioned above entirely explain the advent of "critical" thinking in ancient Greece. It has been argued that Greek rationality, the peculiar rationality we associate with *historia*, was a product of the *polis* or city-state in conjunction with the other factors mentioned above. What was unique about the *polis* was a central square or public space called the *agora*. Although it appears for the first time in the Greek colonies (whose social structures were radically different from those of the Mycenean world, founded on the Bronze Age Greek culture), its essence originated with the old warrior assembly, in which each man could speak freely on condition that he enter the circle and place himself *en mesôn*, that is, at its centre (e.g., Homer, *Iliad* 18.502–5, 19.173; *Odyssey* 2.10–11). After a series of economic and social transformations (beyond the scope of the present discussion),[85] this assembly of equals became the *agora* of the city, where all the citizens (although initially only the aristocracy) could debate and discuss the affairs of the community. The *agora* is thus the circular, centred space that permitted all the citizens to affirm themselves as *isoi* (equals) and *homoioi* (peers), and to enter with one another into a relation of identity, symmetry, and reciprocity – in sum, to form together a united cosmos. Without generalizing too much, the *agora* is the symbol of a spatial structure radically different from the one that characterizes the Oriental monarchies and the Mycenaean world. Power (*kratos*, *archê*, and *dunasteia*) is no longer situated at the top of a ladder. Power is disposed *en mesôn*, in the centre, in the middle of the human group (see Naddaf 2005, 82–6). This, of course, fostered the notion that one could openly debate almost any issue without fear of punishment by god or man. What counted were persuasive arguments based on reason and observation as reflected in the word *historia*. The political experience offered both new models for cosmology (thus the cosmos could now be seen in terms of a balanced relationship or contract between its equal, but opposite, forces or elements, as noted below) and the possibility of challenging deeply held assumptions about "nature."

SELF-KNOWLEDGE, INVESTIGATION, AND CHALLENGING THE TRADITIONAL MYTHMAKERS

I'd now like to turn briefly to some of the philosophers of the earlier period under consideration. I'll begin with Heraclitus of Ephesus (ca 540–480 BCE) and work backwards. Heraclitus has the first literary reference to the Delphic maxim "know thyself" (DK22B101, 116). There are also a number of references in Heraclitus to self-knowledge (DK22B101, 112, 113, 116), the unexamined life (B123), care of the self (B123), and the *psuchê* as the "true self" (B118, 77, and below). In fragment DK22B101, Heraclitus uses the complex reflective in context: "I searched for *myself* (*edizêsamên* <u>*emeôuton*</u>)." A useful fragment to read with this one is DK22B45, where he says,

"You'd never discover the limits of the soul (*psuchê*) although you travel every road; so deep an explanation (*logos*) does it have." *Psuchê*/self and *nous*/mind are inseparable.

Before I turn to the Milesians, the very first philosophers, I must say something about their younger contemporary Xenophanes of Colophon (ca 575–475). Unlike the Milesians, Xenophanes wrote in verse to express the new secular spirit. He offered a sweeping critical assessment of the traditional poetic view of the gods (DK21B10–16) and replaced it with a radical new notion of God that seems to have drawn its inspiration from Anaximander's conception of the primordial substance (DK21B23–6).[86] Moreover, he insisted that "it's not through divine revelation but by searching (*zêtountes*) that men discover (*epheuriskousin*) what is better (*ameinon*) in time (*chronôi*)" (DK21B18). He also claimed that all things originate (*phuontai*) from earth and water (DK21B29), and that fossils and shells found inland and on mountains suggest that the sea must have once covered what is now dry land, and that humanity must have been generated from similar conditions (DK21A33). But my point here is to draw attention to the kind of mindset that did not – and, the evidence suggests, could not – emerge in any other social setting until then.[87]

Meanwhile, Xenophanes gives his personal thoughts (*emên phrondid'*) (DK21B8.2) as a first-person narrator or reflexive voice when discussing the truth about his life in exile: "I (*egô*) know how to speak truly (*etumôs*) about these things" (DK21B8.4–5). Or again, "I (*egô*) tossed about, bearing *myself* (<u>*emauton*</u>) from city to city" (DK21B45, trans. Lesher). I note this to insist once again on the importance and originality of the reflective self in early Greek thought.

I'd also like to mention Xenophanes and Heraclitus in another essential context. Both of them challenged publicly the idea that Homer and Hesiod, the iconic oral poets, had any claim to "truthful knowledge." Recall that Homer and Hesiod were considered divinely inspired, and their works were the closest thing the Greek had to a sacred text. This is a perfect example of a self-reflective individual contesting the group mentality grounded in myth. Moreover, until this *public* scolding of the two great poets, there was nothing to indicate that Homer and Hesiod were understood other than *literally*, as was the case with all sacred texts or sacred oral accounts before then! It was only when Xenophanes and Heraclitus drew attention to the consequences of a *literal* interpretation that allegoresis (allegory as an interpretative mode), a radical new way of interpreting Homer and

Hesiod, was introduced by their defenders. In sum, in reaction to the critics of Xenophanes and Heraclitus, we now have "traditional" intellectuals who insist that the works of Homer and Hesiod must be interpreted allegorically. Thus, for example, the battle of the gods in Homer should be understood as a clash of the natural components of which the universe was composed and by which it functioned according to the Milesian philosophers (see below). Thus, Homer and Hesiod were saying the same thing as the first natural philosophers. This is the origin of what I'll call literary criticism.[88]

ANAXIMANDER OF MILETUS AND THE FIRST SECULAR THEORY OF EVERYTHING

I'd now like to say a few words about the first intellectual pioneers with whom we associate the advent of philosophy. Few working in biological anthropology, evolutionary psychology, and related sciences seem to even be aware of these thinkers or of the degree to which they embody the *Homo philosophicus*. They are, in fact, a kind of culmination of this new *Homo* – not in the sense that philosophy and empirical science no longer continued to evolve, when they were in fact just starting, but because their mindset was so uncompromisingly different from what came before.[89] I'll restrict myself to only a few examples, and I'd like to take them first and foremost from Anaximander of Miletus (610–546), the author of the first known philosophical prose treatise, *Peri Phuseôs* (*On nature*).

Let's begin with meteorological phenomena. Anaximander argued that the same natural causes that were behind the formation of the universe are the ones that explain how the present order of nature is maintained. He gave purely "natural" explanations for meteorological phenomena. Take, for example, thunder and lightning, some of the supposedly ultimate weapons of the gods: "Whenever the wind is enclosed in a thick cloud and forcibly escapes because it's so fine and light, then the bursting of the cloud creates the noise, and the splitting creates the flash against the blackness of the cloud" (DK12A23, trans. McKirahan). Anaximander's naturalist explanation became the norm among the intellectual class. This is reflected well generations later in Aristophanes's *Clouds* (ca 427), which has a perfect example of the new mindset. Socrates tries to disabuse Strepsiades of his rustic anthropomorphic conception of the divinity by offering a naturalistic explanation. It's for all intents and purposes Anaximander's. But the point I want to make here is that Aristophanes uses the complex reflexive as an emphatic locution to characterize the phenomena: "lightning ignites *itself* (autos heauton) due to the rush and force of its movement" (*Clouds* 404–7). Without the gods as external causes, nature (*phusis*) is a *self-maker* (*autopoiesis*) or is *self-grown* (*autophuês*), and thus, like a conscious being, it directs the action toward itself (Jeremiah 2012, 184).[90]

The only extant fragment from Anaximander explains how the present order of things is maintained.[91] The order of nature is based on an equilibrium of rights and obligations, an equilibrium that results when the constituent powers or primary opposites act as equals (DK12A9, B1). The natural order of things is the result of a constant interchange between these powers or opposites, the same powers or opposites that were behind the initial formation of the universe. Some would claim that Anaximander's great eureka moment was his insight that the earth was at the centre of the universe because it was not dominated by anything (*hupo mêdenos kratoumenên*) (DK12A26).[92] The earth's position is the most remarkable element in his cosmological representation because it liberated the mind from imaging that the earth needs a material support, which was the norm in *all* cultures till then. Moreover, the position of the earth at the centre of the universe also explains that the celestial bodies make complete circles around it (unknown till then), and his contention that the celestial bodies have separate rings or orbits suggests that he was the first to discover what we now call space.

Less than a century after Anaximander, Anaxagoras of Clazomenae (ca 500–428) offered one of the first great examples of "scientific" knowledge based on the correct interpretation of the empirical evidence that solar eclipses occur when the moon blocks the sun's light (*antiphraxis*) (Graham 2013).[93] Anaxagoras could empirically test his hypothesis, which explains why it was subsequently accepted by his peers.[94]

Finally, I want to draw attention to his argument that living beings are the result of the same natural causes that were behind the formation of the universe. For Anaximander, living beings emerged from a sort of primeval moisture or slime activated by the heat of the sun after the initial formation of the universe. He also claims that humans must have originated from living creatures of another species because they're the only animals in need of prolonged nursing after birth, and that otherwise they would not have survived (Naddaf 2005, 90). We have here also, in my opinion, a correlation between humans as the authors of their own selves and the natural origin of animal species. The accent is on human beings as self-conscious autonomous entities.

The gap here between the new notion of the self and the revolutions it initiated in science and philosophy, to say nothing of the arts, is so wide as to lend credence to some nineteenth-century views that a miracle of sorts occurred.[95] There's nothing similar to this mindset, including in ancient India, where, as I noted above, there's evidence that a reflective self emerged with the notion of the *ātman* as "true self" as early as the seventh and sixth centuries BCE.[96] In fact, beginning in the seventh century BCE in ancient Greece we find the emergence of a number of competing notions of the self, and with them competing notions of the afterlife.[97] And while some of these may be due in part to cross-cultural influences, the advent of philosophy quickly led to a wide range of competing "rational" models of the self as evidenced in, say, the atomist Democritus of Abdera (460–350).[98] This, too, is a direct consequence of the new mindset that emerged with the advent of the reflective self in a political atmosphere that fostered and tolerated competing ideas, competing ontologies. To my knowledge, this did not occur in ancient India or anywhere else before then.[99]

CULTURAL DEVELOPMENT AND THE REFLECTIVE GENE

What I submit in light of a developing consensus in the scientific community that culture can have significant biological consequences – there are few aspects of human biology that have not been shaped by our culture – is that there may have been a cultural and genetic interaction (or gene-culture co-evolution)[100] driven by a number of unique cultural phenomena that occurred in ancient Greece over a relatively short period of time and that became the catalyst behind the emergence of a reflective self and the new intellectual revolution it initiated.[101] But once started, this process brought about a kind of conscious awakening whereby it was recognized that "individuals" in other cultures, when exposed to the new way of thinking with an open mind and corresponding freedom of expression, could join in the cultural renaissance and make their own contributions.[102] Indeed, while is it in our genes to learn from others (see below), "cultural transmission is more complex than genetic transmission and may occur on short timescales, even within a single generation" (Creanza, Kolodny, and Feldman 2017, 7782). So, to be clear, it's not like the new mindset was restricted to the Greeks, or more precisely a small cohort of Greeks. But as long as the existing culture in which one is raised is dominant, as was largely the case in, say, ancient India and Mesopotamia, the myths one is raised with will still determine in large part who one is, though not entirely what one may become. What seems clear is that in the cultures surrounding ancient Greece – and this would also hold for ancient India – just as the social structure remained essentially static for numerous generations, so did their cosmological models, which were more religiously focused, and which are still very much in the popular mind in India.[103]

This raises the following question: Would a Ju/'hoansi tribesman raised from childhood in the modern world and with equal access to formal education and the other trappings of modernity be as proficient in modern professions?[104] I'm interested in this query mainly to insist that it's not human intelligence but culture that is the primary driving force behind human evolution, and that culture is something that can be learned, which also corroborates the claim that human psychology is dynamic rather than static. [105] An excellent example – and I'm sure every anthropologist has a list – is a study by Madden, Palimi, and Bryson, "Information Behaviour in Pre-literate Societies" (2005). This study focuses on the Kope tribe from the Central Highlands of Papua New Guinea. They were hunter-gatherers and subsistence farmers with a technology based on tools derived from plants, animals, and stones, and their first contact with Western culture was in 1930. Madden and his co-authors detail the information used by the Kope, and in so doing provide a perfect example of myth as understood here: it defines their identity, preserves social networks, and even promulgates practical skills, including hunting, house building, and agronomy. But what's significant as it concerns my own thesis here is that one of the co-authors, Joe Palimi, is also from the tribe. Palimi who is also an airline pilot, was educated at a number of Western universities and is every bit as sophisticated as any "sophisticated" Westerner, whatever their ethnic background. I note this point – which may seem rather pretentious to some – because it strongly suggests that the mind since the emergence of BMH around a hundred thousand years ago – and maybe *considerably earlier*, as we saw with the correlation between campfires and storytelling – has not changed in a fundamental way, and this is the case despite the fact that human gene culture, as Wilson

(2017) and others have surmised, has not only been changing, but changing dramatically, as evidenced in the burst of new technologies around thirteen thousand years ago (see above).[106] This may explain that consciousness – or more precisely, conscious reflexivity – is something learned, and almost contagious once it takes root. I'll have more to say on this as it concerns mythmaking, the creation of identity, and tolerance later on. But I should note that studies in human information behaviour show the degree to which even humans from the Paleolithic period (indeed, our earliest ancestors), while not engaged in conscious reflexivity as understood here, were deeply involved in information technologies in order to survive, and the capacity for such is transferable to the technologies of the contemporary world.[107]

What is in our genes is to learn from others – which is not lost on Brisson when he refers to the importance of working in teams or groups and his claim that originality is a kind of illusion.[108] It's all about information sharing, as human psychology does not permit "cumulative" cultural evolution (see Boyd 2011 above). And so, once philosophy emerged in ancient Greece with the Milesians, we find a similar phenomenon of learning from one another, but, in my opinion, in the form of a burst of creative intellectual energy that was the catalyst behind a plethora of competing brilliant ontologies, rather than simply passing down the same information (cosmologies) from one generation to the next, however important this information was for the survival of the human group/community. But this burst of creative energy didn't make the Greeks (or even a cohort) of their stars intellectually superior to others by nature (*phusei*), as Aristotle seemed to suggest. As noted above, much of their creative genius (or what I'll call creative genius) was nurtured in the political system that was proper to the Greeks in conjunction with other factors such as the writing system. But the fact remains that others nourished in the same system with equal opportunities and aptitudes (say, the gifted among other ancient people) may have also performed as well. In sum, while cultural evolution, at least from the perspective of new innovations, is uncontestable, human minds and brains have not changed biologically to the point that a contemporary human who evolved culturally from countless generations of a preliterate Stone Age culture[109] would not perform as well as, say, a contemporary "white" person if afforded the same opportunities.[110] This is also the case, of course, with what Henrich (2020) calls WEIRDS (Western, educated, industrialized, rich, and democratic). They, too, are products of myths, and those born in a Stone Age culture but raised from birth in a WEIRD one would become (or could become) just as WEIRD![111] Many Western prejudices toward non-Western peoples – and I don't mean to imply that other cultures don't have their prejudices too – are, in the final analysis, directed toward the identity of others as others. But one's identity is determined first and foremost by the myths each of us are exposed to from our birth, and which often have been passed down for countless generations.

MYTH, IDENTITY, AND CONTRASTING ONTOLOGIES

This brings me to the last section of this afterword as it concerns myth and identity and our attempts to make sense of the latter. As one can well imagine, there's a wide range of different perspectives on what it means to be human, and anthropological studies provide numerous preliterate notions of humanity that are exotically different from our own. For the Achuar people of the Amazon, for example, what humans and animals have in common is "humanity" (animals eat, drink, sleep, and dress, the way humans do). Indeed, as expected, anthropologists describe a wide range and variety of ontologies concerning what it means to be human.[112] Philippe Descola, a student of Lévi-Strauss, in *Beyond Nature and Culture* (2014), tries to summarize these with reference to categories: animism, totemism, analogism, and naturalism.[113]

1 animism: Achuar of the Amazon but also some other hunter-gatherer and horticultural societies, including the Ju/'hoansi and Kope mentioned above; also popular among the Inuit; animals and plants are people with souls (or interiorities) similar to ours and with their own societies, but made up of very different stuff;[114]
2 totemism: Australian Aboriginals but also some other hunter-gatherer and horticultural societies, including some First Nations in North America, notably along the West Coast; we humans share both physicality (or some of it) and interiority with many other beings, including rocks and landscapes;[115]
3 analogism: pre-modern Europe, including ancient Greece, and China, or traditional agrarian societies; we humans differ significantly both physically and interiorly from other beings, but there are countless penetrating essences, flows, or qualities that link us all to a great web; and

4 naturalism: the modern technological world; the view that we're all subject to the same physical laws and made from the same stuff, but all beings are radically separated by their interior lives.

Obviously, ontologies are not so cut and dried – and Descola doesn't intend them to be –[116] but I list them to draw attention to a number of stark contrasts among our contemporaries, for we can recognize variations on each of these ontologies within our own multicultural contemporary Western societies. But I also draw attention to the fact that all of these ontologies, including naturalism, would fall under what Brisson would characterize as products of myth.[117]

First, naturalism is the invention of myth, since the theory on which science (or the modern technological world) is based consists of a set of irreducible and indemonstrable axioms, pure inventions of the human mind. It's, as Plato would say, a "likely story" (*muthos eikôs*). This is akin, for Brisson, to traditional myths being composed of sentences that are neither true nor false, and/or events that cannot be verified by the auditors. Moreover, if "science" could explain, for example, the nature of consciousness and how it originated – the grail, as Wilson asserts, to be sought in science and philosophy (see above) – would this bring any sort of comfort to the vast majority of humanity? The later would still turn to "myth" to account for their most pressing concerns, and first and foremost, the meaning of life and death. Finally, all members of the "naturalist" tradition are themselves products of myth. We're exposed to myths in various forms from our birth, and it's these myths that shape much of our identity. Even giants of the Enlightenment like Descartes, Newton, Kant, and even the likes of Darwin, identified strongly with their Christian upbring.[118] And while I suspect that the large majority of contemporary scientists, philosophers, and the intellectual class at large consider themselves as atheists or agnostics – at least in Western democracies – their personal identities in one form or another are the products of myth, and often contrasting ones (also see below on the role of memory).

As we saw above with preliterate societies, myth is a socio-biological phenomenon. It was and is vital for the very survival of the group. In the past, members of the group never doubted or questioned their myths, and yet societies slowly evolved, as we noted, with technological innovations and the emergence of agrarian societies and subsequent urbanization. Later, the invention of writing eventually led to a critique, notably in ancient Greece, of the status quo, and then the first real urban democracies. Of course, we in the West think of our own democratic systems, founded on "social contracts," as grounded in anything but myth. But social contracts, as Brisson reminds us, are pure fictions. They're akin to Plato's "noble lie."[119] As Brisson says above, no group of individuals ever got together in a café or elsewhere and came to the conclusion that, "even if we're free, we have to accept the rules of others in order to avoid fighting with one another." And yet the "social contract" is a fundamental part of the identities of individuals and the group to which they belong in Western democracies. It's also grounded, in large part, in the notion that all men are born free and remain free and equal in rights. This is a fundamental tenet, whether written or not, in the constitutions of Western democracies, including those with a monarch as figurehead.[120] Certainly, few Americans would ever think of their Constitution as founded on myth. Nonetheless, it's founded on principles (that all are born free and equal, for example) that are entirely fictitious. Few Americans would contest that their Constitution defines in large part who they are, and what distinguishes them from citizens of other liberal democracies, to say nothing of other political systems.[121] Of course, it's also a fundamental part of the identity of many groups in the United States that they have not been treated as free and equal, and this, too, is very much part of their identity, engrained in them from birth. In this case, they're, so to speak, the victims of the "myths" of others.[122]

Probably nothing plays more of a role in shaping one's identity than one's creed or religion, which are all founded on myths. Since the American Constitution, like the constitutions of most liberal democracies, guarantees freedom of religion – it's enshrined along with free speech in the First Amendment – this, too, is very much a part of American identity. But what happens in a secular state when the most prominent religion or myth is a proselytizing one? Polls suggest that Americans are among the most religious people on the planet, especially when compared to other Western liberal democracies, and evangelicalism, which was a powerful force in the 2016 election of Donald Trump, insists that the myths of the Gospel, the word of God, consist in the doctrine of salvation by grace alone – that is, in having faith in Jesus.[123] Meanwhile, Christianity isn't the only proselytizing religion or myth. Islam, another Abrahamic religion, understands the Quran as the inspired word of God, which may explain why both religions or myths are widespread around the earth.[124] However, while the doctrines or myths of Christianity and Islam preach conversion, most, if not all, of the primary religions often show little tolerance toward those who do not practise the same faith or adhere to the same doctrine when they form the majority in a country. In India, Hindus are becoming ever more nationalist and intolerant, and yet few modern countries have as many traditional myths running so deep in their psyche.[125] And while the norm is to see Buddhists and the myths that identify them as almost preternaturally pacifist, they, too, have their extremists and episodes of intolerance, as we have witnessed in the violent persecution of Muslims in Myanmar.

But as Brisson insists on several occasions during these conversations, the great political ideologies are all grounded in their respective myths. Now, however, we have, as with Plato, conscious creators of "noble lies." Often, the new myths are still grounded in the myths of old. In China, for example, where ultimate authority once rested with the emperor, it now rests with the Communist Party. Moreover, as noted above, scientists in China are first and foremost functionaries of the state, as they were under the emperor. And the state has little tolerance for myths that do not conform to the true ideology, as the Uighur Muslims have so painfully discovered. European democracies, especially Hungary and Poland, have rediscovered (and re-engaged) their Christian roots – their identity myths – in the face of what they see as a new Muslim or non-Christian onslaught.[126] No doubt, there are many Middle Eastern Christians (ironically, where Christianity began) in the mix; but ultimately, it's all about identity politics, or rather myths. The horrors committed by ISIS, meanwhile, are grounded in that group's own mania for creating a new "noble lie," not unlike the experiment initiated by the Khmer Rouge in Cambodia. And then we have the outrageous war between Russia and Ukraine, capable as it is of morphing into a world war insofar as every major power, military alliance, and economy are taking sides and being drawn into the destructive vortex. The origin of Russia's war lies in a medieval myth of Greater Russia, which also includes Ukraine. If Russia has the support of the church, it's because church and state are seen as one; they're products of the same myth. The war is another perfect instance of the darker side of myth.

This brings me back to Descola and his four primary ontologies: animism, totemism, analogism, and naturalism. There are, as noted above, numerous combinations and variations under each primary ontology. But what we have first and foremost are multiple ways of seeing, understanding, and surviving in the world. What they have in common is that they're all products of myth, and as such are socio-biological phenomena. We live in a world where all these ontologies, these myths, coexist and often overlap, creating complex identities (see above). Those living in the modern world, the world where technology reigns supreme, have much to learn from these other cultures. Often the level of sophistication as concerns survival in traditional preliterate societies is nothing short of extraordinary, as we find in detailed anthropological research.[127] As exotic as the myths of the animists and totemists may appear to those living in the so-called modern world, are they any more exotic than the myths the Christian missionaries and evangelists would have us believe in? Indeed, their ultimate aim would be to have the entire world live under their myths (and let's not forget how enormously influential such groups are in the world's most powerful democracy). On the other hand, many scientists believe that their myths should reign supreme. They claim to hold the key to human progress; or, as some would put it with reference to the burgeoning field of AI, we can now determine our own future, which is really another variation on an old myth already found in Plato.

Since the European Enlightenment that began in the seventeenth century, the individual has been the centre of attention. The notion that we're all free and equal is a more recent phenomenon. It's the clarion call of revolutions, but also of capitalism in its most unfettered form. As Brisson argues in some detail in part 4, there's no originality. Humans have always worked in teams and continue to do so. All human endeavours require co-operation; it's a socio-biological phenomenon with myth at its helm. Despite the fixation with freedom and equality, humans have a natural penchant for belonging to groups, and since groups are defined by myths, myths are inescapable. And yet, as Brisson notes, we must escape myths when they become a political instrument for suppressing those who do not believe in the same myths. This is a phenomenon that seems to be more prominent in the world today. In large part, the answer is tolerance, and not just in the spheres of politics and religion, but also science. The study of other cultures, ancient and modern, can teach us that there isn't one "correct" approach or "perfect" culture. We should be prepared to see that our point of view isn't the only one. We should see all interpretations as provisional, something that would fall under myth as a likely story at best. Logic and its rigorous formulae are not always the common currency when dealing with complex ontologies (Lloyd 2012, 41, 43).

THE MELTING POT AND MULTICULTURALISM AS EXPERIMENTAL MYTHS OF TOLERANCE

A key word is tolerance, and this notion has rarely been more wanting than it is today. Tolerance in the United States seems to take the ideal form of a "melting pot," as per the myth of cultural assimilation and acculturation of immigrants.[128] This is certainly a worthy myth in the sense of creating a new identity, but it has always met with considerable opposition since its inception in the early twentieth century. But if the number of interracial marriages, which has been increasing exponentially, is any indication, things are moving in a positive direction; the myth is closely taking hold.[129]

Canada has a different approach from the one summed up in the "melting pot" metaphor. It's called "multiculturalism." Multiculturalism, a myth in the making, a kind of "noble lie," was adopted in 1971 as a policy solution to rising francophone nationalism in Quebec, but also to account for the increase in cultural diversity across the country.[130] The policy of multiculturalism was to be implemented in a bilingual framework: all immigrants were expected to integrate into one or both of the official language communities, French and English. At the same time the state pledged itself, in the words of the 1988 *Canadian Multiculturalism Act*, to promoting "the full and equitable participation of individuals and communities of all origins in the continuing evolution and shaping of all aspects of Canadian society."[131]

There was, and still is, strong opposition to official multiculturalism in Quebec, but not only in Quebec. The primary argument against, I believe, is that it discourages social integration, and many Quebecers see multiculturalism as placing French culture on no more than an equal footing with all other ethnocultural groups. This explains, at least in part, why the Government of Quebec introduced Bill 101, the *Charter of the French Language*, in 1977. The bill was described as unilingual and culturally pluralist. The chief architect of Bill 101, Camille Laurin, argued that in order to live together in the same nation, different ethnic groups must be able to speak and understand each other using French as the common language, although this does not preclude the continued use of ethnic languages and the maintenance of individual cultures (see Laurin 1978).[132] But cultural diversity has its limits too in the eyes of many Quebecers. After Catholicism, which dominated Quebec society for generations, collapsed with the Quiet Revolution,[133] Quebecers wanted a clear divide between church and state, between religion and government. This is the spirit behind Bill 21, which prohibits persons from wearing religious symbols while in positions of authority, notably, judges, Crown prosecutors, prison guards, and police officers (see above). While a majority of Canadians outside Quebec feel that Bill 21 is excessive, many feel nonetheless that the message of multiculturalism promotes excessive accommodation of cultural and religious diversity at the expense of social cohesion and common values and, indeed, that it encourages the creation of ethnic ghettos. Section 27 of the *Charter of Rights and Freedoms*, which ensconces, or seems to, the myth of multiculturalism – Canadianism in the making – stipulates that the *Charter* "shall be interpreted in a manner consistent with the preservation and enhancement of the multicultural heritage of Canadians." The upshot is that many Canadians thus associate multiculturalism with the basic rights and freedoms enshrined in the *Charter*, such as freedom of expression and freedom of religion. The latter explains why many Canadians feel that Quebec's Bill 21 represents a violation of the *Charter*. But the government, the mythmaker, has not provided any legislative framework for multiculturalism policy as it concerns other relevant sections of the *Charter*.

THE TRUE SELF AND THE IMPOSSIBILITY OF ESCAPING MYTH

I'd like to finish with a few words on the notion of the true self. We often hear people talking about the true self or a search for the true self. What follows from Brisson's analysis of myth, and his attempts to make sense of myth, is that there's no "true self" – that is, a self whose identity has not been shaped by myth.[134] Interestingly, a search, which is to say a *conscious search*, for the "true self" could only begin with advent of a reflective self, and this is the case in both ancient Greece and ancient India. In Hinduism, it was first and foremost *ātman* (see above) that was used to designate the "true self," and in Greek, *psuchê* (although *nous* was just as popular, and later became dominant).[135] Both *ātman* and *psuchê* are derived from roots that mean "breath" of "life force," understood as the pervading principle in the universe, or what gave life to everything *before* these words came to designate the true self and to be used with reflexives (although later they could stand alone). It's one's *ātman* or *psuchê* that transmigrates to a new life after death or attains release from the bonds of existence.

While this is the norm in Hinduism and became popularized in Hindu culture, this was not the case in ancient Greece, where such a belief was held only by a minority (discussed, in context, in part 2, though I return to this below), including among philosophers. But even in the case of the latter, in philosophers such as Pythagoras and Empedocles, the true self is still described as a material entity whether or not it inhabits a body,[136] and when it's in a body, its identity is determined by its previous existence and its new reincarnation (of course, this would also be the case in the Hindu tradition). In sum, its identity is still determined by the myths, as Brisson understands them, to which the soul is exposed. As I noted above, while there were a number of competing notions of the self that emerged with the advent of philosophy in ancient Greece, all of which are due to self-reflection, there's never, strictly speaking, a "true self," that is, a self whose identity was not the product of, or determined in large part by, the community or world into which it was born (and from which it departed). If we can talk about a "true self," it's in an intellectual sense. It's the product of an intellectual or contemplative exercise. We already find this, in my opinion, in early Greek philosophy (Naddaf 2019), and it reaches a kind of culmination with Plotinus (205–270 CE), where we find what I'd call the self-conscious, philosophically examined levels of the self in the quest for the discovery of the true self: sensible consciousness, rational consciousness, spiritual consciousness, and mystical experience. In the final stage or level, the "true self" achieves a state of absolute unity with the One.[137] I note this to insist once gain on the degree to which Greek philosophy took on radical new directions and provided the intellectual foundation for all theologies in the Western tradition and beyond (Islam, for example).[138]

That said, for Brisson, our sense of personal identity is built out of the autobiographical memories we consider significant. But this reconstitution can only be at best approximative. More important, because of our sentiments, such a reconstruction would include a number of biases or prejudices. From this perspective, our personal identity is thus, once again, a myth, even if a certain number of its elements are real. They're real but tainted by all kinds of influences or prejudices. For Brisson, collective memory is as biased as personal memory. He feels that Quebecers' collective identity is still tainted by the bias toward the defeat by the British on the Plains of Abraham. He'd argue, however, that all peoples have some collective bias. In the United States, the defeat of the South by the North in the Civil War still figures prominently in the collective psyche of many southerners despite enormous demographic changes. Myths both personal and collective are hard to erase, and even when they are, they're always replaced by new ones, which is one of the tenets of Brisson's philosophy of myth. What humanity needs are myths, as Plato would see it, that will enable us to flourish as individuals and as collectives without, of course, using others as scapegoats.

Notes

INTRODUCTION

1 However, unlike Plato, Jesus didn't write anything, and this absence of a written record is the perfect soil for a myth as there can be no historical verification. But there is, as we'll see, more to the story.

2 I have a research interest of my own here, and this will be contextualized further on in this introduction, as well as in the afterword, in many of the endnotes, and in my own interview with Brisson in part 4.

3 It would be interesting to see this done more often, that is, the biographical formation of exceptional intellectual figures where their lives are inseparable from their work.

4 Hadot is arguably one of the most important figures in the field of ancient philosophy in the modern area.

5 Before I went to Paris, I was at the Université Paul Valéry in Montpellier. One of my professors there, Jacques Piquemal, who knew I was moving to Paris, encouraged me to attend Hadot's seminars at the EPHE. They had befriended one another in the early 1950s at the seminars of Pierre-Maxime Schuhl at the Sorbonne. I note this to insist on the role of chance encounters in one's life narrative; I know I had plenty in mine.

6 Harold Cherniss (1904–1987) was at the Institute for Advanced Studies in Princeton.

7 I also maintained a close relation with Pierre Hadot until his death in 2010. Hadot will resurface on several occasions during these conversations.

8 Louis-André Dorion is a professor of classics and ancient philosophy at the University of Montreal. He has had his own distinguished career in the field. I should note that I had never met a French colleague, including close colleagues of Brisson's, who had actually read the conversations with Dorion. They were thus as uninformed as I was.

9 Because of my own research interests in myth from the pre-Platonic period, and, more recently, as a socio-biological phenomenon (see below), my references and discussion below can be considered as a supplement to Brisson's, but they also substantiate his theory.

10 There is no one simple definition of myth; indeed, the notion is controversial. I summarize and contextualize the different approaches in my introduction to *Plato the Myth Maker* (1999, vii–liii). Suffice to note here that Plato's understanding is largely in agreement with that of ethnologists.

11 The gods of traditional poetry and religion were described as being jealous, conniving, vindictive, adulterous, and cruel, which are also some of the attributes of Yahweh in the Old Testament. For Plato, the gods should be, of course, models to follow. He therefore reforms the traditional notion and argues that gods can only be perfect and unchanging, and that these are the models that citizens should follow. This requires a reformed educational system and a reformed mythology playing a determining role. It's worth noting for the general reader that poetry for the Greeks was not the solitary and individualistic written pursuit that it's generally understood to be today. Poetry was *the* mass medium of the day, the most effective way to capture the attention – and to influence – a large group of people. The poets "performed" their art through acting, music, and dance, typically before a large group of mesmerized people who interacted almost hypnotically or mindlessly with the performer. Traditional poetry, of course, emerged out of an oral culture, and, even after the written word took the Greek world by storm (see below), oral culture remained dominant in Greek society, with the great poets Homer and Hesiod as the primary exemplars. Long after their works were written down, roving poets or disciples continued to enact their colourful interpretations at public events. Moreover, the poems were the primary texts for all Greek school children, as parents believed that knowing Homer's poems by heart and being able to perform them were necessary conditions for becoming a model citizen.

12 This is connected with the tension between myth and reason that's at the foundation of Western philosophy. This tension, which is inseparable from the famous quarrel between philosophy and poetry (the poets, the "traditional" educators in ancient Greece, were the primary mythmakers and transmitters of myth), will resurface again in the course of these conversations. Indeed, I also provide a historical analysis of the origin of philosophy and the reflective self behind it in the afterword.

13 The Atlantis story, which Plato characterizes as "absolutely true" (*alêthinon logon*) (*Timaeus* 26e), will resurface on several occasions in these conversations and endnotes. It's also an integral part of Plato's

account of the origin of the universe or present order of things. The rational will also be contextualized further on.

14 This only happens when a kind of critical thinking emerges that is connected with the advent of a certain kind of writing, and this will be contextualised on several occasions in the conversations and notes.

15 The most recent research in cognitive science argues convincingly that ritual preceded myth as the human ability to mime and re-enact emerged before language itself with *Homo erectus*. See Boyd (2018). Boyd discusses the latest research in the context of the origin of language. See below.

16 The following definition by Henri Frankfort captures well the inherent relation between myth and ritual: "A myth is a form of poetry which transcends poetry in that it proclaims a truth; a form of reasoning that transcends reasoning in that it wants to bring about the truth it proclaims; a form of action, of ritual behavior, which does not find its fulfillment in the act but must proclaim and elaborate a poetic form of truth" (1946, 16).

17 Since imitation or mimesis is at the heart of both myth and storytelling in the ethnological and Platonic sense (the idea is to *replicate* what the audience hears and sees), myths are akin to what Richard Dawkins understands by the term "memes" (derived from the same Greek root as the word "mimesis"), a word he coined in his 1976 book *The Selfish Gene* as the equivalent of gene. Just as genes compete to be copied, so memes compete with other memes across the world to shape our minds/souls and the social structures or cultures in which they reside. Memes (as in the case of genes) may remain seemingly fixed for thousands of generations, as we see in the storytelling among the Ju/'hoansi of southern Africa (Wilson 2017, 35, 66, 85–6). Indeed, the latter may be a perfect example of how myths first functioned in the context of behaviourally modern humans if not earlier (see afterword). There are many factors that cause myths and memes to change, to compete, to mutate so to speak. The primary factor is culture (see below), but the advent of writing, or more precisely, alphabetic writing, led to the emergence of critical reasoning, which, in turn, was the catalyst behind a plethora of competition that characterizes Western philosophy (see afterword) and a whole new attitude toward myth. Plato, for his part, could be considered as a meme-maker, but one who wants to consciously "create" new memes that will establish a fixed society, which, of course, would be the antithesis of what Dawkins has in mind. Meanwhile, although there is a lack of consensus on a definition of culture, there is growing agreement among behavioural scientists that culture does have a number of common

features, including a system of behaviours (and cognitions) that promotes and creates values, ideas, and world views that are shared and transmitted in a community from one generation to the next (see Cohen 2009). This notion of culture has a correlation with myth as understood in these conversations. Indeed, genes also enter the picture in a big way. For an introduction, see Causadias and Korous (2018). The relation between genes, culture, and myth will resurface in the afterword.

18 Storytelling has been defined in a broad sense as "an account of a sequence of events in the order in which they occurred to make a point" (Polletta et al. 2011); see also Smith et al. (2017). In this case, while all myths fall under storytelling, not all storytelling falls under myth. Indeed, storytelling in this broad sense would include most any kind of everyday conversation. Storytelling and its origin and evolution are also of considerable interest for psychologists and cognitive scientists in a large sense (see below).

19 The famous anthropologist Lévi-Strauss has powerfully argued that myths are a subconscious phenomenon. Indeed, there would have been a kind of internal storytelling – the mind accounting for what was happening in the external environment before communication through language originated. Lévi-Strauss's contention seems to be substantiated in the most recent research in psychology and cognitive science on the origin of storytelling, with some arguing that language is basically for telling stories (see, for example, Donald 1991). For an excellent analysis of the most recent research, see Boyd's 2018 article cited above. Brisson, meanwhile, discusses the impact of Lévi-Strauss on his own philosophy of myth on several occasions. I'll have more to say on Lévi-Strauss further on.

20 I'll discuss the socio-biological function in more detail in my afterword, but given what was said above, it's not surprising that cognitive scientists consider storytelling hard-wired.

21 It goes without saying that the recognition of the survival of one's existence or self in the beyond in one form or another is grounded in myth, but it's easy to imagine the ritual before the story. The different human attitudes toward death will figure prominently in these conversations. Indeed, for Brisson, the need to confront death is a driving force behind myth, and the choices range from accepting it to fighting it. I'll have more to say on the "self" and its meaning in the context of myth in the afterword.

22 I'll also have more to say on the San Ju/'hoansi, a quintessential egalitarian society, in this context in my afterword.

23 For Wrangham (2009, 14), fossil evidence suggests that the discovery of fire goes back to the start of human evolution by the habilines that became

Homo erectus, and thus as early as 1.5 million years ago for some. The newest evidence suggests that archaic humans practised pyrotechnology as early as 800,000 years ago (Stepka, Kolska, and Natalio 2022). But by then, fire making may have been simply routine, although the convention among specialists is that the evidence suggests the control of fire only became widespread around 400,000 years ago. Cooking food, meanwhile, dramatically changed the human anatomy. The change in diet necessitated an entire change in the gastrointestinal system. This is a prime example of the effect of culture on biology. How far back this goes is a matter of scientific debate, but it seems that the human anatomy, as far as anatomically modern humans are concerned (see afterword), hasn't changed essentially in well over 200,000 years. This includes, of course, the vocal apparatus, which must be connected with spoken language. Dor captures the effect of culture on biology with the following formula: "First we invented language. Then language changed us" (2015, 4). Indeed, language, he notes, altered not just our cognition, but also our emotions, behaviour, and our relationships to our own experience and to others. There are, meanwhile, two competing views on the origin of language and speech capabilities: language emerged suddenly, as evidenced in the extraordinary changes in human behaviour around 40,000 years ago; and language and speech originated hundreds of thousands of years ago, as evidenced in the skeletal remains and structures related to speech production. I believe that the best current fossil and genetic evidence for the evolution of spoken language – evidence relating to tongue, ear, and mind – supports the latter contention. More to the point, it suggests that speech had begun to develop by about half a million years ago, in *Homo heidelbergensis*, the common ancestor of *Homo sapiens* and *Homo neanderthalensis* (Dediu and Levinson 2013; see also Dunbar and Gowlett 2014). I haven't seen any changes to this evidence, but I'm aware that research is fluid. Wilson claims that "those with a better capacity for language enjoyed higher survival and reproductive rates" (2017, 88). Wilson would fall in the camp that sees spoken language as a later development. Meanwhile, there has been the claim since the birth of philosophy that language is necessary for human existence. Indeed, the Greeks saw a correlation between speech and reason. They are, in fact, derived from the same root, **leg-*.

24 Brisson is not just a great admirer of Plato, but a caretaker of sorts in the form of overseeing most everything that is published on Plato in every language. This is the aim of the Platonic bibliography that Brisson oversees (discussed in context in parts 2 and 4). It's fair to say that

most of the publications on Plato are academic, and many of these in the context of tenure and promotion. This will also be addressed in these conversations.

25 The influence of Plato in other cultures will be discussed in part 4.

26 Brisson's own "pocket book" translations and editions of Plato's dialogues in French (with over a million copies sold) will be discussed in context in part 4.

27 Plato's Atlantis story will be discussed in part 2.

28 Whitehead ([1929] 1985, 39). Whitehead didn't mean that Plato got the contours of philosophy figured out so that subsequent figures have just filled in the gaps, but that Plato was a towering figure for an entire way of thinking about fundamental questions. The title of the 2018 dissertation by Nathan Dufour Oglesby is a play on Whitehead's famous quip: "Footnotes to Footnotes: Whitehead's Plato." The dissertation, which is available online, is well worth the read.

29 See Heisenberg (1958). Plato's *Timaeus*, as noted above, was the main competitor to the biblical Genesis until the birth of modern physics. Of course, Plato was not aware of Genesis, and would not have held it in high esteem if he were. Nonetheless, they would both fall under what Plato would call "likely stories," with the difference that his account is more likely as he was the first to mathematize the universe and use what we would now consider a scientific method. This will resurface in context during the course of the conversations.

30 Popper will be discussed in context in a series of notes, notably in part 2.

31 I'll touch on the notion of the individual, another largely Enlightenment phenomenon (but with ancient Greek precedents), in the context of the American Constitution further on.

32 The heavenly bodies are the primary source of human benefits; they're the markers of time and thus the source of number, a providential sign if ever there was one in Plato's eyes.

33 As the story goes, Greek almost became the official language of the United States. For a succinct synopsis, see Gregory Pappas, "The Classical Education of the Founding Fathers; Was Greek Almost the Official Language of the United States?," *Pappas Post* (blog), 4 July 2015, https://www.pappaspost.com/the-classical-education-of-the-founding-fathers-was-greek-almost-the-official-language-of-the-united-states.

34 For a recent detailed survey, see "When Americans Say They Believe in God, What Do They Mean?," Pew Research Center, 25 April 2018, https://www.pewforum.org/2018/04/25/when-americans-say-they-believe-in-god-what-do-they-mean.

35 "We the People of the United States, in Order to form a more perfect Union, establish Justice, insure domestic Tranquility, provide for the common defence, promote the general Welfare, and secure the Blessings of Liberty to ourselves and our Posterity, do ordain and establish this Constitution for the United States of America."

36 Michael Lipka, "5 Facts about Religion in Canada," Pew Research Center, 1 July 2019, https://www.pewresearch.org/fact-tank/2019/07/01/5-facts-about-religion-in-canada.

37 It's akin to the American "In God We Trust" on its currency. For an overview of what Americans mean when they say they believe in God, see Pew Research Center, "When Americans Say They Believe in God." It may be unsurprising to some that accordingly to this study, 70 per cent of Republicans believe in the God of the Bible, in contrast to 45 per cent of Democrats.

38 Obviously, religious freedom is protected under the *Charter of Rights and Freedoms*, but that's another story, on which I'll have more to say in the afterword.

39 Eros, or love, meanwhile, as Plato reminds us in his dialogue the *Phaedrus*, is also a divinely inspired madness (*mania*), a gift that has not only nurtured the great works of art but that also enables the soul to apprehend, if educated correctly, a vision of God (265b). In the *Phaedrus*, Plato also provides an unforgettable description of the soul qua "self" confronting the different facets of love or eros in the form of a myth of the nature of the tripartite soul (*Phaedrus* 245c–246d). In *Phaedrus* 246a–256d, we find a charioteer (the rational part of the soul) trying to control a pair of winged horses representing the appetitive part of the soul (bad) and the emotional part of the soul (good). It's as relevant now as it was then because human nature, being what it is, hasn't changed, or hardly!

40 In fact, the archetypes of all beings are endowed with both sexes, and this will be discussed in context and in more detail in part 2, as will the intermediaries between gods and humans, women and men, and living and dead.

41 Plato also advocated vegetarianism for some of the same reasons.

42 *Logos*, or reason, is "rooted in myth" in the sense that it's a special way of seeing myth as traditional stories. There is no *logos* as Brisson understands it without writing, but not all writing systems lead to the birth of reason – that is, to a critical approach to traditional stories. With the alphabetic script (discussed in the afterword), inconsistencies were slowly seen and pointed out, and this led to more rapid changes in storytelling or approaches to seeing the world and the society in which one was raised.

But the political institutions of the polis are also a catalyst here as these institutions allowed open debate in the private and public spheres (see afterword).

The primary reason for which the word *logos* was able to perform the function of "reason" is found in the root of the word. *Logos* is derived from the root **leg-*. The fundamental meaning of the root is that of "gathering," "picking up," "choosing" (see Chantraine 1974, 625). In sum, *legein* was not originally a "saying" verb ("say, speak," whence *logos* as "word"), but a term that translated the activity and laws of the mind (see my introduction to *Plato the Myth Maker* in Brisson 1999, ix–x.). If *legein* was later to become a saying verb, this was due to its figurative meaning of "recounting, telling over, reckoning up" – one of the essential aspects of the verb "say." However, contrary to *legein*, *logos* retained in Attic Greek the rational values of the root **leg-* with the meanings "account, reason," and applied them to the concept of speech. This explains why one can reduce the numerous meanings of *logos* to two: speech and reason. The subjection of the first to the second explains why *logos* could, and did, take on the sense of "rational discourse," that is, a discourse that is argumentative and open to criticism, a discourse that can be logically and empirically verified.

43 For a historical analysis of how allegory or allegoresis – that is, allegory as an interpretative mode – originated, see Naddaf (2009).

44 This is akin to what some see as postmodern philosophy.

45 It's fair to say the Wachowskis' cult movie *The Matrix* draws its inspiration from the cave analogy in the famous choice between the red and blue pills, between perception and reality, between the revelation of the truth and being content to watch the shadows on the cave wall, the true reality for the cave dwellers. What is fascinating and disturbing in the new world of fake news, conspiracy theories, and science denial is the insistence by its promoters that their truth is the only truth, the revelation of which is likened to a quasi-mystical experience, as Lee McIntyre observes in his well-documented recent book *How to Talk to a Science Denier: Conversations with Flat Earthers, Climate Deniers, and Others Who Defy Reason* (2021). If their actions weren't driving a political agenda, science deniers may be less worrisome. In Brisson's theory of myth (as summarized best in part 4), the world of fake news and climate denial would fall under rumour rather than myth.

46 Plato aptly claims in the *Laws* that education is training the child to feel pleasure and pain, to love and to hate correctly, before he/she can understand the reason why (653c–d). Today, the claim is that non-conscious

actions are shaped by the conscious variety. Indeed, it's a question of survival. The unconscious processes of the brain must operate according to conscious intentions and goals that were nurtured during childhood and adolescence. Plato was the first, as far as we know, to consciously take advantage of this on another level to create a new society. The level of consciousness in the case of Plato is from an evolutionary perspective far more advanced. It's a reflective self-consciousness, the genesis of which I'll describe in the afterword.

47 Conflicting in that his preference for the city versus the rural world in which he was raised also plays an important role in his narration of his life story and thus in his psychological makeup.

48 The importance of consciousness is fundamental here. It's becoming aware of who we are, of who I am, and taking hold of one's destiny – becoming aware of our myths in order to avoid manipulation, but also to play the game if need be, if one sees that the myth as something constructive to offer.

49 Quebec's Bill 21, which is not just relevant to Canada and Quebec, is a ban on religious symbols. It's full title is an *Act Respecting the Laicity of the State* (French: *Loi sur la laïcité de l'État*). It was tabled by the ruling Coalition Avenir Québec on 29 March 2019 and passed on 18 October 2019. The act bans new hires in the public service in positions of coercive power (for example, police officers, prison guards, Crown prosecutors, judges, school principals, teachers) from wearing religious symbols. It also mandates that one's face must be uncovered to give or receive public services. It has considerable support among the province's francophone majority, but less among the non-francophone minority. Support in the rest of Canada seems to be uneven. Indeed, it changes from province to province, with older areas of the country being more in favour. Although Bill 21 could be challenged based on the *Canadian Charter of Rights and Freedoms*, the law invokes the notwithstanding clause (*la clause nonobstant* in French) in section 33 of the *Charter*, which allows the federal Parliament or provincial legislatures to override certain parts of it.

More recently (25 May 2022), the National Assembly of Quebec passed by a wide margin Bill 96, which is, for many, a more draconian version of Bill 101 (see above). Bill 96 and the law it enacts prohibits the use of any language but French in the province's workplaces, large or small, public or private, provincially or federally regulated. It's enforced by a language police that can compel documents without a warrant. It shows the degree to which language is seen as indispensable for the survival of Québécois culture. Needless to say, anglophones in Quebec are outraged. But recent statistics indicate that while the number of people speaking French at home in Quebec has increased, the percentage of Quebecers speaking French at home has dwindled, in large part because of immigration to the province. In fact, with increased immigration, one in four Canadians in 2021 claim a mother tongue other than French or English. See "While English and French Are Still the Main Languages Spoken in Canada, the Country's Linguistic Diversity Continues to Grow," Statistics Canada, 17 August 2022, https://www150.statcan.gc.ca/n1/daily-quotidien/220817/dq220817a-eng.htm.

50 The conversations don't hide the admiration for a number of cultural traditions inherited from the British.

51 I'll contextualize this phenomenon, an integral part of myth, in the notes and in my afterword.

52 In some respects, the ultimate aim of the *Canadian Charter of Rights and Freedoms* is to create a mythology proper to Canada: that as Canadians we're all equal, whatever our ethnic background, creed, and historical origins, in the Canadian mosaic. This is the rationale behind the Canadian invention of "multiculturalism." I'll have more to say on this notion in the context of the *Charter* in my afterword.

53 Another point to which I'll return in the afterword.

PART ONE

1 Brisson's post-1999 publications are discussed in part 4.

2 The Treaty of Paris in 1763 brought an end to the Seven Years' War (1756–63). By the terms of the agreement, Britain obtained the French possessions of Île-Royale (Cape Breton Island), Canada (Quebec), the Great Lakes Basin, and the east bank of the Mississippi River. The French settlers remained because they were allowed to maintain their language and the Catholic religion. Moreover, until then, there was an English or French troop offensive approximately every thirty years, and they thought that the next time the French would win. But with the outbreak of the French Revolution in 1789, France was incapable of intervening beyond its own borders. When the calm was re-established, Napoleon embarked on the conquest of Europe. His dream was definitively destroyed at Waterloo in 1815. France would no longer attempt an offensive in North America, which left Quebec under the domination of the Catholic clergy, which continued to live under the Old Regime. Indeed, the revolution was also against the church. This important historical fact will resurface in context below, for it explains much of Brisson's own narration.

3 Limbo was for the Catholic Church at the time an abode where the souls of dead infants, or others, went if they died before baptism. These cases consisted of individuals who died in original sin but who were free of grievous personal sin. Limbo is thus neither heaven nor hell, but an abode in or on the border, as the Latin *limbus* (border) implies.

4 Maurice Duplessis (1890–1959) was premier of Quebec from 1944 until his death in 1959. A controversial figure in Quebec politics, he created the conservative Union Nationale party in 1935, which dominated Quebec politics. Duplessis was a champion of a strong Catholic education and family values, and was opposed to secular social development. He was notoriously anti-union and legendary for his creation of a strong patronage system that many argue got out of hand. But he was also a nationalist at heart, as we can see with the adoption of the Quebec flag in 1948.

5 For more on the meaning of Mass and its mythical antecedents, see the appendix at the end of part 1.

6 Jean de Brébeuf (1593–1649) was a French Jesuit missionary who went to New France in 1625 and worked mainly among the Hurons, learning their language and culture (he was a gifted and renowned linguist). He was captured by the invading Iroquois in 1649, and according to the reports, brutally killed. He was canonized in 1930 and retains an iconic status among the Québécois.

Marie de l'Incarnation, born Marie Guyart (1599–1672), for her part, was an Ursuline nun who experienced her first vision of Jesus at the age of seven. Inspired by further visions of Jesus and the Virgin Mary, and by reading the *Relations des Jésuites de la Nouvelle-France*, she determined to devote herself to missionary work in French Canada. As one of a group of nuns sent to establish the Ursuline Order there, Marie arrived in Quebec in 1639, where she founded a convent and school for girls, including Indigenous girls, to teach them the Catholic religion and French culture. This effort at assimilation eventually failed. She was also an excellent linguist and wrote catechisms in Algonquin, Huron, and Iroquois. Her personal writings contain her experiences and observations during her time in New France and thus constitute an important source of its early history. She was a key figure in the spread of Catholicism in New France, and, like Jean de Brébeuf, is a cultural as well as religious icon. She was canonized in 2014.

7 The classical course in Quebec was a program overseen by the high schools, and it led to the granting of a BA (baccalaureate in arts). The course generally lasted for eight years subsequent to university studies in preparation for both the priesthood and liberal professions. Each year

had a different name: Éléments Latins, Syntaxe, Méthode, Versification, Belles Lettres, and Rhétorique. These first six years were followed by two years of philosophy: Philosophy I and Philosophy II. Classical studies was inherited from the French tradition that went back to the sixteenth century. It was transported to New France by the Jesuits. The first five years of classical courses became the five years of high school in the current educational system in Quebec. The year devoted to rhetoric was discontinued, and the two years of philosophy became the two years of pre-university college education, or CEGEP (originally a French acronym for Collège d'enseignement général et professionnel). As we will see, the seminary in Terrebonne didn't go beyond rhetoric.

8 Jean Lesage (1912–1980) served as premier of Quebec from 1960 until 1966. As leader of the Liberal Party, he introduced a series of reforms, many of them connected with the so-called Quiet Revolution. During his term in office, the role of the Catholic Church was considerably diminished, the prosperity of French-speaking Quebecers grew significantly, and national consciousness increased. Indeed, Lesage made French the language of work, and eventually championed the notion that Canada is a bilingual nation with two founding peoples. The government under Lesage also created a modern and national health-care system, and a modern democratic school system open to the entire population, which is reflected in a number of Brisson's conversations. Moreover, Hydro-Québec, whose accomplishments became a source of pride among Quebecers, was nationalized. Other considerable successes under Lesage included the creation in 1965 of the Caisse de dépôt et placement du Québec, responsible for administering the assets of the Québec Pension Plan (the Quebec equivalent of the Canada Pension Plan), but also for guaranteeing economic benefits for Quebec society through investments, when needed, in key industries.

9 René Lévesque (1922–1987) was part of the cabinet of Jean Lesage before founding the Parti Québécois in 1968 and serving as premier of Quebec from 1976 until 1985. He was the first political leader of Quebec since Confederation to try to achieve the province's formal political independence through a referendum. Lévesque was the leading figure behind nationalizing Hydro-Québec and then expanding it during his term as a minister in the Lesage cabinet. His own government's signature piece of legislation was Bill 101, that is, a Quebec *Charter of the French Language*, the goal of which was to make French the normal and everyday language of work (but he was a pragmatist and insisted on protecting the English language and school rights). The aim of Bill 101 was also to

encourage immigrants, who would be required to attend French schools in order to integrate themselves into the majority francophone culture (Bill 96, passed in 2022, and which prohibits any language but French in the province's workplaces – public or private – is, for many, a more draconian version of this). His government was also the first in Canada to prohibit discrimination on the basis of sexual orientation in the province's *Charte des droits de la personne* in 1977. Many regard Lévesque as the father of modern Quebec, but that seems to be a stretch. Interestingly, he seemed more culturally attached to the United States than to France.

10 The French sociologist Marcel Mauss (1872–1950) famously argued in *The Gift: The Form and Reason for Exchanges in Archaic Societies* (1925) that gifts are never truly free but bring about reciprocal exchanges. Mauss was fascinated with the question of knowing what power resides in the object given that causes its recipient to pay it back, as numerous examples in human history and culture demonstrate. The answer is that it involves a law of obligations infused with spiritual mechanisms. Gift giving engages the honour of both giver and receiver. The giver gives not merely an object but part of himself, and so the act of giving creates a social bond with an obligation to reciprocate on the part of the receiver. Exchanges are made between groups rather than individuals; in other words, the phenomenon of gift giving is understood as such by all members of the society or social group.

For Mauss, gift giving is one of the necessary conditions in building social solidarity and the individual sense of belonging to a particular group, and it's here that Brisson finds support in Mauss's acute anthropological observations as to why francophone Catholic Quebec has never fully integrated into Canada. They simply haven't felt recognized and respected by the anglophone community. Indeed, the ultimate demand – and some would say the minimum demand – on the part of the francophone population in Quebec to get them to sign on to the Canadian Constitution was to recognize Quebec as a "distinct" society and to enshrine this status in the Constitution, which has yet to be achieved. Brisson, for his part, makes the perspicacious observation further on that this lack of recognition of francophone Catholic Quebec by the anglophones is a consequence of the radical isolation in which they lived following the fall of Quebec in 1759. To resist the British Empire, they lived in a kind francophone Catholic ghetto controlled by the church, which included forcing women to have as many children as possible. This explains for Brisson the considerable delay in many areas of social development (prior to this, Quebec francophones were as entrepreneurial as other colonial groups in North America).

Brisson claims that he's a product of this ghetto, in which secular France as well as protestant England were considered evil. The people of French Catholic Quebec saw themselves as a kind chosen people, the vanguard of Catholicism.

I should note that the group mentality to which Mauss is referring is understood as natural, while what the church did in Quebec is closer to what Brisson would call the Platonic model. The church *consciously* endeavoured to indoctrinate every facet of society through an educational model that would prevent those under its control from thinking for themselves.

11 This is an association that strives to uphold and defend Catholic values.

12 The Society of the Priests of Saint Sulpice (Sulpicians), who had their start in Paris in 1641, were in Montreal almost from its origins (the city was founded in 1642). They established a seminary there in 1657. The Sulpicians were quite opposed to the Jesuits, who were all-powerful in Quebec. They were both missionaries and educators. The main focus of the Sulpicians, inspired by the Council of Trent (1546–63), was the formation of the diocesan clergy, or the education of priests and parish work. They thus place a great emphasis on academic and spiritual training, and members commit themselves to a *continual development* in these areas.

The Order of Preachers (Dominicans), to which the famous philosopher-theologian Thomas Aquinas belonged, are a mendicant Catholic order founded in France in 1216. Their primary purpose was to leave the cloisters behind and preach the Gospels in the vernacular language. They're active both in preaching and the contemplative/intellectual life. The Dominicans established themselves in Quebec in 1873.

The Society of Jesus (Jesuits) were founded in Paris in 1534. They taught and teach not only the tenets of Catholicism but also the classics. They were the first missionaries in New France, arriving in Port-Royal in 1611 and in Quebec in 1625. The Jesuits established their first seminary in Quebec in 1663 and henceforth founded a number of post-secondary institutions. They were also linguists, explorers, and ethnographers. Jean de Brébeuf (see above), who arrived in 1625 and died as a martyr in 1649 at the hands of the Iroquois, remains their most famous member in Quebec.

13 Brisson is of the opinion that French cultural nationalism is first and foremost an instrument in the service of economic policy.

14 Napoleon sold Louisiana to the United States in 1803 for fifteen million dollars. At the time, Louisiana stretched from the Gulf of Mexico to what is today the Alberta border, and covered around 828,000 square miles (or around 1,775,000 square kilometres).

15 Aristotle seems to have two distinct projects in his *Metaphysics* that shift between a general sense of being and a particular sense of being. The general sense is that of ontology, or the science of being qua being; the particular sense is that of the most eminent kind of being – that is, the divine – and constitutes the science of theology since it includes the discussion of unmoved movers, which are Aristotle's gods. God, for Aristotle – that is, the ultimate God – is thought thinking itself, or eternal bodiless contemplation, and thus has little, if any, relation to the Judeo-Christian sense of God.

16 Brisson's point is that all natural environments are hostile for a population without technology and medicine. To ward off death and catastrophe, such peoples must relate stories or myths.

17 When a population/group becomes conscious of death, they begin to organize a ritual around the funeral. There are an astounding variety of cultural approaches to death in the contemporary world. Corpses, for example, are burned, buried, and eaten (raw or cooked), and funerals are occasions for weeping, laughing, fighting, and even sexual orgies (Huntington and Metcalf 1979). The question is when do responses to death become culturally meaningful? We know that this phenomenon is not proper to *Homo sapiens*, but is also found in some form in Neanderthals (see Pettitt 2013, 79–89). The mortuary evidence suggests that Neanderthals already had a wide range of different practices.

18 I return to the Neoplatonic philosopher Plotinus (204–270 AD), and other post-Platonic philosophical currents, in several notes in part 2 and the afterword.

19 Since this book is directed to a wider audience, it's worth putting the famous Atlantis myth into context, since most everyone has heard of it, but – Plato scholars and *aficionados* aside – few may be aware that it's Plato's invention. It also plays a fundamental role in Brisson's theory of myth.

In the preamble to the *Timaeus* (17b–19a), Socrates (one of the interlocuters) first gives a brief summary of what appears to be the ideal city of the *Republic*. Then, he says he would like to hear the story of the "real" city corresponding to the theoretical description, that is, a city so conceived, brought to life, and shown in action as fitting into the "concrete" world of war and negotiations. To this effect, Critias evokes a story that, although appropriate to Socrates's request, is said to be "absolutely true" (20d and 26e). The story relates an extraordinary event, a war fought nine thousand years before by an earlier Athens against a great and aggressive power based on an island called Atlantis. Socrates's ideal city will be shown to exist in the primitive Athens, which, by providential coincidence, has a socio-political structure and institutions similar to those of the ideal state. Primitive Athens defeated the Atlanteans and restored freedom to the Mediterranean but was subsequently destroyed in a great natural catastrophe, which also engulfed Atlantis.

It is agreed that Critias will relate the whole story, but not immediately. Before proceeding, one must know the origin of these well-bred men, these Athenians of old, in order to know why they behaved in such a distinguished manner. This explains why Critias's story (and thus Socrates's request) is prefaced by an account of the origin and nature of the universe and humanity by Timeaus. In sum, it's impossible to know why the primitive Athenians behaved in such an admirable way without knowing, first, the nature (*phusis*) of man, and since the latter is dependent on the nature of the universe, a cosmogony (or cosmology) is the obvious starting point. This was the case, I should note, with all accounts, mythical or rational, that pretended to explain the origin of the present order of things. For a detailed contextual analysis, see Naddaf (2005).

PART TWO

1 *Memoirs from Beyond the Grave* (*Mémoires d'Outre-Tombe*) by François de Chateaubriand (1768–1848) was published posthumously in two volumes in 1849 and 1850. It provides a fascinating account of the political and historical events of the author's time by someone who travelled widely and operated as a politician, diplomat, historian, as well as a writer. The reference here is the opening paragraph of book 8, chapter 1 of the *Mémoires*. Contrary to what this quotation suggests, Chateaubriand, who is often considered the founder of French Romanticism, appears not only fascinated with the great expanses but in love or enchanted with what they have to offer, and numerous passages express his admiration for the Native tribes who also saved his life on more than one occasion. The reference to the uninhabited shorelines of the Great Lakes (with a special emphasis on Lake Erie) is, in his own words, the result of the nations of the lakeshore having been exterminated by the Iroquois two centuries earlier. It's a very different world today.

2 Established in 1868, the École Pratique des Hautes Études is one of those uniquely French institutions. Its main purpose is to promote academic training through research. Many distinguished scholars have taught or lectured there rather than in the university system. I trained with Pierre Hadot at the EPHE in the religious studies section, which also included ancient philosophy. Hadot was there before being elected to the Collège

de France, another uniquely French institution. There are some very good online articles on the EPHE for those who may want more details.

3 The Cité internationale universitaire de Paris was established after the First World War by André Honnorat as a meeting place for graduate students, researchers, and intellectuals in the spirit of peace and friendly co-operation. Since 1925, around forty residences, most of which belong to individual countries, including Canada and the United States, have been built there. The campus is also a large private park, which is rare in Paris. I also spent several years there as a graduate student.

4 The École Normale Supérieure (ENS) in Paris is one of the most selective and prestigious institutions of higher education in France. It's outside the framework of the public university system. The ENS was conceived during the French Revolution and was intended to provide the nascent republic with a new body of professors trained in the critical spirit and secular values of the Enlightenment. During their studies, ENS students hold the status of paid civil servants. This arrangement is, if anything, unique. The ENS will resurface a number of times during the course of these conversations.

5 Ancient Greek is a language that belongs to the Indo-European family. Indo-European languages are a group of languages whose lexicological, morphological, and syntaxial elements have resemblances between one another of such a nature that they can be reduced to the same base root. The presupposition is that each group of comparative elements originates from diverging evolutions from original forms now extinct. By extension, one qualifies as "Indo-European" peoples who use an Indo-European language: Indians, Persians, Greeks, Scythians, Romans, Celts, etc. This initial definition implies no notion of "race," since populations of extremely diverse origins can speak the same language.

During the twentieth century, Émile Benveniste and Georges Dumézil proposed that peoples who spoke Indo-European languages shared a similar, tripartite or tri-functional ideology. This tripartition implies a clear distinction between religious and political power, physical force, and material abundance, with India providing the most ancient and complete model. This theory has had a profound influence on several of Brisson's theses.

6 Simone Pétrement was a specialist of Gnosticism, and Simone Weil was a philosopher and left-leaning political activist who still has a large following. She was only thirty-four when she passed away.

7 To be *agrégée* – that is, to have successively passed the *agrégation* in the French educational system – entails passing a highly competitive exam (Sartre failed his the first time) after which the recipient is entitled to be

a professor in a high school or on a university faculty. Every discipline, including philosophy, has its own *agrégation*.

8 Brisson recently noted that, fifty years later, young French scholars publish in English, and organize conferences completely in English (see also note 9 below).

9 Brisson notes that the situation has changed a lot since then. In every field, the common language has now become English, and many French intellectuals, and European ones too, have thus considerable trouble showing their originality except through a mediocre English. The consequence is that the originality of the French, German, and Italian traditions is reduced each and every year. Brisson believes this is a shame, for it constitutes an erosion of other traditions and gives the impression that there's no longer but one point of view in space and time – the English one. I also address in context the phenomenon of English as the lingua franca in several notes in part 3.

10 Brisson was elected to the CNRS in 1974. It was to be his world for his life as a researcher. It's another one of those unique French institutions, and a few words about the organization are in order. Jean Perrin, who was awarded the Noble Prize in Physics in 1926, was at the origin of the merger of the Caisse nationale de la recherche scientifique with the Office national des recherches scientifiques et des inventions in 1938 under the name Centre national de la research scientifique appliquée, which became in 1939 the Centre national de la recherche scientifique. The CNRS really took off after the Second World War. The organization was then orientated toward fundamental research. But in 1966 an important structural mutation began within the CNRS with the creation of associate units. These were university laboratories that were supported by the human and financial resources of the larger institution. These laboratories are connected to the CNRS by an affiliation agreement. With the associate units, the CNRS, covering all scientific disciplines, could help all French research. When Brisson was elected, the CNRS included thirty-five sections, the first being mathematics and the last philosophy. They were elected by a commission that included 21 members: 7 representing the CNRS unions, 7 representing the university unions, and 7 appointed by the government. An elected member had to submit a report every year, but the risks of being expelled were minimal. One could work without feeling any of the various pressures felt by university professors, who envied CNRS scholars in that respect.

11 This would also, of course, apply to technical skills like that of carpentry. The carpenter transmits his skills to an apprentice by showing him/her

what do. A musician, to use a different example, can communicate information through the intermediary of another language, the language of music.

12 What Brisson means here is that philosophy, contrary to, say, medicine or accounting, cannot be separated from one's personal experience. In sum, philosophy is not objective like the science of physics. This is very much the narrative of these conversations.

13 The main thrust of Brisson's point here is that the individual lives in a community that follows rules transmitted through tradition, and that philosophy since Plato has been seeking to evaluate or assess these rules and to change them.

14 Diès ([1927] 1972, 2:433).

15 It's interesting to note the degree to which the understanding of sexuality in ancient Greece is different from ours. It didn't imply any notion of fault, and, in particular, it didn't take into account the identity of an individual. A certain number of social rules had to be followed. But there were no moral interdictions related to such and such an act. Moreover, the same individual could be married and have children and still have relations with a young man.

16 The Plato bibliography lists the editions and translations of the philosopher's works, as well as the books and articles devoted to his life and works. First published by Harold F. Cherniss, then by Luc Brisson (with the help of his collaborators Hélène Ioannidi, Frédéric Plin, and Benoît Castelnérac), it covers the period from 1950 to 2017 and now includes more than fifteen thousand titles.

These titles constitute the data used by Pythia, an electronic bibliographical project conceived and directed by Benoît Castelnérac. The Internet version of this project was developed by computer specialists under the editorial supervision of Denis Arnaud of Vrin publishers. Pythia is a powerful search engine that allows users to find a book or article, its title or contents, very quickly; moreover, many titles are provided with a description. Pythia also enables very rapid searches for Greek terms (more than six hundred), notions (a thousand keywords in French and English), and even the passages in Plato's work dealt with by the inventoried passages. Since the results of all these searches can easily be exported, the teacher or researcher who is preparing a class or working on a publication will find in Pythia an effective and complete tool. The electronic version will be subject to continuous work, to ensure that the search engine is in good working order, and that the bibliographical data are accurate and up-to-date.

17 *Philosophie grecque*, under the direction of Monique Canto-Sperber (1997).

18 For a detailed contextual analysis of Plato's use of myth, see Brisson (1999). In my introduction to that volume, I show the originality and importance both of Brisson's method and of Plato's analysis and place the work in the context of contemporary debates over the origin and evolution of the oral tradition, before as well as after the advent of literacy in ancient Greece.

19 I'll discuss the iconic poets, Homer and Hesiod, in context in the afterword.

20 The Greek expression *gennaion pseudos* (*Republic* 414c1) is generally translated as "noble lie." The lie is also characterized as a *muthos*, or myth. The lie or falsehood is not only that all the citizens are autochthonous (Greek: *auto* [self] + *chthon* [earth or soil]) – that is, sprung from the earth – but that the entire society, in its present form, emerged in the same way. Consequently, the citizens are raised to believe in and defend the present social order at any cost. The society itself is tripartite: it consists of three separate classes (producers, soldiers, and philosophers/rulers), who are also characterized as bronze, silver, and gold. Moreover, the classes must never be mixed, for mixing would lead to the destruction of this divinely inspired social order.

It's important to note, though scholars rarely do, that the Greek adjective *gennaios* (*a*, *on*) can mean both "true to one's birth" *and* "high birth" or "high born." In the context of the *Republic*, it could thus be interpreted as a lie about being "true to one's birth." From this perspective, it can mean all three classes are true to their origin, or simply refer to a lie about being high born. In the first case, *gennaion* is connected with all three classes, whereas in the second case, *gennaion* is connected (or could be) with only the ruling class.

There's more on the famous "noble lie" in part 4.

21 For an analysis of the origins of allegory, and its history prior to Plato, see Naddaf (2009). This essay was originally meant to serve as the introduction to Brisson's *How Philosophers Saved Myths: Allegorical Interpretation and Classical Mythology* (2004). However, I got bogged down with other projects, and the translation was already in press by the time I finished.

22 Plato's philosophy was considered a theology according to Neoplatonist philosophers, based on an interpretation of the second part of his dialogue the *Parmenides*. Brisson, for his part, believes that the second part of the *Parmenides* is instead making a reference to the historical Parmenides and his contemporaries.

23 The revelation is that Plato's theology, which includes his *Timaeus*, is in agreement with the other theologies – the theology found in the iconic

poems of Homer and Hesiod, in the Orphic poems, and in the *Chaldean Oracles*. They were all equally understood as divinely inspired and thus as revealing the same truths. The Orphic poems will be discussed in the context of Brisson's research further on.

24 Brisson (1976). A detailed summary of the myth of Tiresias can be found in chapter 4, entitled "Mediators," in Brisson, *Sexual Ambivance: Androgyny and Heraphroditism in Graeco-Roman Antiquity* 2002, 115–45.

25 In structural anthropology and literary criticism, mythemes are fundamental generic units of narrative structure (normally involving a relationship between a character, an event, and a theme) from which myths are thought to be constructed. Myths that share several mythemes can lead scholars to conclude that they share a common source.

26 Snakes were understood to be the guardians of primordial powers that lurk within Gaia/Earth.

27 Tiresias fulfilled his function as diviner for the royal house of Thebes during the seven generations it was in power. But the main function of a diviner – and Tiresias seems to be the prototype here – is to establish relations between the world of the gods and the world of human beings.

28 According to the Greek tradition that goes back to the *Iliad* and the *Odyssey* and of which Plato was well aware, at death a human's psyche or soul separates from the body, but not in a radical way. Although it leaves the body, the psyche remains a quasi-corporeal entity, always associated with a corporeal element. This quasi-corporeal entity, the soul, is the source of motion for its temporary host.

In Homer's *Iliad* and *Odyssey*, even if the principle of life called "soul" (*psuchê*) isn't strictly speaking corporeal, it remains connected with blood and breath. In these two poems, the psyche, which is located within the body, is not directly observable as such during life, but only once it leaves the body. The soul is connected with a breath (*Iliad* 23.98) that can exit through the mouth (*Iliad* 9.409) or with a vapour that rises from the blood that flows from a wound to the chest (*Iliad* 16.505) or to the side (*Iliad* 9.322). That's why Achilles can complain about "risking his soul" (*Iliad* 9.322).

In the *Iliad*, we find descriptions of two famous deaths: that of Patrocles, killed by Hector (16.505), and that of Hector, killed by Achilles (22.362). "Even as he [Hector] spoke, death that ends all had already enfolded him. His soul left his limbs fleeting to Hades, bewailing its fate, abandoning manliness and youth." When the soul leaves it, the body is no more than a cadaver, a pile of flesh that decomposes. The soul, for its part, is presented as an image (*eidolon*) of the late person (*Iliad* 13.72, 11.476,

24.14; *Odyssey* 11.83, 20.355), its *alter ego*, as Achilles describes it when he evokes the soul of Patrocles, who asked him to organize a funeral in his honour: "Look you now, even in the house of Hades is the spirit and phantom (*psuchê kai eidôlon*) somewhat, albeit the mind (*phrenes*) not anywhere within; for the whole night long hath the spirit (*psuchê*) of hapless Patrocles stood over me, weeping and wailing, and gave me charge concerning each thing, and was wondrously like his very self (*autôi*)" (*Iliad* 23.102–7, trans. Murray in Loeb Edition). Even if this image is his alter ego, when it leaves the body it animates, the soul is deprived not only of physical force but also of psychological force, for it no longer has the capacity to think. Achilles can no longer grasp the soul of Patrocles (*Iliad* 23.102–7) any more than Ulysses can hold his mother's arm in the house of Hades (*Odyssey* 11.205). And it's only *after* drinking the blood of the slaughtered animals (blood is the source of consciousness) that the seer Tiresias, who unlike the other souls is still conscious in Hades, can now predict the future of Odysseus (*Odyssey* 11.90–6), and the other dead, including Odysseus's mother, can be questioned by him.

In this context, death constitutes for the individual a considerable diminution, even if something can indirectly outlive him, that is, if he was successful in passing on his genetic capital through his children or in living on in the memory of his family, friends, or community. But as such, this individual only continues his existence in the form of a shade or spirit that leaves the interior of the body, a breath of air that, under the earth, vegetates for an indeterminate time. Reduced to the state of a shade, the soul seems, with the unique exception of Tiresias, incapable of self-awareness, incapable of agency, incapable of change. Without practically any individuality, such a soul cannot thus be subjected to a system of rewards and punishments destined to correct in another world the injustices committed or suffered in this world.

29 Even though the mouse's closeness to the earth is less evident than that of a snake, the mouse remained a chthonic animal, sometimes even represented as born from the earth. Meanwhile, the transformation into a mouse adds the transgression of another opposition: that between human beings and animals. This version of the myth introduces us to a bestiary of dual sexuality and divination that is composed of a whole set of animals, all linked to dual sexuality.

30 The Phoenix is the bird of fable that repeatedly gave itself life, since it was at once its own father and its own mother.

31 In modern English, as in French, the word "bisexual" refers to a person who has sexual relations with both men and women. In antiquity, where

such sexual behaviour was regulated by a certain number of more or less explicit customs, the problem of "bisexuality" or "dual sexuality" concerned the simultaneous or successive possession of both sexes (i.e., female and male genitalia) by a single individual. That's why the term "dual sexuality" may be preferable to "bisexuality." Brisson (2002) provides a detailed analysis of the rich source material in its historical and intellectual contexts.

32 For Diotima, the ultimate object of love is the Beautiful, which coincides with the Good and the One, whatever its identity. This seems to begin with Plato, but will flourish with Neoplatonism, examples of which Brisson cites in context further on.

33 The discussion of Orphism and related texts also provides a number of pertinent examples of simultaneous dual sexuality, which are fundamental to an Orphic world view. I note this in case the reader misses the context.

34 Hesiod's *Theogony* (ca 700 BCE) has often been called the Bible of the Greeks. It was considered to be divinely inspired, and was meant to be sung as an incantation. Along with Homer's iconic poems, it provided the Greeks with standard theogonies and profiles of the divine personalities.

35 We only have fragments from the original work, to which there are a number of references. The date when the *Sacred Discourses in Twenty-Four Rhapsodies* was written is difficult to determine. The word "rhapsodies" (*rhapsôdia*) suggests that the discourses were recited, as in the case of the Homeric poems, which were also divided into twenty-four books (see below). Brisson (1995) provides a detailed review of the opinions on the topic. For a more recent overview, see Meisner (2018).

36 These will be discussed in context below.

37 The six generations are those of Phanes, Night, Ouranos, Chronos, Zeus, and Dionysus. According to Proclus, *Commentary on Plato's Timaeus* III, 168 17–25 Diehl, "Orpheus taught that these gods are kings who preside over all things, in conformity with the perfect number." For 6 = 1 + 2 + 3 = 1 x 2 x 3.

38 This is the oldest known extant Greek papyrus, and the first discovered in Greece itself. According to the archaeologists, the burning of the roll (see below) took place around 300 BCE. The date of the papyrus, based on the type of writing, is more difficult to determine. The text, which seems to be a dedication, is written in an Ionian dialect, but there are also a number of Atticisms, possibly due to the intermediaries who ensured its transmission. The preserved text consists of an "allegorical" commentary on an Orphic theogony, but the theogony must be older. It probably dates to the fifth century BCE, if not the sixth. This is based on the author's

allusions to other people, notably to Diogenes of Apollonia, Anaxagoras, and the atomists Leucippus and Democritus, all of whom flourished in the fifth century BCE. But the only explicit reference is to Heraclitus (ca 540–480), who is mentioned by name in the fourth column. The scholarship on the Derveni papyrus is considerable, and, as one would expect, there are conflicting interpretations. Brisson, for his part, argues that the philosophical interpretation corresponds to the beginnings of Stoicism (Zeno of Citium [ca 334–262] is the traditional founder of Stoicism) and is thus more recent than what the mainsteam commentators claim (i.e., that it's prior to Plato). There are two reasons for this according to Brisson. First, the use of etymologies and the association of divinities with physical phenomena that we find in the Derveni papyrus begins with early Stoicism. Second, Heraclitus is presented not as a philosopher of perpetual change, as Plato and Aristotle interpret him, but as a philosopher of *logos* (reason), which is a Stoic interpretation.

39 Kronos is born from the union of Ouranos and Gaia. The six generations here are Night, Protogonos, Ouranos, Kronos, Zeus, and Dionysus.

40 I discuss this in some detail in Naddaf (2009).

41 The text says that Chronos made or fabricated (*eteukse*) a silver-plated egg. The use of the verb *teukhô* suggests, not the sexual act, but a craftsman-like activity, for the egg is described as silver-plated. This clearly implies that the egg is not a product of generation and that the sexuality of the beings who preceded the egg was still undetermined.

42 Phanes is derived from the verb *phainein*, "to shine, to make shine; to appear, to make appear." When he emerges from the primordial egg, Phanes illuminates all things. By allowing all things to appear in full light, he inaugurates the process of distinction that constitutes the Orphic theogony, a process that up until then had been thwarted by the darkness in which everything was merged. Phanes, the god who separates and makes distinctions, is also the one who unifies and intermingles. He's the principle of all disjunction and all distinction, all union and all mixing, the ancestor of all the gods, the father and creator of all things. In the *Rhapsodies*, he's also known as Eros, Protogonos, Metis, and Erikepaios.

43 And so in Greek mythology, Athena was born from the head of her father, Zeus. Athena is associated with many things, including wisdom and warfare. It's not by chance that those who used cunning and intelligence in warfare rather than brute force were favoured.

44 The important point in the case of Erikepaios is its identification with Phanes, Eros, Protogonos, and Metis, all of whom are also dual-sexed gods.

45 Brisson's reference here is to Marcel Detienne's thesis in his essay "The Orphic Dionysos and Roasted Boiled Meat," in *Dionysos Slain* (1979). According to Detienne, the Orphic myth in which the Titans dismember, boil, roast, and sacrificially devour the infant Dionysus is articulated in a culinary code whose message is to attack and subvert the whole politico-religious system. That system was allegedly based on the blood sacrifice of animals and the community's feast on their cooked flesh. He insists that the myth's insistence on boiling followed by roasting contradicts the mandatory sequence of the state sacrifice, where food had to be roasted and then boiled. For the Orphics, to create this myth was, for Detienne, to deny a history of culture from bestiality to civilization, which was symbolically condensed in that sacrifice, and which represented man's mediatory position between gods and beasts. Cooking meat civilized humans, distinguishes them from beasts, and thus puts them in a mediatory position between gods and beasts, but also reaffirms a radical separation between humans and gods. Since the myth of the foundation of the first blood sacrifice by Prometheus is found in Hesiod's *Theogony* (535–616) – an account that explains its place, function, and significance in the religious and political life of the Greeks – Brisson and Detienne argue that Orphism is a critique of Hesiod's *Theogony*, the official theology of the polis, and the orthodox view of the city concerning its relation with the gods and the animal world.

Orphism is above all a protest movement on the religious level. It's opposed to the distance between gods and humans. Since traditional religion is founded on a Promethean kind of sacrifice that is inseparable from a certain kind of cuisine that constitutes the paradigm of the division between gods and humans, to change the dietary regime, as we find in Orphism, is to contest the traditional set of relations between humans, gods, and beasts. The myth of Dionysus as we find it in Orphism also teaches the refusal of any blood sacrifice, because this ritual reproduces in a concealed way the crime of the Titans against Dionysus. The true union between humans and Dionysus, in which they participate, cannot be consummated until they recognize their filiation with the Titans and they purify themselves by abstaining from meat. This is also the only means for the Orphics to practise their initiation, which repeats the murder of Dionysus by the Titans, and to escape the cycle of birth and death that continues with successive reincarnations in the form not only of humans but also of beasts. From this perspective, eating meat, murder, and cannibalism correspond. It's only by avoiding this triple crime that humans will be able to unite with the gods, with Dionysus assembling, in himself, the synthesis of all the other gods (see also below).

46 This is reflected in the following postulate from Diogenes Laertius (I, Proem 3), upon which the Orphic theogony rests: "All comes from one and is resolved into it." But it's important to draw the reader's attention to the fact that Hesiod's theogony or succession myth is an exception. All theogonies or succession myths prior to Hesiod are circular, as we see, for example, with the *Enuma Elish* creation myth. Such myths involve the periodic renewal of the present order of things. They're grounded in ritual, a renewal ritual related to fertility. It's the absence of ritual that explains why Hesiod's theogony involves a permanent order. For a detailed account, see Naddaf (2005, 37–57). Meanwhile, in the succession myth that Brisson is analyzing, we can see that every stage of the myth is consciously manipulated. In this regard, it's not unlike, say, Plato's Atlantis myth as a conscious creation. The *Enuma Elish*, on the other hand, is still working at the level of the unconscious, as every member of society would relate to the theogony, and understand it literally. The theogony in the *Sacred Discourses* and its Orphic antecedents are directed at, and consciously created for, a small number of initiates.

47 Both Hesiod's theogony and the Orphic theogony imply a cosmogony and culminate in an anthropogony. Prometheus and Dionysus are the central characters in these anthropogonies, and the episodes in which they appear explain the origin of the human condition, and in particular their relation with the gods and how they should sacrifice to the gods (see note 45 above).

48 The Dionysian or Bacchic Mysteries (like the famous Eleusinian Mysteries) had an agrarian origin, connected as they were with grapes and wine. It's unclear when Dionysus became connected with mysteries (although there's evidence that Dionysus is already a god of mysteries in the sixth century BCE.) As in the case of the famous Eleusinian Mysteries, which can be traced to the seventh century BCE, they imply individual initiation into a secret cult and a happy afterlife. But they have strong bonds with the Orphic Mysteries, which also appear on the scene in the sixth century. The parallels between the Bacchic and Orphic Mysteries are so close (both Orpheus and Dionysus descended into Hades and returned) that often one talks as if they're the same thing. But there are also a number of major differences. How the initiates lived their lives was of no consequence for the initiates, or *mustai*, of the Dionysian Mysteries. Moreover, for the Orphics, immortality could *only* be achieved through laborious efforts that lasted throughout one's life, which was not part of any Dionysian Mysteries. Finally, Dionysian festivals connected with the mysteries were everywhere in the Greek world, and had the status of an Athenian polis religion.

49 Around the same time Orphism appears on the scene, we also have the appearance of Pythagoras of Samos (ca 570–510). The first explicit reference connecting the two (DK36B2) is in the lyric poetry of Ion of Chios (ca 490–430). Pythagoras and his followers, like the Orphics, believed in the immortality of the soul, metempsychosis, vegetarianism (that is, dietary restrictions connected with metempsychosis), primitive taboos, ritual purification, and initiations to assure a better lot for the soul in the next life. But Pythagoreans also differed from the Orphics in a number of important ways. Most important of all, the Pythagorean community subjected its members to a complete formation, integrating scientific knowledge (including astronomy, mathematics, and music) with a complex of ethical, metaphysical, and religious principles so as to assure salvation, or one's unity with the divine.

50 Since Platonism is constantly resurfacing, it may be useful to give some explanation of the doctrine for those who do not have a background in ancient philosophy and culture. There are at least two different kinds of Platonists – those who were interested in his work, and those who also subscribed to his doctrine. There's thus a difference between those who commented on Plato's work and those who were his followers. Here are some of the primary traits connected with the latter sense, which is the most relevant here.

First, while interpretations of Plato's doctrine were quite liberal (see below), there's nonetheless a fidelity as concerns the heart or core of Platonism, which consists of a twofold distinction. The first distinction is that being as a whole consists of two levels of reality: intelligible entities and sensible entities that are copies of the former. This is the case however one wants to define these entities and their mutual relations. This, in turn, explains the relation in a human being between the body and the soul, or what moves the body. The soul survives the body and is susceptible to retribution according to its former life. Moreover, in this soul, a faculty must be postulated that is more or less distinct from the rest of the soul. This faculty is capable of apprehending the objects whose existence is independent of the things in the sensible world and that cannot be perceived through the senses, that is, the forms or intelligible entities. It's obviously this second distinction that constitutes for most people the primary trait of Platonism, insofar as the survival of the soul after death interests most every human.

The determination to defend these two tenets against rival doctrines constitutes another trait of Platonism. The fidelity of Platonists naturally implies a confrontation, an opposition that in each case is inseparable from a strong influence in return. So it can be said that the history of Platonism corresponds to the history of its relations with other schools of philosophy and with Christianity. First at Athens, but also in the entire Roman Empire, there's opposition to Aristotelianism in the case of the Old Academy, to Stoicism in the New Academy, then a reaction to a Platonism too inclined toward Aristotelianism and Stoicism in the case of Middle Platonism, then a critique of Middle Platonism, and finally a more acute opposition to Christianity, at first dissident and then orthodox in the case of Neoplatonism. Obviously, as we can see from Brisson's conversations, there are also the influences of Orphism and Pythagoreanism, or rather Neo-Pythagoreanism. What was central to the latter was the mystical properties of numbers and the notion that the soul had an inherent desire for a mystical union with the divine.

51 Calliope was the first of the Muses born from the union of Zeus and Mnemosyne.

52 Brisson is here referring to Kant's forms of sensibility (space and time) and the twelve categories of understanding (e.g., unity and plurality), which are, for Kant, a priori or pure concepts. Kant, nonetheless, still works at the level of phenomena. He must take into consideration the ideas of reason – that is, the ideas of the world, soul, and God, to which no objects of sense correspond. These ideas can only be associated with the Christian faith (Kant was a Pietist). In sum, even the most "critical" philosophy cannot escape myth.

53 *Chôra* is often translated as "space" but is a far more complicated notion, as one can infer from what follows. Plato's famous description is found in *Timaeus* 52b–53c, where it's also inseparable from his description of the receptacle (another name for *chôra*) and its contents before the intervention of the Demiurge. There will be more on the Platonic notion of *chôra* in part 4.

54 To construct a model, one must decide which elements are involved, and at what time. These decisions differ from cosmology to cosmology, and consequently the definitive results change accordingly.

55 Brisson and Meyerstein (1995). The meaning of the title is the following. Reason is never as powerful as when it recognizes its limits. A reason that doesn't understand its limits falls into extravagance and causes catastrophes. This work has not been translated into English.

56 Brisson's point here is that when Plato, Kant, and Heidegger (his prime examples in this book) question values, each of them begins with a critique of myth they consider primary and then tries to devise a rationally based theory of values, but these only end up being rebuilt on another

myth. Brisson's leitmotif in *Puissance et limites de la raison* is, with a few variations, that philosophy, as the exercise of reason to reach truth, is only a detour between two myths (Brisson and Meyerstein 1995, 128, 158). The word "myth" is here taken in its broad sense to designate a set of unjustified and unjustifiable propositions that are advanced for the sake of persuasion alone, and thus are independent of any preoccupation for the truth (31). Myth plays with our feelings!

PART THREE

1 The first edition had been prepared by G.S. Kirk and J.E. Raven in 1957. At the time it was arguably the best critical history of Presocratic philosophy in the English language.
2 It may be surprising, but those with a position at the Centre national de la recherche scientifique have no teaching obligations, nor do they have an office or particular study location. There are, nonetheless, seminars they must attend or organize among themselves. They were also expected to supervise doctoral theses (I'll discuss this in relation to Brisson in more detail in part 4). Otherwise, as Brisson notes, they have a salary and work on whatever they please within their particular section of the CNRS. It's quite unique, like so many of the other French institutions noted above.
3 The Quebec government offices are the Government of Quebec's official representations around the world. They're overseen by Quebec's Ministry of International Relations.
4 See part 2, note 20 on the noble lie above. It will also be discussed in part 4.
5 Because of the considerable influence of Karl Popper's book *The Open Society and Its Enemies* (1945), considered by many to be among the most important non-fiction books of the twentieth century, it's worth putting the book into some context as it concerns Brisson's argument. It will also give the non-specialist some more insight – assuming one now needs more – into Plato's influence on Western culture and beyond.

Popper detects the emergence of what he calls an "open society" in the democratic Athens of the fifth century BCE. He claims that Athenians were the first to subject their own values, beliefs, institutions, and traditions to critical examination. However, reactionary forces were averse to the rapid social change that an open society had unleashed. These forces wanted to turn back the clock, and Plato emerges as the philosophical champion of the "closed society" and lays the foundation for totalitarianism. Thus, in his *Republic*, Plato, Popper argues, invents an intricate system that would thwart all political and social change and turn philosophy into an enforcer, rather than a challenger, of authority, as his mentor Socrates had done. Popper argues that there are several biases that support Plato's defence of a closed society, but it's holism, in particular, that is related to Brisson's comment. Holism can be understood as the view that comprehension of entities requires understanding them as wholes. It suggests that such entities have qualities that cannot be reduced to their constituent parts. This perspective is often held to be true for biological and social systems in particular.

Plato's holism, for Popper, is reflected in his view of the Greek polis, or city-state, as prior to, and in a sense more real than, the individuals who inhabit it. In conjunction, a just state requires individuals to sacrifice their needs to the interests of the state. Popper saw this as extremely dangerous. In fact, the perspective that any collective social entity has needs that are prior and superior to the needs of actual living persons is the central tenet of all totalitarian states. In the case of the Nazis and the Bolsheviks, it was the needs of race and of class aims and interests that supplant the needs of individuals.

Without making light of Popper's influential thesis – and it has many opponents among Plato scholars – Brisson's point is that Popper's thesis is anachronistic because the notion of the individual as Popper understands it didn't exist in ancient Greece, and, in fact, is a relatively recent phenomenon (I don't entirely agree with Brisson on this, and this should shine through in the afterword). Brisson is here thinking, in particular, of the famous studies by the French sociologist Louis Dumont (*Homo Hierarchicus: The Caste System and Its Implications* [1970] and *From Mandeville to Marx: The Genesis and Triumph of Economic Ideology* [1977]). For Dumont, the word "individual" has two meanings: the empirical agent or particular human found in all societies and cultures, *and* the rational autonomous being peculiar to our modern ideology or to Western civilization, as evidenced in the values of equality and liberty (which, to simplify, emerges during the Enlightenment, but originates with Descartes's *cogito* argument and the discovery of the disengaged self, and the moral source as within us that Kant later made famous). Dumont argues that the people of India (one of his areas of expertise) are individuals in the first sense but not in the second (or, rather, most today in India still see themselves as naturally belonging to a traditional hierarchical society). Indeed, he claims that this is the case for all traditional or hierarchical societies past and present. They have a collective idea of "man." Dumont also uses Plato's *Republic* as a paradigm. The stress is placed on society as a whole; there's only a "collective" human being, meaning that each particular person has a given place in the organization of society and its ends, and, by extension, the global order and its ends. Or, as Plato puts it, the purpose of the model society under construction is to make the entire society or citizen body happy, not particular individuals or groups (*Republic* 420b). In such a traditional society, it's not possible to exercise violence to coerce individuals in the modern sense, because such independent "individuals" do not exist. Even then, I don't mean to imply (speaking for myself here rather than Brisson) that aggression is non-existent among members of the same traditional society. The biological anthropologist and primatologist Richard Wrangham, in his recent book *The Goodness Paradox: The Strange Relationship between Virtue and Violence in Human Evolution* (2019), provides a fascinating account of how members of a traditional society deal with a rogue member, and this seems to be part of our biological evolution.

On the other hand, in contemporary Western democracies, society is made up of individuals, as a result of the Enlightenment in conjunction with the Industrial Revolution and the advent of true capitalism. The individual is autonomous, a complete moral being. But even when separated from the whole, the state still exerts an influence, a coercion, on each individual. Indeed, a new form of subjugation emerges. Political systems meant to be officially egalitarian employ discipline to construct non-egalitarian relations, as Michel Foucault has so well demonstrated. Prison becomes the new norm to impose discipline, but on the individual, not on the group (albeit at times on individuals that seem to belong to a group). In conjunction, individuals can be "destroyed" by stopping them from working, from expressing themselves, or from engaging in politics. Nazism and Bolshevism (Western phenomena that are also products of the Enlightenment) take this to a whole new level. Society is again made up of individuals, but only insofar as these individuals conform to the dominant ideology. Otherwise, they're seen as threatening groups or classes (real or imaginary) against which extreme violence and indoctrination on a massive scale must be employed. Concentration camps and gulags are perfect examples of this. Brisson, for his part, sees himself as having been raised in a traditional "closed" society whose members would have looked after one another. As a reminder, he was raised in a close-knit village community nurtured by Catholic dogma.

6 On the origin and role of the Cité internationale universitaire de Paris, see part 2, note 3 above.

7 Pierre Laporte (1921–1970) was a French-Canadian lawyer, journalist, and politician who was the deputy premier and minister of labour of

Quebec before being kidnapped and assassinated by members of the Front de libération du Québec during the October Crisis. Laporte's body was found in the trunk of Paul Rose's car.

8 An insightful analysis of the consequences of English as the lingua franca is Minae Mizumura's *The Fall of Language in the Age of English* (2015). The work is a clarion call to consciousness about the role of language, and about what it means for the fate of national languages at a time when English has become the world's dominant "universal" language. Interestingly, she dedicates a chapter to the fall of the French language, which was at one point the preferred language, written and spoken, of the cultured elite around the world. Mizumura has a decidedly nationalist attitude toward language that echoes in some respects the language laws in Quebec. But she has a more extreme position in that she'd like to restrict the teaching of English in the Japanese educational system to those who intend on making a profession of English as, for example, translators.

For those who followed the news from Hong Kong, and the District Council elections (held in November 2019), it was interesting to see the ballot boxes labelled "ballot box" in both Chinese and English, and many of the pro-democracy leaders (and their opponents) sporting Western first names. Actually, they have complete Chinese names too but appear to go by "Michael" etc. for public purposes. This would be anathema, the ultimate insult, for Mizumura.

9 I have no idea how things have improved in the francophone universities in Quebec, but recent articles in Quebec papers seem to confirm Brisson's lament. In 2017, the paper *La Presse* revealed that in 2016 nearly 50 per cent of those training to work as francophone teachers in Quebec failed the mandatory French-language exam required to get their teaching certificate. But I don't think this is restricted to Quebec. I believe most would argue that the literary skills of those completing high school a century ago were on average much better than those of students today, and this would include many university students. The number and percentage of students now attending university in Canada is astonishingly high. Today nearly 30 per cent of Canadian adults hold a university degree.

When I began my teaching career at York University, a close colleague in the Philosophy Department at the University of Toronto once told me that in his experience around 20 per cent of the students were A students, while the rest were all over the map. This has also been my experience except in advanced undergraduate seminars. Meanwhile, a new phenomenon in Canadian universities – although this is not restricted to Canada – is the dizzying increase in the number of non-anglophone foreign students.

In some universities, there are now more foreign than domestic students. The primary reason is that universities are cash-strapped. All universities in Canada are public and under provincial jurisdiction, but the operating grants from the provinces have been steadily decreasing (in some provinces, it's now under 30 per cent), and to make up for the shortfall, universities often compete for foreign students, who pay a tuition that may run from twice to six or more times the domestic rate (which, for a basic undergraduate degree, can run from $2,500 to $8,000 – modest by American standards – depending on the province. Although there's an entrance exam, many if not most of the students, as bright as they may be, struggle with the language.

10 Because in most Western countries Latin, if not Greek, was still quite prominent in the school system up to fifty years ago, and still the norm a hundred years ago, I suspect the students were better prepared for an undergraduate university degree in the humanities. This is discussed at more length in the following note.

11 Latin was the language of international scholarship until well into the eighteenth century. Some saw the decline of Latin and Greek as a worrying trend, a sign of decadence. Thomas Jefferson wrote in 1782, "The learning [of] Greek and Latin, I am told, is going into disuse in Europe. I know not what their manners and occupations may call for: but it would be very ill-judged in us to follow their example in this instance" (*Notes on the State of Virginia* [1787], in Peterson 1974). The decline of the classical languages is complex. One reason was the rise of science and the realization that the Greeks and Romans had been astoundingly surpassed. But it was only in the twentieth century that universities, at least anglophone universities, began to drop the Latin requirement for all students seeking undergraduate admission. At Oxford and Cambridge, the requirement lasted well into the 1960s. In France, it was mandatory in middle school till 1968, the year of the great upheaval. Latin still has a prominent place in the Italian school system.

12 And so Aristotle's treatise on moral philosophy in his *Nicomachean Ethics* is still a major competitor with any ethical theory today.

13 To combat the low birth rate, Quebec introduced in the late 1990s a subsidized child daycare system that remains the envy of the rest of the country.

14 It's worth reminding an anglophone audience that until the 1970s, the Canadian business elite thought that a francophone Quebecer could not be qualified to manage a company. How could one not react to such arrogance! Thanks, in large part, to the Caisse de dépot et placement du

Québec, the Quebec national pension plan, there has been a dramatic shift in such attitudes. Quebec now has a considerable number of francophone business leaders, whatever their competency in English as a second language. Moreover, Quebec is now one of the economic engines of the country with one of the lowest unemployment rates.

15 In my opinion, a testimony to the distinction between francophone and anglophone cultures in Canada can be found in watching and comparing the evening national news on the CBC (Canadian Broadcasting Corporation) with its francophone equivalent, Radio-Canada. Even the coverage of international news stories can be quite different. But the most astounding difference is when a Québécois cultural figure, largely unknown in anglophone Canada, passes away. It may take up much of the opening news report on Radio-Canada, while in the anglophone world, an equivalent figure would be relegated to a clip toward the end, assuming such a story made the cut at all.

16 The initial interviews were conducted in 1999; today, Brisson has now lived in France for almost fifty years.

17 For Brisson, the cultures of ancient Greece and Rome are dependent on the culture of India, as we find in the studies to which he alludes above. This is confirmed for him in the Sanskrit language. I should note that Brisson does not mean to imply that the Western science and philosophy that originated in Greece in the early sixth century BCE are or were dependent on the culture of India.

18 The famous Greek expression *homoiôsis theôi kata to dunaton* appears in Plato's *Theaetetus* 176b1–2.

PART FOUR

1 The new French translation and edition of Plotinus's *Enneads*, in nine volumes, was published by Flammarion between 2002 to 2010, with a volume appearing each year. While Brisson and Jean-François Pradeau were the main editors, the work involved other scholars, including Richard Dufour, Jean-Marie Flamand, Francesco Fronterotta, Matthieu Guyot, Jérôme Laurent, Laurent Lavaud, Pierre-Marie Morel, Alain Petit, and Thomas Vidart. The edition is a massive undertaking that assembles the fifty-four treaties of Plotinus in the chronological order in which they were edited by Plotinus's pupil, Porphyry. Each of these volumes has an extensive introduction and copious notes. On Plotinus, see note 136 in afterword.

In addition to this collaboration, Brisson worked with Jean-François Pradeau on a translation and edition of Plato's *Laws* in two volumes

(2006), and on Plato's *Politicus* or *Statesman* (2003). They're both published in the GF series noted above. Both have extensive introductions and copious notes.

Brisson also served as joint editor, with Olivier Renaut, of a collection of fifteen essays for Academia Verlag entitled *Erotique et politique chez Platon* (2017). He also worked with Arnaud Macé and Anne-Laure Therme to edit *Lire les Présocratiques* in the Quadrige Manuels series published by Presses universitaires de France (2012), and, in the same series, with Francesco Fronterotta to co-edit *Lire Platon* (2006).

2 *Études platoniciennes* is an annual, peer-reviewed, open access journal founded in 2004. Each issue focuses on a theme or work relating to Plato and the Platonic tradition. Each issue also features the "Bulletin Platonicien," with its reviews of recent books, and the "Bibliographie Platonicienne," which lists all the publications in the field. *Études platoniciennes* promotes pluralism of languages, disciplines, and methods of reading.

3 *Sentences*, Greek text, French translation, interpretative essays, and extensive commentary by Luc Brisson *et al.*, 2 vols. (Paris: Vrin, 2005).

4 Just to be clear, when Brisson mentions the translation of Plotinus that he undertook with Pradeau and others in 1995, he's referring to the translation of Plotinus's *Enneads* in the Garnier-Flammarion series.

5 Brisson is saying that it's very different from doing a translation alone, which can often lead to peddling a single interpretation. His own editions offer lengthy introductions and copious notes to try to address competing interpretations.

6 Thus footnotes in editions like those of Plotinus should alert the reader to the variety of interpretations on offer.

7 The most recent research in evolutionary anthropology supports Brisson's claim here. Creativity and innovation are rooted in a collective brain, even if some individuals are more creative than others. As Henrich notes, "the great feats produced by those geniuses, generally represent recombinations of ideas or concepts already circulating within their communities or networks" (2023, 418). In conjunction, the latest anthropological research claims that it is in human nature, and thus in our genes, to learn from others "unconsciously." This will be discussed in context in the afterword.

8 Brisson's edition of Plato's *Apology or Defence of Socrates* in the Garnier-Flammarion series has sold well over 500,000 copies.

9 Almost two-thirds of Brisson's edition of Plato's *Symposium* in the Garnier-Flammarion series consists of an introduction, notes, and indexes (noted in context above). This is also the case with his other contributions to the series.

10 For the general reader, I should note that Plato's *Symposium* is arguably one of the greatest works on love ever composed.

11 Brisson's point is that Agathon and Pausanias were living together in what we'd call today a common law relationship, even though it didn't conform to the custom of the time.

12 Brisson is here referring to the archaic, and even classical, Athenian notion that education was connected to homosexuality. From this perspective, education is considered the transmission of power, knowledge, or virtue that passes from a recipient who is full, the master or lover (*erastês*), to a recipient who is empty or less full, the disciple or beloved (*eromenos*), through the intermediary of physical contact by simple phallic touching or penetration and then ejaculation in the sexual union. The origin of this association between sexuality and education is related to an initiation ritual that was practised by the Dorian warrior class during which the older males transmitted their powers (essentially of a military and moral order – that is, the virtuous qualities of an accomplished warrior), which were thought to reside in the male sperm, to the younger males in the course of copulation. The older males in this tradition were expected to be more interested in the qualities of character than of physical beauty.

Plato takes up this idea but subjects it to a devastating critique. He now sharply contrasts the seduction involved in such sexual relations with the seduction at work in education. Although seduction obtains in both sexual relations and education, the nature of that seduction is now completely different in each. The type of seduction at work in education is only interested in the soul, and it has as its aim a way of life that seeks wisdom.

13 The feminine model is found in the figure of Diotima, a priestess, in the *Symposium*. She's portrayed as better informed about male desires than males themselves, because she can explain in what consists the correct practice of pederasty (*paederastia*), which deals with the soul rather than the body. Education is no longer considered an acquisition of a competence relative to material things, but a conversion toward the intelligible in general, and toward beauty in particular, which the soul contemplated before it gained a physical body. And Socrates, by his questions, enables the soul, pregnant with this knowledge, to give birth. Thus teaching, rather than transmitting knowledge, is in fact a matter of making a soul conscious of the knowledge it already has in itself. In this context, teachers are assimilated to divinities who preside over childbirth, and they lead the soul of the disciple to give birth to beautiful discourse about knowledge and virtue. This segues into references to the mysteries and culminates in what it truly means to be a philosopher.

14 For a succinct overview of Strauss's philosophy, including the context of what follows, see Batnitzky (2021).

15 Brisson is not implying, of course, that all right-wing people in North America identify with Strauss. Nor is he implying that the far-right groups that are thriving in European countries, and in particular in eastern Europe, are not radically opposed to relativism. Indeed, there's some irony in the fact that many members of the Far Right adhere to an ideology grounded in the same mistrust of relativism as, say, some Muslims.

16 Friends and associates of Socrates, who we can characterize as aristocratic reactionaries.

17 I should note that Plato thought that prayers should always be supported by one's rational judgment (*Laws* 687e). The gods cannot be swayed by pleading or presents.

18 On the other hand, there are a number of works now devoted to Plato as a model for contemporary ecology, with widely different perspectives. See, for example, Ophuls (2013).

19 This was discussed in the context of Orphism and sacrifice in part 2, including in several related notes.

20 This poses a problem for contemporary interpreters. The fact that the highest knowledge for Plato is the result of an intuition makes the communication of it difficult, for the experience of truth remains individual. Since truth is extremely difficult to communicate, it runs contrary to democracy, which is founded on discussion. This is one of the primary criticisms against Plato.

21 In the Jewish, Christian, and Islamic worlds, law is imposed from the outside in a revelation that is fixed in writing or in the written word. Interestingly, the written word also plays a fundamental role in Plato's law code in the *Laws*, but the code is the final result of trial and error involving the human intellect in the pursuit of the best constitution to enable humans to flourish, which is to say attain happiness. It's not imposed on humans by an exterior power or almighty God.

22 As we see in book 3 of the *Laws*, the lessons of history are a primary factor in determining which law code will be the most appropriate to human flourishing as Plato understands it.

23 *Chôra*, or space, a controversial topic in Plato's cosmology, was discussed in a different context in part 2 and corresponding note.

24 See part 1, note 15.

25 As Plato notes in the *Timaeus* (48a), his creation myth, the generation of the universe is a mixed result of the combination of reason and necessity. Since the Demiurge is not all-powerful, as in the case of the Abrahamic

God, there will always be aspects that are outside of God's control; that is, the victory of reason over necessary, also considered an errant cause, is never complete, although the Demiurge crafted the best possible world under the circumstances.

26 The entire universe for Plato is a living animal, a living organism, that must be understood and respected. Indeed, for Plato, we must work with the resources at our disposal and avoid the kind of superfluousness that an avidity for wealth promotes. The most famous example of Plato as a feminist is the fact that women can also be philosopher-queens, the counterparts to the philosopher-kings, in the ideal city of the *Republic*. In the *Laws*, both girls and boys attend school, and women have access to the highest offices of the state, and must perform military service.

27 What I mean by humans existing for a reason is that their raison d'être for Plato in the *Timaeus*, his cosmogonical myth, is that they must make the motions of their souls conform to those of the world soul, which is a living model of perfection and harmony. Since humans are by nature social and political animals, this can only be achieved in the context of a reformed city-state, which, in principle, must also have a corresponding eternal model. As for humans being part of the world furniture, what I mean here is that, for Plato, humans are included in the eternal form on which the sensible world is modelled. We don't find this in any previous cosmological accounts, rational or mythical. In, say, the famous *Enuma Elish* creation story, where humans are created to be the slaves to the gods, this is presented as an afterthought. In Hesiod's creation story, we first find the gods and humans feasting together. But the humans here are strictly male. It's only later that woman is created (the famous Pandora myth), to punish Prometheus for offending Zeus. In all the Presocratic rational accounts of the origin of the present order of things, humans evolved after the formation of the universe. There's a possible exception with Anaxagoras, for whom the seeds of everything now existing were inherent in the original mass from which the universe evolved. For a discussion in a wider context, see Naddaf (2019).

28 Plato doesn't use the word *muthos* (myth) in the example of Gyges. The accent is on the lesson that one can or should learn from the story that is an integral part of myth, and why Brisson uses the term here.

29 I always found the Gyges ring story a favourite to get students engaged. For what would they do, as in the story of Gyges, with a ring that would make them invisible? What would they do with such power? In fact, what they say they'd do is a good indication of how they were raised and the values they hold dear. Gyges, a Lydian king, for his part, overthrew the legitimate

king and married his wife. Interestingly, the first time the word *turannos* (tyrant) appears in the Greek language is in reference to Gyges (Archilochus of Paros, ca 650 BCE). The story, without the reference to the invisible ring, is first related by famous Greek historian Herodotus (ca 490–425 BCE) in *The Histories* (book 1.2–19), which relates the struggles between a small, divided Greece and the mighty Persian Empire.

30 For Plato, the perfect model requires that there be three classes of citizens (philosophers, guardians/military, and producers), as we saw on several occasions above, and notably in the myth of the metals. The question is how to create a living model of perfection, or what is seen as perfection. What will be point zero in the real world? For Plato, the best of the guardians will become philosophers. Once this is initiated, then the question is how to sustain it. That's where the importance of raising them, and educating them, in one big family comes into play. Moreover, origin myths and testing by a select few from childhood will always be necessary.

31 Plato's idea – and he's well aware that it will be controversial – is that the children of the philosophers and guardians, which includes men and women (there are philosopher-kings and philosopher-queens), will be raised and educated in one big family (this is not the case for the productive class). Mothers and fathers would never get to know who their biological children are. Only a select few would know this. The titles "son," "daughter," "brother," "sister," "mother," and "father" would be applied to children born within a precise time frame. This will prevent relevant groups having sex with one another (*Republic* 461d–e). Socrates points out that a city will attain the most unity when all the citizens feel pleasure and pain at the same events, and that this is possible only if they all say "mine" and "not mine" in unison about the same things in the same way. Socrates (the spokesperson) lists a number of advantages of communal life as it would be experienced in the ideal state. There would be no need of lawsuits and mutual accusations, and no dissensions would arise because of differences of wealth (*Republic* 464d–65c). Indeed, wealth is perceived with some contempt as it's connected with the lowest part of the soul.

32 In Plato's ideal city of the *Laws*, he introduces private property, but private property that can be exploited but never sold. There will be 5,040 lots of land (a number with an important mathematical significance), and this number will never change. There will be four property classes, and the owner of a *kleros*, or family lot, can never accumulate more than four times the maximum amount of wealth that was initially mandated by the legislation, or, alternatively, never have less than one-quarter the minimum amount initially mandated by the legislation. From this perspective,

the lowest amount of wealth can never be more than sixteen times the maximum. In any event, the owner of a *kleros* can never acquire more land. Nor can he sell or rent it. The *kleros* must be transferred to one of his sons, and if he doesn't have a son, then it reverts to the state. Again, there's apprehension toward wealth acquired for the wrong reasons (i.e., for its own sake). Obviously, there's no community of wives and children, but everyone is exposed to the same education. It's in this dialogue that the philosopher-kings and -queens are replaced by the rule of law, another Platonic first!

33 In book 10 of Plato's *Laws*, we find the first arguments in Western philosophy for the existence of God. There are, in fact, two: the cosmological argument, and the physico-teleological argument. Plato's arguments are directed at what we now call reductive materialism. He calls these arguments the best and finest preamble the law code could have. Until *Laws* 10, it's assumed that everyone believes in God/gods, and the entire law code was based on their existence. And then we hear of modern theories that think/argue otherwise.

That said, it's also important to note that in the famous Greek expressions *theous nomizein* or *theous ou nomizein* – that is, "to recognize the gods" or "not to recognize the gods" – the verb *nomizo* is directly related to *nomos* (law or custom). To be an atheist didn't mean to refuse to adhere to a revealed doctrine by an all-powerful being, as we find in the Abrahamic religions, but simply not to recognize the gods of state and the myths concerning them. The number and nature of these gods and corresponding myths could change from city-state to city-state. While Socrates was accused of atheism in the *Apology*, he was anything but an atheist. He simply didn't believe in the traditional gods of mythology – that is, the traditional gods of most of his compatriots, the gods recognized by the customs and laws of Athens. For a discussion of the origins of atheism in a wider context in ancient Greece, see Naddaf (2019).

34 Just to be clear, this is not the same notion of criticism as when one is critical of another for various reasons. Even in Stone Age preliterate societies, such as the Ju/'oansi of southern Africa, who seem to have had the same egalitarian social structure and storytelling technique for 100,000 or more years (see introduction and afterword), complaints and criticism are not uncommon. But in this case, they're motived by envy or jealously during mostly daytime talk. See, for example, the fascinating study by Wiessner (2014). Brisson is using "criticism" in the sense of an argument in favour of cultural relativism, or at least to highlight that there are various competing cultural positions, as we find prominent in

Herodotus. The philosopher-theologian Xenophanes of Colophon (ca 575–475 BCE) made similar arguments a century before Herodotus.

35 Criticism, which is closely connected with the birth of philosophy in ancient Greece, also gave birth to cultural relativism, which played a prominent role in the Greek Enlightenment and was a catalyst behind Plato and Platonism.

36 I should note that Brisson is referring here first and foremost to confronting death from a traditional perspective – that is, the innumerable myths that humans devised to account for death, which may be as old as language itself. If, on the other hand, we were to examine how, in the face of death, one ought to live one's life, then we get into philosophy as a way of life and encounter a plethora of different philosophical positions and arguments on confronting death. For example, the Epicureans, Stoics, and Platonists espoused ways of life and approaches to death that were inseparable from how they viewed man's place in the universe, which, in turn, was closely connected with their perspectives on the origin of the present order of things.

37 In the Greek polytheistic tradition, punishment is limited in time and space, and one always has an option of asking another god to help you.

38 In Hesiod's *Theogony*, Zeus as the most powerful of the gods imposes a new socio-political order, but this order is limited to the Greek people.

39 The question, then, is what ethical guidelines or theory would be the most appropriate to follow in order to replace, first and foremost, the most important constraint in the religious toolbox, that is, the fate awaiting the adherent in the afterlife for not abiding by God's law? One possibility would be a meta-system as we find in the eighteenth-century philosopher Emmanuel Kant (see above), which is dominated by the famous categorical imperative, a supreme principle of moral law that is unconditional or absolute for all agents, the validity or claim of which does not depend on any ulterior motive or end. The categorical imperative captures the duty dictated by our reason and is best known in its first formulation in his *Grounding for the Metaphysics of Morals*: act only according to the maxim whereby you can, at the same time, will that it should become a universal law.

40 For the Amazonian myths in which Lévi-Strauss specialized in his field work, see below.

41 All these Catholic doctrines are myths for Brisson in that they're all connected with sacred and unverifiable stories that are considered true for the believers, and that determine, in large part, how and why they should live their lives as practising Catholics. Such thinking is basic to all myths

as defined by Plato, but also for ethnologists and cultural anthropologists who have studied storytelling in all preliterate peoples.

42 As societies became more sophisticated and complex with the slow transition from hunter-gatherer to farming/agriculture-based societies that involved new forms of co-operation, different kinds of gods were introduced/generated, including the belief in moralistic high gods, which are absent from hunter-gatherer societies. Cross-cultural data shows that larger and more politically complex societies tend to have more supernatural punishment and moralistic deities. See Purzycki et al. (2016); also see Smith et al. (2017).

43 I'm using "myths" here in the sense of immigrants arriving with the myths that enabled them to identify with a particular group, and, more precisely, with a particular religious group. This includes, of course, the different branches, denominations, or sects associated with Protestantism.

44 It was on the occasion of the marriage of the Catholic King Charles IX's daughter, Margaret, to the Protestant Henry III of Navarre (Henry IV). Many of the most distinguished Protestant noblemen had gathered in Catholic Paris for the occasion. As the story goes, the king ordered the killing of a number of Huguenot leaders, including the Admiral Gaspard de Coligny. It's estimated that anywhere from five thousand to thirty thousand Protestants were massacred.

45 Of course, the Crusades, which were initiated by western Europeans (and the Latin church), are also explained by the fact that Muslims on several occasions tried to impede pilgrimages to Jerusalem, which had a history dating back to the fourth century, and thus long before the "Holy Land" was conquered by the Muslims. In the eyes of the most devoted Christians, and those who could afford it, the pilgrimage, which was long and dangerous, offered rich spiritual rewards, if not a key to the gateway to heaven itself. One can only imagine the consequences if there was opposition to pilgrimages to Mecca. It's worth the reminder again that the Christian Byzantine Empire remained on the borders of the Holy Land until the fall of Constantinople in 1453 (in sum, it lasted a thousand years after the fall of the Western Roman Empire). For an interesting and entertaining account of the pilgrimage in the late Middle Ages, see Chareyron (2005).

46 I can well imagine that some would contest this given what is currently happening in, say, Hungary and Poland, where religion is used to further the interest of a political party.

47 The reference here is to the final section of part 2.

48 For a summary of Detienne's position on myth as "rumour," see Detienne (1980). Detienne sees *muthos* as synonymous with *phêmê*, the main meaning of which is rumour and is already found in Hesiod's *Works and Days* (760–4), in a passage where it's used on several occasions in the strong sense of what we generally associate with rumour, noise/confusion/talk that spreads, which is intimately connected with its Latin origin (*rumor, rumoris*). For Detienne, the myth qua rumour can be used to highlight the absurdities of others, or, in a more positive sense, as in "let what we're saying spread like a charming rumour." For the use of *muthos* prior to Plato, see my introduction to Brisson's *Plato the Myth Maker* (1999, vii–x).

49 I addressed the different interpretations of the meaning of *gennaion pseudos*, or "noble lie" (*Republic* 414c), in part 2, note 20.

50 We find the first clear formulation of the social contract theory in Plato's *Republic* (358e–359b). The reference is probably to a sophistic theory from the late fifth century BCE. Rousseau, for his part, argues that laws are binding only when they're supported by the will of the people. His famous claim that "man is born free, but he's everywhere in chains," challenged the traditional order of society, and was a catalyst, or one of them, for the French Revolution. Rousseau was obviously influenced by La Boétie (see below).

51 In *The Politics of Obedience: The Discourse of Voluntary Servitude*, La Boétie (1530–1563), in his youth (he was only thirty-three when he died), asks the question that most of us have thought about at one time or another – and I don't just mean intellectuals. During his time, most every state was dominated by a tiny minority who lived by rules or laws that were different from everyone else and who maintained a monopoly on these laws and thus the authority to rule everyone else. This is slowly, but surely, becoming the case in many Western democracies, which are now ruled by what Plato calls the "money-making" part – that is, the lowest part of the soul – which is for the new tiny minority the *sine qua non* for authority. How could such a state, La Boétie asks, have any staying power, since it could be toppled at any time if people withdraw their consent? He then investigates the mystery as to why people do not withdraw such consent, given what is obvious to him – namely, that everyone would be better off without the state (or such a state). Is it, he asks, because of cowardice, tradition, and so on? He believes that the tyrant (enlightened dictators, as Plato would call them, don't seem to enter into the picture) has nothing more than the power that we confer on him. He would never come after you, he notes, if he didn't have your

co-operation. La Boétie goes on to make a case as to why people *ought to* withdraw their consent immediately. He urges all people to rise up and cast off tyranny simply by refusing to concede that the state is in charge.

La Boétie seems to be replying to Machiavelli (1469–1527), who, in *The Prince*, argued that it was better for a ruler to be widely feared than to be greatly loved. Machiavelli bases his theory on what men do rather than on what they *ought to* do. Thus, his observations leave aside the questions of religion and morality. Unsurprisingly, Machiavelli was also influenced by the great Athenian historian of the Peloponnesian War, Thucydides.

52 Brisson doesn't mean to imply that the conquest of democracy wasn't realized without a great fight, but only that it's founded on a social contract, which is a modern myth. Many are not aware of the relation between Rousseau (1712–1778) and the social contract, but the social world of our democracies is modelled on its consequences.

53 For an interesting analysis, see Kobe (2018).

AFTERWORD

1 The intent of this section, which may appear unrelated to the overall theme, is to draw the reader's attention to the very foundation of the correlation between the evolution of *Homo sapiens* and storytelling/mythmaking. I have profited considerably from the public symposia of the Center for Academic Research and Training in Anthropogeny.

2 There's evidence of *Homo erectus* in Indonesia as early as 1.7 million years ago and in Europe as early as 1 million years ago.

3 The Acheulean culture or tool kits are characterized by the biface with hand axes and other large cutting tools. The Oldowan tool kits that preceded them include hammerstones, stone cores, and sharp stone flakes.

4 There are four recognized systems of inheritance that influence evolutionary processes that are important to note for a general audience: genetic inheritance (passing of genes encoded in DNA from one generation to the next); epigenetic inheritances (stress sensors on a mother in pregnancy that can be passed down to the next generation); behavioural inheritance (passing of behavioural actions and knowledge that are not unique to humans from one generation to the next); symbolic inheritance (passing down ideas and symbols that influence the way we live that are proper to humans and can potentially affect the transmission of biological information from one generation to the next). I borrow these categories from Fuentes (2017, 6–7).

5 There was a group of small-bodied hominins that also have their origin in *Homo erectus* that became isolated on the island of Flores in Indonesia and only became extinct around 60,000 to 100,000 years ago (see Fuentes 2017, 44). This begs the following question: What was the main factor that enabled them to survive without spoken language for countless generations? Indeed, how did they get to the island to begin with?

6 Denisovans are a mysterious hominin species named after the Denisova Cave in Siberia (Russia) that left behind substantial traces in our DNA and share a common ancestor with Neanderthals and *Homo sapiens*.

7 The comparison of Neanderthal and anatomically modern human DNA suggests that both lineages diverged from a common ancestor, and paleoanthropologists claim that the most likely ancestor is *Homo heidelbergensis*, and that this occurred between 350,000 and 400,000 years ago. The Heidelbergensis-Neanderthal line lived from 400,000 to around 40,000 years ago (30,000 by some accounts) in North Africa, much of Europe, the Middle East, and parts of central Asia. Those in this lineage developed increasingly complex stone and then wood tools, built shelters, learned to control fire, adapted to different environments, crafted small pieces of art and jewelry, and buried their dead. They exhibited innovation, ingenuity, and collaboration (they also later mated with *Homo sapiens*). If the Neanderthal and *Homo sapiens* lineages separated at least 400,000 years ago, and both were innovators (I discuss the mythmaking San Ju/'hoansi in this context separately further on), this says something about the cognitive aptitudes of *Homo heidelbergensis*, which, in fact, had close to the modern brain size. Indeed, it was around this time that technological innovations began to expand (see Fuentes 2017, 227–8).

8 Genetic analysis indicates that "all people living today share a common archaic *Homo sapiens* ancestor less than about 320,000 years ago" (Reich 2018, 18). Meanwhile, the oldest *Homo sapiens* evidence to date from fossils is from Jebel Irhoud in Morocco and dating to around 300,000 years ago (see Hublin et al. 2017, 289–92).

9 For the evolution of the human brain shape of BMH, see Neubauer, Hublin, and Gunz (2018). If the brain cases were similar to ours in size and shape 100,000 years ago, this suggests they had the same capacity of intelligence, and so a *Homo sapiens* from 100,000 years ago would perform just as well in our contemporary society with the correct opportunities. Indeed, this may be the case long before 100,000 years ago. I'll have more to say on this intriguing topic further on in the case of the San Ju/'hoansi. Of course, this begs the following question: When did mythmaking begin?

10 The argument for 100,000 years ago is that for the first 200,000 years after AMH first appeared, tools and artifacts remained surprisingly simple, although this is much contested. The paleontologist and evolutionary biologist Nick Longrich (2022a) provides a good synopsis. Some specialists place the dating of BMH around 65,000 years ago with the appearance of more advanced technology, such as complex projectile weapons, fish hooks, ceramics, sewing needles, and, indeed, seafaring (the evidence for the latter being the arrival of *Homo sapiens* in Australia around 65,000 years ago). But it's highly unlikely such mastery appeared abruptly. Meanwhile, others yet again place BMH around 40,000 years ago, when representational art begins or rather takes off (cave paintings, ivory goddesses, lion-headed idols). For a useful synopsis of innovations based on recent research, see Longrich (2022b). One of the best accessible books on the topic is Fuentes (2017).

11 I don't mean to imply that BMH emerged abruptly. There's always incrementalism. So, before BMH left Africa, the seeds associated with their development were already germinating. Indeed, the evidence suggests that the mental capacities associated with BMH are found in southern Africa around 100,000 years ago in the form of the manufacture of compound paints and adhesives in the descendants of the San or Ju/'hoansi hunter-gatherers of southern Africa today (see below). I'll have more to say on the Ju/'hoansi in this context further on, as the genetic evidence confirms that they're the oldest *Homo sapiens* lineage. Moreover, just as we now know that *Homo sapiens* interbred to some degree with Neanderthals after their arrival in Europe, *Homo sapiens* have likely interbred with other *Homo* species before they left Africa and during their dispersion around the globe. Indeed, the evidence suggests that there were early *Homo sapiens* living in the Middle East by 130,000–100,000 years ago, and so potential interaction with other human species long before the major dispersal out of Africa (ca 80,000 years ago). I discuss language in context further on. Language, of course, is the medium by which myths are created and conveyed.

12 There were a number of migrations, as attested in evidence of AMH in other parts of the globe over 100,000 years ago.

13 There's the seeming Eurocentric thesis that true BMH only emerged in Europe after the arrival of *Homo sapiens* around 46,000 years ago. At this time, Neanderthals were still thriving, and their subsequent annihilation or disappearance circa 40,000 years ago is inseparable from the dominance of more innovative *Homo sapiens*. Meanwhile, there's now evidence of *Homo sapiens* in southern Europe as early as 210,000 years ago (Harvati et al. 2019).

14 Again, the dating is obviously fluid, as it depends on what counts as a threshold for BMH. As Fuentes (2017, 228) notes, even before the emergence of AMH around 300,000 years ago, there's evidence of stone tools at a level of craft and symmetry beyond their basic need between 500,000 and 300,000 years ago (see also above), and this is the case in different locations around the globe. For an analysis and discussion of Neanderthal creativity and subsequent *Homo sapiens* creativity often during the same period, see Fuentes (2017, 229–37). But in all fairness, there's nothing that even approximates the artifacts left by BMH later than 40,000 years ago – the cave paintings at Chauvet circa 35,000 years ago are nothing short of extraordinary. Indeed, there's a convention among cultural anthropologists and the like that around 40,000 years ago major changes began to occur in the mind, as attested in cave art, and then dramatic social changes began to occur around 12,000 years ago with the advent of agriculture (dating, of course, is fluid). Urban societies began to emerge around 7500 BCE, and we find, between the hunter-gatherer and the advent of urban societies, chiefdoms where the social structure is already hierarchical (but based in kinship), with the chief whose position is hereditary at the apex of the social pyramid. I understand the term "civilizations" to refer to the first city-states or large urban centres, which may have eventually housed up to 50,000 people or more and of which Uruk (ca 4500 BCE) is considered the first. It was presided over by a king or king-priest and included large, highly decorated temple complexes, which later served not only a religious role, but also economic, administrative, manufacturing, and trading functions. In sum, as organization became more complex, urban centres became more centralized, and myths were created to account for the origin of the new societies and way of life (see Naddaf 2005, chap. 2). Meanwhile, as sites became more complex, so did the technological sophistication, with the number of specializations increasing exponentially (contrary to a hunter-gatherer society, where all members of the group had to learn everything to survive). Around 3500 BCE, meanwhile, bronze metallurgy was developed in Mesopotamia and with it the so-called the Bronze Age started. Around the same time proto-writing was invented, and then took off (more on writing below). In fact, the wheel, the sailboat, the plough, the chariot, and astronomy/astrology (difference below) all emerged in Mesopotamia around this time. It's important to note, meanwhile, that many of these inventions, including writing, later emerged independently in several other areas of the globe in similar urban settings (including China, Egypt, and India). Since there were very few major technological innovations until the so-called

Neolithic Revolution, it seems that human gene culture began to change more dramatically around this time. Obviously, as the society changed with the discovery or invention of new technologies, including agriculture, so did its myths, and, with these myths, the self/subject connected with these societies and myths changed accordingly.

15 I noted earlier that spoken language was preceded by a mimetic language, which is still prominent in some contemporary Stone Age cultures (see, for example, Lewis 2014, on contemporary Pygmy culture). Meanwhile, one linguistic anthropologist, Daniel Everett, has argued in *How Language Began* (2017) that since there's strong evidence that *Homo erectus*/archaic humans migrated to islands in the Pacific as early as a million years ago, they could only have reached them by seafaring means, and the kind of organization this requires (the minimum group size is calculated at twenty individuals) could only be achieved with verbal language. Everett makes similar claims premised on the evidence found in Gesher Benot Ya'aqov circa 780,000 years ago (see below), which archeologists reveal has a sophisticated culture for the period. Everett has few followers in the scientific community. Otherwise, as it concerns the theme of this volume, how long was verbal language around before mythmaking emerged?

16 I think the word "invented" is too strong. It suggests that language was consciously contrived, whereas it evolved over time. Language, meanwhile, changes us, but this must have occurred at a very slow pace as evidenced in the tardy development of culture till around 100,000 years ago. Was this, too, myth related, that is, being unconsciously satisfied at a cultural level with the world in which groups were residing?

17 See also note 19 below. The anthropologist James Suzman (2017a) sees the Ju/'hoansi as the closest living analogues to how our *Homo sapiens* ancestors lived during the first 290,000 years of their history. He provides a vivid portrait in *Affluence without Abundance*.

18 There were earlier *Homo sapiens* migrations out of Africa well before 100,000 years. See Hublin (2021) and note 13 above.

19 This is based on the largest genomic study ever conducted among Khoe and San groups. The study reveals that these groups from southern Africa are descendants of the earliest diversification event in the history of all humans – some 100,000 years ago, and thus well before the "out of Africa" migration of modern humans. The study also shows that the northern San separated from the southern San (Ju/'hoansi) as early as 25,000–40,000 years ago. While the southern San are essentially hunter-gatherers, the northern San are also pastoralists and farmers.

The former – and thus the Ju/'hoansi – have maintained the older culture. For the scientific study, see Schlebusch et al. (2012). For a synopsis in context, see Suzman (2017a, 21–33).

20 The spectacular rock paintings were initially dated much earlier, but whatever the dating, it attests to the work of extraordinarily talented individuals.

21 It also confirms that human innovations (cave painting and bows and arrows, for example) emerged independently in different locations around the globe.

22 In all fairness, as soon as any culture is exposed to another – and Western culture isn't exactly just any culture, but an omnipresent one – the members of another group are going to be affected. See, for example, the essay by the anthropologist James Suzman in *The Atlantic* on the more destructive side when the Ju/'hoansi were forced to confront Western culture (Suzman 2017b). But I should also note that, as the Ju/'hoansi created new innovations, as in the case of the bow and arrow, they would've fabricated myths to account for these innovations. The stories would then be passed down essentially unconsciously from one generation to the next as a survival mechanism.

23 See references to Henrich in this context below. It's not my aim here to weigh into a debate where I have little expertise of my own. I'm more interested in the emergence of storytelling/mythmaking and the formation of identity among members of a discrete group or social unit and those in their immediate vicinity. I will say that Henrich's research certainly substantiates my thesis.

24 I don't mean to imply that each and every member of a society is a clone of the other; rather, each and every member has a particular function to fulfill without which the group/community would not be able to survive. Being socio-centric is inherent in the myth. Indeed, it's inherent in human nature, and thus in our genes, or at the very least, in our biology. On the other hand, there will always be some who are more gifted or creative than others in many capacities, including telling stories!

25 Otherwise, the self will always change according to the social situation or dominant culture in which it finds itself with other selves, and the normal course of everyday life. As I note below, I do agree that human psychology is dynamic. I'll discuss below in the context of anthropology the different kinds of ontologies and corresponding selves in the contemporary world.

26 In grammar, "reflexive" denotes a pronoun that refers back to the subject of the clause in which it's used – for example, "myself," "themselves." I'll have more to say on the role of the reflexive below. Suffice it to say here

that the Greeks were the first to use reflexives critically or as an object of reflection (think of knowing one's own self: *gnothi sauton*), and in this usage the person is no longer referred to as the body.

27 I'll have something to say on Indologists and the use of the reflexive in ancient India further on. But I'm referring first and foremost here to those specializing in cultural and evolutionary anthropology, evolutionary psychology, cognitive science, and related disciplines (see below).

28 *Phusis*, or nature, will be explained in context further on. Suffice to mention it concerns a new way of understanding the universe where natural causes are substituted for supernatural causes, and the conviction that we should never be bound to the uncritical acceptance of a particular position.

29 In the case of the Greeks, the same genius is exhibited in their literature and art.

30 What's interesting to observe when examining the evolution of society in ancient Greece is how the corresponding virtues or excellences (*aretai*) shifted considerably. What was a virtue in one society could, and did, become a vice in another. We thus find the Homeric conception of heroic virtue as summarized in advice Peleus gives to his son Achilles: "Always be first and best, and ahead of everyone else" (*Iliad* 11.784). Heroic virtue is first and foremost about individual pre-eminence and the pursuit of one's own self-interest as willed by the gods, and as a reflection of a polytheistic way of life. With the emergence of the Greek *polis*, or city-state, heroic self-interest is seen as a vice, and the members of the state are seen, and must be seen, as equals, as equal selves. The very survival of the state depends on it. For a relevant discussion of the historical and conceptual roots of the idea of virtue, see MacIntyre (1981).

31 The norm among contemporary philosophers is to claim that the nature of consciousness is connected with the mind-body problem (or mind-body dualism) as we find it espoused in Descartes (1596–1650). In sum, the mind and body consist of radically different (and incompatible) substances or entities, neither of which is reducible to the other: mind is a thinking and unextended substance, and body is an extended and unthinking substance. There's thus no single natural order. However, since the theory of evolution, the philosophical question has become a scientific one. How to account for mind and thus the origin of consciousness in evolution? Formulated this way, consciousness is connected first and foremost with subjective experience, but also, and above all, with introspection, which was Descartes's way of verifying to his own mind that there was indeed a mind-body dualism. From my perspective, the *conscious* dichotomy, or at least the problem of *consciously* accounting for consciousness, is as old

as the birth of philosophy in sixth-century Greece, and it's intimately connected with the invention of conscious reflexivity, which is late (I'll provide numerous examples in context below). In his entry on "Consciousness" in the *Stanford Encyclopedia of Philosophy*, Van Gulick (2022) claims that "Questions about the nature of conscious awareness have likely been asked for as long as there have been humans." I have no idea how he can make this kind of claim. It implies a kind of introspection on the nature of consciousness itself, which is late. It's about a lot more than telling myths. Van Gulick, of course, is not alone. As we see in Boyd (2018) and Christensen (2020) and their reviews of the scientific literature regarding the evolution of storytelling and consciousness, our earliest ancestors were always engaged in critical thinking within their own minds and among members of their social group.

32 But, for Damasio, only after the brains that existed in countless creatures for millions of years "developed a protagonist capable of bearing witness did consciousness begin and only after those brains developed language did it become widely known that minds did exist" (2010, 18).

33 "Organisms make minds out of the activity of special cells called neurons," and "minds emerge when the activity of small circuits is organized across large networks so as to compose momentary patterns" (Damasio 2010, 18, 19). So, I'm tempted here to say we are returning in some respects to the origin of life and its relation to consciousness. But consciousness as Damasio defines it is a much later biological phenomenon that is first and foremost human (see below).

34 Pleasure and pain would be examples of primordial feelings.

35 The autobiographical self is defined in terms of biographical knowledge pertaining to the past as well as the anticipated future or again as *slowly* incorporating social and spiritual dimensions (Damasio 2010, 11, 24). It's only with the emergence of the autobiographical self that consciousness strictly speaking originates, but again it's the final stage, which is late (see below), that Damasio equates with a reflective self.

36 In some respects, Damasio uses the terms "robust self," "reflexive self," and "rebellious self" interchangeably (2010, 306–11), but there's also a biological and cultural progression to each (306–15).

37 The prominence of symbols for some scientists is what separates BMH from AMH (see above). Damasio, meanwhile, seems to imply that human language – by which he means the ability to produce words and string them together in sentences – originated *after* humans were capable of complex symbolic communication and culture such as burials, cave painting, and even some sophisticated tool making (2010, 313). This

runs contrary to current research in a number of fields, including evolutionary anthropology, evolutionary psychology, and cognitive science (see above on the origin of language). The most recent research, according to Boyd (2018, 6), suggests that speech (and thus the seeds of storytelling) began to develop about 500,000 years ago in *Homo heidelbergensis*, the common ancestor of *Homo sapiens* and *Homo neanderthalensis*. I'll have more to say on the correlation between language and storytelling below.

38 This would bode well with the contention noted above that language was invented for storytelling.

39 See, for example, Wiessner (2014). Since language, and thus a primitive storytelling, may have developed as early as 500,000 ago (see below), human minds/selves must have undergone numerous transformations as the processes of cultural exploration through storytelling would have produced new behaviours, which, in turn, affected individual cognition that at some point would have been somewhat "genetically accommodated" (Dor and Jablonka 2014; see also Suzman 2017).

40 Damasio claims that an intense exchange of ideas led to neurobiological developments (2010, 311), which suggests the powerful effect of culture on biology. I'll have more to say on the important relation between culture and biology further on. I don't want to imply that hunter-gatherer cultures or any *Homo sapiens* cultures are less "intelligent," but only that what Damasio calls the full-fledged conscious autobiographical self has yet to emerge. The capacity is *always* there.

41 In this regard, Damasio (2010, 307) draws his inspiration from Jaynes (1976), who argues that something dramatic happened to the human mind during the events that separate the narration in the two iconic poems. I also argue that something occurred during this relatively short period that explains the emergency of conscious reflexivity and a new notion of the reflective self or person, but my arguments are grounded in several factors not addressed and/or contextualized by others (see below).

42 Damasio doesn't mention the Greek alphabet specifically, but after mentioning the appearance of writing around five thousand years ago, he notes the following: "by the time of the Homeric poems, which are likely to be less than three thousand years old, autobiographical selves had *undoubtedly* [my italics] come to human minds" (2010, 306). I'll have more to say on the role of alphabetic writing and the emergence of the reflective self below.

43 In his otherwise insightful and interesting book *The Creative Spark: How Imagination Made Humans Exceptional* (2017), Fuentes doesn't even give Greek philosophy, science, and culture a footnote. In a like way, those

working in the origins of Greek philosophy and science rarely venture into contemporary scientific research in the fields noted above. A notable exception is G.E.R. Lloyd.

44 Greek city-states (*poleis*) were relatively small entities that were ruled by citizen assemblies rather than kings at this time. I'll discuss in context the role of the *polis* in the creation of the new mindset further on.

45 I argue in a recent article (Naddaf 2023) that what all these ontologies have in common is the *conscious* conviction that the seeds of human consciousness, cognition, and value were inherent in the originative principle.

46 This receives more attention in several contextual notes in part 2.

47 Charles Taylor and others connect the origin of the Western concept of the individual with a Christian notion of the soul in individual relationship with God that emerged in the Middle Ages, but which has its roots in Saint Augustine (354–430). Part of Taylor's own thesis (1989) is that we cannot understand who we are except in dialogue with others; in other words, our narrative is constructed in dialogue with other members of the community or society. So, there's some kinship with Brisson's notion of myth.

48 See introduction, note 11.

49 It's also important to note that poetry was always sung, a phenomenon common to most ancient societies, and still continuing in the more traditional ones. Indeed, most texts considered "sacred" are still sung or chanted (e.g., the Quran, the Torah, the Mass, the sutras).

50 We're dealing here with the collective memory of a society and *not* that of the individual, which many contemporary scholars and psychologists seem to take for granted, including Boyd (2018) and Christensen (2020). From this perspective, song is a vital form of discourse that not only onserves all the information that a community has of its past but also transmits that history from one generation to the next. The memory that presides over poetic inspiration is both impersonal and collective, meaning it does not concern the past of the individual singer-poets.

51 To be clear, I do see a difference between the *Iliad* and the *Odyssey* as far as the narration is concerned. The *Odyssey* is reflecting major changes in migration witnessed during the period, and there are references to eighth-, if not seventh-century, events. The seeds of a new sense of the self are already emerging due to the advent of the alphabet. But we're a long way from the reflexive self that will dominate the intelligentsia and lead to the birth of philosophy and science, as we'll see below.

52 I make some allowance for ancient India below, but even then, there's a sharp difference.

53 "Inspiration" is an action noun derived from the Latin verb *inspirare*, meaning "to blow or breathe into," and denotes the action of blowing, breathing, or inspiring.

54 We still find this in the English word "pneumatic." The Greek word *pneuma* is one of the popular words for breath.

55 In sum, it's not Penelope's reflective self or conscious agency that is behind the ploy. She literally believes a god is the source. The ploy is to frustrate the suitors who have invaded her household in the absence of Odysseus.

56 This can, of course, be qualified. There are passages in Homer where there's a kind of double determination, where an event is motivated by both god and man (*Iliad* 15.603–4). There are also examples of conflicts that seem to be resolved through selves (e.g., *Iliad* 23.602–3), but even here the hero is still working within the bounds of society; that is, only gods and heroes (part divine, but mortal) are "selves" because, in the Homeric world view, and following the principle of scalarity, they are at the top of the ladder. The average person is not autonomous (*autokrates*) in the same way, but they will be after a series of social and intellectual developments (see below). For an important discussion in context, see Jeremiah (2012, 43–66).

57 The best analysis in my opinion is still Onians (1951). The Greek terms identified here often have several English translations. Thus, for example, *thumos* (from *thuô*, "seething, breathe violently") is sometimes translated as "heart" as well as "anger," "temper," "spirit," and "desire," for the heart is the location or organ where these conscious phenomena occur.

58 This has been vigorously contested by Gill (1996) and Williams (1993), and it's worth noting that numerous scholars have since rallied around them, whence my use of "controversial" above. I think this is mistaken, and I'm not alone. It seems to me that many scholars imply that the human psyche or the notion of a person has not evolved since the Neolithic period – indeed, since the advent of BMH in the Upper Paleolithic, if not earlier (see above). This is not the same as claiming that preliterate Stone Age people could not integrate and flourish in the contemporary world if provided with the same opportunities (I'll have more to say on this important point below). Meanwhile, Gill insists that while there's no unified "I" in Homer, there's a complex of functions that are unified by their interaction, and thus there's really no change in the notion of the self in Greek thought as a whole. He thus distinguishes the "subjective-individualist" approach from the "objective-participant" approach, and argues that the latter, which is concerned with public rationality, is what is proper to the Greek world. The first real change is the modern Western

notion that begins with Descartes in the seventeenth century and would constitute the "subjectivist-participant" approach. But as Jeremiah has argued, the increasing concern with the advent of philosophy with interiorizing reflexivity (see below) certainly had a strong component of the subjectivist-individualist attitude. Moreover, as Seaford (2017 and 2020, 55) has judiciously noted in his opposition to Gill, can there be a concept of the self in Homer if there's no word for it, or if the concept isn't formed enough to generate a word? I'll have more to say on this point when discussing the new notion of *psuchê* and the advent of reflexivity further on in light of Jeremiah's research and analysis. I should note in passing that I'm not claiming the Greek notion of the self is the same as Descartes's notion of the self as a single, private reasoning and feeling "I." Meanwhile, one of the main arguments of Brisson's theory of myth, and one which my introduction and afterword endeavour to substantiate, is that human beings are by nature socio-centric and products of myth, and so the Cartesian notion of the self as independent of society is an illusion.

59 For an interesting overview that considers both the anthropological and the philosophical in the context of the difference between the dividual and the individual, see Smith (2012). The Greek notion isn't, as I understand it, considered. Even with the advent of the reflective self in ancient Greece, and the famous Protagorean notion that "man is the measure of all things" (ca mid-fifth century BCE), individuals remained largely socio-centric.

60 With this in mind, Bremmer's study on the evolution of the notion of *psuchê* in ancient Greece is quite revealing. He applies the research of the Swedish anthropologist and Sanskritist Ernst Arbman on the Vedic soul belief in India to the development of the Greek notion of the soul/*psuchê*. Arbman showed that the concept of the *ātman*, or unitary soul, in India was preceded by a duality, and the eschatological and psychological attributes of the soul had not yet emerged (Bremmer 1983, 9). The duality consisted of a free soul, an unencumbered soul representing the individual distinctiveness, and a body soul endowing the soul with life and consciousness (and which consisted of parts). Bremmer equates the free soul with the Homeric *psuchê*, and the *thumos*, *nous*, etc., with the body soul. He concludes that the early Greek notion of the soul must have been a dualistic one, and thus that the unitary notion of the soul can only be found *after* the Archaic period (66). According to my own analysis, the Greek notion of a unitary soul would have emerged *during* the Archaic period given the traditional dating of the period (ca 776–480). Meanwhile, this could suggest that the notion of a unitary soul in India preceded it. Jeremiah has pointed out that the development of the unitary conception of the soul in Sanskrit is

also "complemented by a development in its pronominal reflective system" (2012, 63). Indeed, the word *ātman* is itself (or became) a reflective pronoun with a referential connection to the reflective "self" of the human being. Jeremiah concludes, "We may thus propose that in both these languages a development in the reflexive system is linked to a development in the conception of the person, and also the development of culturally important reflexive categories" (64). I'm not sure when or how the notion of the *ātman* as the inner self or reflexive self/soul in Hindu thought emerged. Specialists seem to suggest around the seventh century BCE, when similar changes in the socio-economic environment were developing; see texts cited by Jeremiah (2012, 64n50) and Seaford (2011, 2020) (more on Seaford below). Be that as it may, the *ātman*, or Indian notion of the reflexive self, didn't culminate in the kind of philosophy and science we find in ancient Greece beginning in the sixth century (see below). Indeed, the Upanishads are sacred literature, and dominated by what I'd characterize as the supernatural. And the society in which it's prominent is deeply hierarchical. From this perspective, one could say that not all self-reflective selves are equal. Such selves also need to be nurtured in a society where one (i.e., a citizen) can express oneself without any fear or retribution by god or man.

61 Reflexivizations such as "know thyself," which reconstitute the nature of the person, are *entirely* absent in Homer.

62 This is consistent with the fact that Homeric gods are themselves "physical" entities, which explains their physical descriptions and physical interventions, including sexual intercourse with humans. All this is to be taken literally, and not metaphorically or figuratively, but a conscious differentiation will also occur after the discovery of the self and the advent of philosophy. I'll give a telling example later in the context of the birth of allegorical interpretation.

63 Anyone reading the Sumerian poem the Epic of Gilgamesh for the first time (the poem dates from around 2100 BCE, but the version we have was committed to writing much later) would also be tempted to see the hero's quest for immortality in this light. But Gilgamesh is still an example of the Homeric man. The accent is put on living in the present.

64 Seaford insightfully argues in his recent essay "The *Psuchē* from Homer to Plato" (2017) and in *The Origins of Philosophy in Ancient Greece and Ancient India* (2020) that the concept of the inner self or *psuchê* as the immortal organ of consciousness – the same notion of the conscious reflexivity I'm referring to – is the effect of the monetarization of the Greek polis in the sixth and fifth centuries. There's thus no sense of

the inner self or unitary organ of comprehensive consciousness in Homer (contra Gill and Williams; see note 58 above) or anyone else before the invention of coinage. Again, he provides a barrage of seemingly insightful analogies, in particular in Heraclitus, and again claims that this occurs at the unconscious level. While I wouldn't exclude that coinage also played a role in the psychology of the citizen body and the movement toward more democratized systems of government, the economic expansion of the Greek city-states and revolutionary change was already in the air well before the dates that Seaford ascribes to the introduction of coinage. Indeed, if we can believe Hesiod (*Works and Days*, 19–26), competition was already at a fever pitch in his time – that is, during the opening decades of the seventh century. The notion that "wealth makes the man" was already common currency!

65 It seems that Greek mercenaries were a common sight all around the Near East during the first part of the Archaic period, and it was travel to the various locations that also nurtured new ideas. We know Egyptian pharaohs hired Greek mercenaries in the early seventh century, and shortly thereafter we find the first Greek emporium in the Nile delta seeking fame and fortune.

66 As Jeremiah notes, even when "recognition of a unity of person is evident in the use of personal pronouns and names" (already emerging in Homer), this does not mean that they're used critically or as an object of reflection (2012, 12). The self is not objectified as a "curiosity of thought" (12).

67 Unless otherwise indicated, I'll be using Jeremiah's translations with some minor changes. Jeremiah (2012) has a barrage of examples from the early lyric, iambus, and elegy period, as well as from the Presocratic philosophers, tragedy and comedy. The examples from Archilochus's and Solon's use of *nous*, or mind, are my own.

68 This is the spirit behind Archilochus abandoning his shield in the reference above.

69 I don't wish to imply here that there were no coherent world views before the advent of philosophy, but they're radically different from those that emerge with the birth of philosophy. I contextualize these in my forthcoming chapter "Cosmological Models and the *Peri Phuseos* Tradition," in volume 1 of *The Edinburgh Critical History of Western Philosophy*. The penultimate version is available on my academia.edu website at https://www.academia.edu/25128934/COSMOLOGICAL_MODELS_AND_THE_PERI_PHUSEOS_TRADITION.

70 I should, however, qualify this. We're still not at the sense of introspection as we find in, say, Descartes and modernity – that is, introspection in the

sense of a dispassionate observation of one's own mental states. For some, this Enlightenment notion of introspection is at the foundation of Western individualism and the conviction that one is the sole proprietor of one's capabilities, and that these capabilities owe nothing to society. The Western notion that each human is equal and free is discussed in context in part 2 in relevant notes.

71 Solon appealed to no other power than his own sense of what was just: "I wrote down the laws alike for base and noble, fitting straight judgements to each" (frag. 36.18–20 Edmonds). Solon presents the benefits and sanctions of law as human, and since the laws were written down, it meant they were available for all to see.

72 There's no doubt that Solon is already well aware of the difference between the literal and the figurative. Dikê, or Justice, is consciously personified.

73 The DK references are used widely in books and articles on the early Greek/Presocratic philosophers. The abbreviation refers to H. Diels and W. Kranz, *Die Fragmente der Vorsokratiker*, 6th ed. (Berlin: Weidmann, 1951), which is the standard edition. Each Presocratic philosopher is assigned a number, and each fragment of each Presocratic is also assigned a number, which is preceded by the letter *B*. Thus, the number for Democritus is 68, and Democritus's fragment 174 is referred to as DK68B174.

74 This is a critical point that is entirely ignored by specialists in evolutionary anthropology, evolutionary psychology, cognitive science, and related disciplines. In my opinion, it creates a weak link in Henrich's popular *The WEIRDest People in the World* (2020). The iconoclastic Greeks don't even get a footnote. For Henrich, the notions of individuality and "guilt" only emerge with Christianity!

75 It seems to me that the ancient Indian example of the *ātman* (discussed in several notes below) doesn't fit the description in the same uncompromising way, as religion continues to play a fundamental role. I don't wish to imply that the new reflective self led to the Greeks being less sociocentric, but the two came together in a new way, as we find in the birth of democracy and the free and open discussion concerning which political regime and corresponding virtues are best.

76 What I understand by philosophy in ancient Greece and how it's exhibited in Anaximander of Miletus (see below) is without parallel in ancient India. Seaford's 2020 book misses the point as it's limited in its scope to the claim that something non-plural underlies the world pluralities.

77 For a more detailed analysis, see Naddaf (2012). An English version is available on my academia.edu website at https://www.academia.edu/37980043/Historia_in_Early_Greek_Writing_and_Thought.

78 For an explanation of DK references, see note 73 above.

79 A linguistic analysis of the word *phusis* shows (1) that the fundamental and etymological meaning of the word is that of "growth" – it's derived from the root **phû-* (to grow) – and (2) that as an action noun ending in *-sis*, it includes three things: the origin, the process, and the result – that is, the whole process of the growth of a thing from its birth to its maturity (for a detailed analysis, see Naddaf 2005, chap. 1). The expression *historia peri phuseôs* (investigation into the nature of things), which appears later, captures the new scientific revolution. These accounts or investigations were attempts to understand the history of the world from a naturalistic perspective. They're what some would call today theories of everything. Indeed, the evidence suggests that the primordial substance whence everything came also contained the seeds of consciousness, cognition, and value. This is akin to Thomas Nagel's claim in *Mind and Cosmos* (2012).

80 Vlastos captures the spirit of the new age in the following statement: "Regardless of many disagreements among themselves, the *phusiologoi* are united in the assumption that the order that makes our world a cosmos is natural, that is to say, it's immanent in nature; all of them would account for this order by the natures of the components of the universe without appeal to anything else, hence, without appeal to a transcendent ordering intelligence" (1975, 24). Now, this statement could give the impression that the *phusiologoi*, or "natural philosophers," were reductive materialists, although this isn't the spirit behind Vlastos's assertion. As he notes elsewhere, the word *theos* (God or divine) is often employed to qualify *phusis*, and the word *theos* is found more often than the word *phusis* in the Diels/Krantz index *Die Fragmente der Vorsokratiker* (Vlastos [1952] 1993). I discuss the relation between God and nature in the early Greek philosophers in context in Naddaf (2019). God is synonymous with or related to first principles.

81 There's no better example of this than in Parmenides of Elea (ca 515–450), the father of deductive logic for some, but also a keen observer of the nature of the universe for others (see Graham below).

82 Seaford (2004), and more recently (2020), makes an insightful and original argument for the role of money in the birth of philosophy and science in ancient Greece. Seaford emphasizes that the Ionians were the first to use coinage, and that they did so at the same time they produced philosophical cosmology. He connects the origin of Greek philosophy with the sublimination of monetary value. More to the point, he argues that early Greek philosophy arrives at the idea of the world as a single substance underlying the plurality of things by projecting *unconsciously*

the substance of monetary value onto the cosmos – although strictly speaking he never explains how the mechanism functions. In the case of Anaximander, Seaford thus focuses on the extensive analogy between coined money and the principle of the unlimited (*apeiron*), and then goes on to consider the origin of Anaximander's cosmology, but not his model, which would be far more challenging for his thesis. Against the socio-political factors, which I discuss below, he claims that the Greek city-states were more distinct from other polities in their economies due to coinage/money than in impersonal law, public spaces, and freedom in public debate, which I consider fundamental.

This is not the time to engage with this intriguing thesis. But could the effects of coinage have been ingrained in the Greek psyche so quickly? Indeed, Seaford also argues that coinage was behind the notion of a unified mind. The dating would suggest it would've been almost coeval with the use of coinage. I suspect that the invention of coinage and the monetarization of ancient Greece may have had something to do with the direction the Greek *poleis*, or city-states, were moving toward. This would, of course, explain why their neighbours were initially uninterested in coins. Otherwise, I agree with Seaford – and science now confirms it – that cultural factors can have a determining effect on human minds, on our biology, on our genes!

83 I discuss Havelock's thesis in my introduction to Brisson's *Plato the Myth Maker* (1999).

84 I do agree with Havelock that the Greek alphabet is a cultural event that had a major impact on our cognition. It may have caused neurobiological developments that were eventually genetically accommodated (see above). However, as I note below, there are other factors at play; most notably, the advent of the *polis*, a unique Greek institution, that nurtured literacy.

85 I discuss these in some detail in Naddaf (2003).

86 On Anaximander's primordial substance, the *apeiron*, see note 91 below.

87 Xenophanes also gives us one of the earliest uses of *psuchê* in the sense of the true self (DK21B7).

88 For a detailed analysis, see Naddaf (2009). Christensen (2020, 283–5) contends that Homeric poetry is consciously using allegory and indulges in its interpretation. I'm aware he's not alone. As one can see above, I argue that this only begins with Homer's detractors after the birth of philosophy. But I don't exclude that epic can be therapeutic. All myth has by definition some kind of therapeutic quality.

89 In his aptly titled book *Anaximander*, the Italian theoretical physicist and science historian Carlo Rovelli (2011) provides an excellent evaluation of how radically different Anaximander's cosmology is from the world views

of his predecessors, and he uses numerous comparisons with contemporary science to make his point. Rovelli explains in detail why Anaximander is the father of one of the greatest conceptional revolutions, on a par with those of Darwin and Einstein (112–13; see also 180–1). I note this for the evolutionary psychologists, anthropologists, cognitive scientists, and the like for whom there's little if any change in the human psyche from Homer to the advent of philosophy, to say nothing of the evolution of the human mind prior to Homer. Historians who focus on the origins of ancient Greek philosophy and science largely agree, but Rovelli uses a plethora of different pertinent examples to make his point. Let me add that with the advent of philosophy we have *for the first time* astronomy as opposed to astrology. Astrology is about a correlation between a celestial event *and* a terrestrial event, about omens that occur in the sky, about interpretating the will of the gods. It was only with the Greeks that the celestial bodies were studied for their own sake and to learn about what we see in the universe. For a detailed discussion, see Naddaf (forthcoming), where I examine in context the norm among mythical models of the cosmos before moving to the revolutionary changes that emerge with the early Greek cosmological models.

90 I discuss Aristophanes's *Clouds* in the context of the origin of atheism, another Greek phenomenon of the period, in Naddaf (2019).

91 Anaximander chose the word *apeiron* to designate his originative first principle, or *phusis*, as *archê*. The term led to the spilling of considerable ink. It suggests an enormous mass that is both spatially and qualitatively indefinite, and he picked the word, following my own analysis (Naddaf 2005, 65–70), because it was the best he could find to account for the physical phenomena that were too complex to reduce to a precise element.

92 Aristotle (*On the Heavens* 295b10) makes a similar claim when he states that Anaximander held that the earth is at rest (*menein*) at the centre (*epi toi mesou*) of the celestial sphere because of its equilibrium (*dia tên homoiotêta*) – that is, because it's equidistant from all the points on the circumference (*homoiôs pros ta eschata echon*).

93 Graham (2013) sets out to explain that the Presocratics were not just great theorizers; some developed methods to tests their hypotheses. Graham convincingly argues that heliophotism (the moon derives its light from the sun) and *antiphraxis* (the moon blocks the sun's light) were empirically tested, passed the tests, and by having done so constitute the first examples of "scientific" knowledge based on correct interpretation of empirical evidence. Graham sees Parmenides (the first to discover heliophotism) as behind the most creative burst of scientific energy until then (96) and

Anaxagoras "as the Einstein of his age" (4). I consider Anaximander of Miletus as the wonder child for reasons I summarize above (Rovelli, a theoretical physicist, arrives at a similar conclusion, as mentioned above in note 89). I provide a detailed review of Graham's enlightening book in Naddaf (2016b).

94 I provide some examples and details in Naddaf (forthcoming).

95 This doesn't detract from the great achievements of other cultures and civilizations that preceded the Greeks or were their contemporaries. Nor do I wish to imply that there are no other ways of doing science. In fact, some would claim that the difference between science as it began to be practised in the "second" Enlightenment in seventeenth-century Europe and the Greek Enlightenment are radically different. I sympathize with Lloyd's claim that the notion of science should cover "every attempt systematically to investigate the phenomena, to observe, classify, predict and explain them" (2012, 3–4). Given this broad definition, Lloyd emphasizes the pluralism in the ways people have gone about the tasks of understanding. In considering the roots of scientific reasoning, Carruthers (2000) argues that there's no difference between the cognitive abilities of the hunter tracking prey and the scientist drawing inferences from data. What is different, however, is the extent to which scientific activity can draw on external resources; in particular, the prop of the written word. A preliterate hunter-gatherer, for example, cannot learn from the writings of a zoologist. He can only draw on his experience and the experience of those in his tribe who have taught him. But his teachers, in turn, are drawing on the collective memories of a limited community. Zoologists, by contrast, have learned a great deal from the recorded observations of preliterate trackers from many hunter-gatherer societies. I empathize with Carruthers, but there's considerably more to the scientific mind, as Rovelli reminds us (see above note 89 above). Indeed, without the birth of philosophy and science that emerged with the reflexive self, and which were due in large part to cultural factors unique to Archaic Greece, it's probably that contemporary humans would be living in a very different world. Meanwhile, I'll have more to say later regarding Carruthers's observation in the context of myth and how it structures our particular identities.

96 While *ātman*, a Sanskrit word meaning "essence, breath, soul," is a central idea in all the Upanishads, scholars are divided about when they were composed. The "earliest" Upanishads, which are pre-Buddhist, are placed in the seventh and sixth centuries BCE, and some scholars place them in the 800 to 300 BCE range (e.g., Phillips 2010). Some of the later Upanishads were composed as late as the fourteenth and fifteenth centuries CE.

97 I discuss many of these in this context in Naddaf (2016a).

98 For Democritus, reality consists of only atoms and the void, and the reflective self or soul is composed of spherical fire atoms. Moreover, for Democritus, although for the first time there's no reference to the primordial substance as divine, he still claimed that the images of the gods of traditional religion were in some sense real, and that the gods could speak to us and predict the future (68 B 166). This is also the case for his follower Epicurus (342–271 BCE). Like Democritus, Epicurus claimed that the self is just a combination of soul atoms that on death are dispersed, so there's no immortal soul, and fear of death and punishment in the afterlife are nonsensical, and thus not to be feared – something he claimed that most were obsessed with. Nonetheless, he argued that nature (*phusis*) implanted in us an "innate" notion of gods, what Epicurus called *prolêpsis* – that is, something preconceived in the mind (Cicero, *On the Nature of the Gods* 1.43). And Epicurus sees the forms of the gods as anthropomorphic because no people see them otherwise (Epicurus, *Letter to Menoeceus* 123–4; Cicero, *On the Nature of the Gods* 1.19, 49). This suggests once again the degree to which traditional myths were still embedded into the Greek psyche. But it also attests to the extraordinary level of secularization in a free-thinking society. For an excellent analysis of different notions of the self from antiquity to the present, with a particular emphasis on the ancient Greeks, see Sorabji (2006).

99 But the fact remains that, as Brisson notes, while almost every Greek philosopher was promoting a way of life meant to nurture the soul qua self and liberate it from fear of death, they all required intellectual exercises that were beyond the scope of the average person, who still feared the Homeric notion of the afterlife, or some equivalent. This is, in large part, why Christianity was so appealing. Faith became the road to salvation, and it was open to all. Needless to say, a new form of the self and identity began to emerge with these new myths, as well as corresponding virtues. But in every culture in which Christianity took hold, pagan myths hardly disappeared, which made one's identity more complex.

100 For a variety of ways genes are related to culture, see Causadias and Korous (2017), and Dor and Jablonka (2014). As Dor and Jablonka note, "the collective processes of cultural exploration produced new behaviours which in turn changed individual cognition in ways that were eventually partially genetically accommodated" (17).

101 In sum, just as language (which arose from an adaptive predisposition) impacted human development on every level, cognitively and emotionally, and thus our genes and/or our biology, so did the advent of the polis and

alphabetic writing impact our genes and/or our biology, or our cognitive abilities. To use Dor's formula, "First we invented language. Then language changed us" (2015, 4). In this case, the invention of writing changed us yet again, but alphabetic writing more dramatically as Havelock (1982) notes27p4(see above).

102 For a comparison of the ancient Mesopotamian views of the world that remained essentially static and the ancient Greek views, see Naddaf (forthcoming).

103 India has remained essentially a traditional society with a fascinating culture grounded in myths with which an enormous number of Indians identify. In fact, much of the social unrest is connected with the intolerance of the Hindu majority toward minority groups, or, for the case at hand, a battle over whose myths are to be deemed superior. For the record, I don't mean to imply that in ancient Greece the new mindset became the norm as it concerns a critical approach to traditional myths. We see excellent examples of this in Aristophanes's *The Clouds* (see Naddaf 2019). Indeed, even today the number of people in Western democracies who maintain a literal interpretation of the Bible (or sacred books in general) is surprisingly high, even as they inhabit a world dominated by modern technology. Nonetheless, conscious reflexivity is still the norm, even if not always active!

104 We are, of course, all BMH and descendant from the same AMH. I discussed this in context and in more detail at the opening of the afterword.

105 I don't mean to imply that anyone can become an expert at most anything. Clearly, we all have different aptitudes, as Plato notes in the *Republic*, something that scientific research shows is often genetically determined, although sheer will is sometimes certainly a determining factor too (Stetka 2014).

106 It's a good example, once again, of the degree to which psychology is dynamic rather than static under certain conditions. The Kope example also reinforces the claim that culture has more likely been the primary driver of human adaptation rather than our genes. This would not exclude that it's in our genes to learn from others, as we find in Boyd, Richardson, and Henrich (2011). See also Waring and Wood (2021).

107 See Spink and Cole (2005). On the role of oral tradition in forager groups and its essential place in survival, see Sugiyama (2011). What is in human nature and thus our genes is "to learn from others, powerfully and unconsciously" (Boyd, Richardson, and Henrich 2011, 10924). It's all about information sharing. Or, as the anthropologist Joseph Henrich reminds us elsewhere (2016, chap. 2), no single individual could figure out in his or

her lifetime the skills, abilities, or know-how necessary for survival in any of the immense diversity of habitats; in sum, survival is not dependent on specific genetic adaptations. Human psychology, Henrich insists, does not permit "cumulative" cultural evolution. What counts is social learning rather than "intelligence" strictly speaking. But no one would deny that normal human development depends both on biological and cultural inheritance. As Tomasello (1995, 5) reminds us, a human child understands that other human beings are like him- or herself, and so tries to understand things from their point of view. Tominson (2018, 17) claims that the early hominin technologies didn't change "across huge periods" because the fashioning of artifacts "did not involve agency," which is to say they were fashioned unconsciously. It's part of what Tominson calls mimesis. I see this phenomenon as enduring a lot longer than Tominson seems to imply. I claim that if unconsciousness endured for so long in human history, and indeed continues to rule in some respects, it's largely because of myth.

108 The notion of working in groups and why originality doesn't really exist is contextualized in part 4.

109 As discussed above, the evidence from skulls and genes suggests that *Homo sapiens* were behaviourally modern even before they branched out geographically over 100,000 years ago.

110 To cite the late Black American baseball star Hank Aaron, "a man's ability is only limited by his opportunities." But it's also clear that Aaron had aptitudes that others didn't. On different aptitudes, see related notes above.

111 Ultimately, Henrich, in his much-praised book *The WEIRDest People in the World: How the West Became Psychologically Peculiar and Particularly Prosperous* (2020), is arguing that Western psychology is different or odd compared to the rest of humanity, and he walks us through the history of how this came to be, which he traces first and foremost to Christianity. I'm arguing with historical examples and textual analysis that a similar phenomenon occurred in ancient Greece, one that nurtured the advent of philosophy and Western science. A cohort of Greeks became "psychologically" different and odd, which is attested in reflexives and wildly different competing ontologies and ways of seeing the world. What both views have in common is the claim that those nurtured for generations in a psychologically different culture can adapt to the new culture and mindset if they are nurtured in it from youth. As I noted elsewhere, it is telling that the ancient Greek culture, let alone the period under consideration here, is entirely ignored by Henrich and in reviews I've seen till now.

112 Ontology is about how things are, and, in philosophy, goes back to the ancient Greek founder of ontology, Parmenides of Elea (see above); it's about what is, what is not, and what may be. Ontological anthropology seeks to open us to other realities, to alternate ways of seeing the world. It's both a critique and an exploration of other realities seen through the eyes of other cultures, from preliterate Stone Age societies to the world of artificial intelligence; an attempt to understand how things could be otherwise good for others. But such anthropology also exposes different kinds of selves!

113 Descola (2014) also identifies six modes of transaction, which then create twenty-four combinations. Of course, as critics point out, reality is not so neat and tidy, and he misses much in his categories. I certainly see Greek philosophers as having some peculiarities of their own, and, more important, the notion of living in conformity with nature, which is prominent in most Greek philosophers, would appeal to a wide range of people in the contemporary world, and not just environmentalists. Many of the latter would hardly identify with naturalism as Descola understands it.

114 These are also, as I understand it, individual spirit beings that help to perpetuate life, and since animals and plants are the source of one's food, such a perspective seems commonsensical.

115 The Inuit also recognize that non-living things, including landscapes, have a spirit.

116 The ancient Greeks, for example, have a radically different ontology than the Chinese, although they do have commonalities that would fall under analogism. Moreover, the Greek polis, which was a necessary but not a sufficient factor behind the advent of philosophy (see above), was foreign to China. The emperor dominated the state of affairs. Indeed, he was the intermediary between the state and the cosmos, not unlike what we find in ancient Mesopotamia.

117 Descola sees naturalism and its champions as an ethnocentric Euro-American phenomenon and the epitome of imperialistic arrogance. Henrich describes what he sees as the origin and development of this Euro-American phenomenon in *The WEIRDest People in the World* (2020).

118 One of the foundations of Descartes's philosophy is that God is not a deceiver. Descartes of course was raised and remained a Catholic. Isaac Newton (1642–1727) was obsessed with seeking to reconcile Greek mythology with the Bible, which he considered the primary authority on the early history of mankind. Or again, he was fixated with alchemy and his belief that Greek myths encoded the alchemical recipes he was seeking. For Newton, discovery was still recovery! Kant was a faithful Christian

Pietist till the end. As the story goes, Charles Darwin, an "inspired genius" we could say, delayed the circulation and publication of *On the Origin of Species* for a generation after he discovered his theory of natural selection. He remained throughout his life a deeply pious and religious man. Nature, he could argue, works in mysterious ways, and it doesn't exclude a divine force behind the scenes. But what was most troubling was that the vast majority of Darwin's European contemporaries, including naturalists, still had a "literal" interpretation, as Simonton (1999, 33) correctly observes, of the opening books of Genesis, and thus believed that creation had only occurred around 4000 BCE, and with it all the species.

119 The relation between myths and noble lies is discussed in context on several occasions during the conversations.

120 La Boétie's notion of voluntary servitude is discussed in the same context – that is, qua myth – in part 4. His observation that almost every state was dominated by a tiny minority who lived by rules or laws that were different from everyone else, and who maintained a monopoly on these laws and thus the authority to rule everyone else, still seems like a common practice in many states, including in some liberal democracies.

121 The modern conception of citizenship emerges with the American and French Revolutions.

122 And I say "myths" and not "rumours" (the difference is contextualized in part 4) because slavery and its aftermath, in the case of Black Americans, is grounded in anything but rumour. Escaping the myth as understood here requires far more than being only *conscious* of an undeniable fact. On the other hand, much of the recent and ongoing turmoil in American politics is occasioned by rumour. That the 2020 presidential elections were rigged against Trump, and numerous other accusations by his supporters, are based on fantasies, not myth. Rumours are fleeting, and not part of one's identity as understood here. Rumours are fabricated to malign an individual or a group, but not exclusively, as the intention could be quite the opposite.

123 As I noted before, Brisson's critique of the myth of Catholicism and Christianity was a catalyst behind his efforts to make sense of myth. In the case of Trump, his supporters developed a kind of crush on him (some would call it a fetish) and claimed he's entitled to rule under the same principle as the divine right of kings – in other words, that he is appointed to rule by God.

124 What we find in the Middle East is all three of the Abrahamic religions, so-called religions of the Book, in a kind of eternal conflict, with competing myths and corresponding identities offering conflicting interpretations of the same God.

125 India is, in fact, made up of dozens of unique cultures and competing myths.

126 Poland is in a world of its own. It never ceased to be a deeply Catholic society, even under the Marxist regime, which was viewed with contempt. Now the battle that is tearing the country apart is between secularism and religious fanatics. It's a return to the foundation myths!

127 For some fascinating examples, see Boyd, Richardson, and Henrich (2011).

128 It's certainly the antithesis of what Plato had in mind in the myth of the metals, discussed in context on several occasions during the conversations and in several corresponding notes.

129 A 2021 Gallup poll suggests that 94 per cent of Americans approve of interracial marriage between Black and white people. See Justin McCarthy, "U.S. Approval of Interracial Marriage at New High of 94%," Gallup, 10 September 2021, https://news.gallup.com/poll/354638/approval-interracial-marriage-new-high.aspx. In 1958, it was 4 per cent. According to Pew Research Center, in 1967, just 3 per cent of married couples were interracial. Now it's 20 per cent. See Erica Pandey, "The Rise of Interracial Marriage – and Its Approval Rating," Axios, 6September62022,https://www.axios.com/2022/09/07/approval-of-interracial-marriage-america.

130 This is discussed in context in the course of several conversations, and Brisson has some rather discerning observations. The *Canadian Charter of Rights and Freedoms*, mentioned above, is an outcome of this policy. I'll note in passing that the origins strictly speaking of the policy can be found in the Royal Commission on Bilingualism and Biculturalism (1963–69).

131 Prime Minister Pierre Trudeau claimed that while there were two official languages, there was no official culture. His son, Prime Minister Justin Trudeau, makes a similar claim when he contends that Canada has no "core identity." These claims are relevant to the meaning of myth in the current context. As Louis-André Dorion observes in part 3, Canada is a country without a mythology.

132 Some have argued that multiculturalism was contrived to put the brakes on Quebec's aspirations to separate, as the sizable "ethnic minorities" in Quebec would invariably vote against separation. This was in fact Premier Jacques Parizeau's claim when the referendum on separation was lost in 1995. For Bill 96, a more recent version of Bill 101, see introduction, note 49. Meanwhile, Statistics Canada reports that in 2021, one in four Canadians declared having a mother tongue other than English or French. With the pace of immigration increasing dramatically (Canada has the fastest immigration intake in the Western world), it's unclear what

the consequences may be for the official languages, or, again, for what it means to be Canadian.

133 I touched on this above, but it's also discussed in context during the conversations and in several notes.

134 The true self would have little to do with the protoself or core self as Damasio describes them (see above). Meanwhile, I suppose that one can be a true self in the material world in the sense that one conforms to all the expectations of the society in which one is living in order to assure its survival; in that case, maybe those living in a preliterate culture would then be closer to the mark. But in this case, it's the non-reflective self. Indeed, can a true self be anything but socio-centric?

135 For the role of *psuchê*, or soul, in early Greek philosophy, see Naddaf (2019). This essay also discusses the origin of atheism in ancient Greece.

136 We find an incorporeal mind, self, or soul for the first time in Plato. But the individual soul or self is still shaped by the myths of the society in which it lives. As noted on several occasions, this is something that Plato realizes to his advantage. But there are contexts in which we can talk about a "true self" in Plato. One of these is when the Demiurge first creates human souls in the *Timaeus*, that is, before they inhabit a body for the *first* time. In this case, we can conjecture that *all* human souls were the same. Of course, this is all part of Plato's "mythical" account of the creation of the universe.

137 *Plotinus,* the founder of Neoplatonism, inspired by his reading of Plato, developed a complex spiritual cosmology that involved three foundational elements: the One, the Intelligence, and the Soul. The One is a supreme transcendent entity that is beyond the categories of being and time (thus similar to Plato's famous Form of the Good in the *Republic*). The four levels or stages above are summarized by Hadot (2009, 84–5). I should note that I don't have the expertise to make a value judgment on ancient India as concerns the intellectual ascent described here. Suffice to say that the Greek tradition is not deriving its inspiration from ancient India.

138 I'm understanding by theology (*theo-logia*) here not simply discourse (*logos*) on God, but a rational discourse on God (or science of divine things, as the Greek philosophers understood it). *Logos* means both speech and reason (see introduction, note 42).

References

Backwell, Lucinda, Justin Bradfield, Kristian J. Carlson, Tea Jashashvili, Lyb Wadley, and Francesco d'Errico. 2018. "The Antiquity of Bow-and-Arrow Technology: Evidence from Middle Stone Age Layers at Sibudu Cave." *Antiquity* 92 (362): 289–303. https://doi.org/10.15184/aqy.2018.11.

Batnitzky, Leora. 2021. "Leo Strauss." In *Stanford Encyclopedia of Philosophy* (Summer 2021). https://plato.stanford.edu/entries/strauss-leo.

Boyd, Brian. 2018. "The Evolution of Stories: from Mimesis to Language, from Fact to Fiction." *Wiley Interdisciplinary Review: Cognitive Science* 9 (1): 1–16. https://doi.org/10.1002/wcs.1444.

Boyd, Robert, Peter Richardson, and Joseph Henrich. 2011. "The Cultural Niche: Why Social Learning Is Essential for Human Adaption," PNAS 108 (S2): 10918–25. https://doi.org/10.1073/pnas.1100290108.

Bremmer, Jan. 1983. *The Early Greek Conception of the Soul*. Princeton, NJ: Princeton University Press.

Brisson, Luc. 1974. *Le Même et l'Autre dans la structure ontologique du* "Timée" *de Plato*. Paris: Klincksieck.

– 1976. *Le mythe de Tirésias: Essai d'analyse structurale*. Leiden: Brill.

– 1995. *Orphée et l'orphisme dans l'Antiquité gréco-romaine*. Aldershot, UK: Variorum.

– 1999. *Plato the Myth Maker*. Translated, edited, and with an introduction by Gerard Naddaf. Chicago: University of Chicago Press.

– 2002. *Sexual Ambivance: Androgyny and Hermaphroditism in Graeco-Roman Antiquity*. Translated by Janet Lloyd. Berkeley: University of California Press.

– 2004. *How Philosophers Saved Myths: Allegorical Interpretation and Classical Mythology*. Translated by Catherine Tihanyi. Chicago: University of Chicago Press.

Brisson, Luc, and F. Walter Meyerstein. 1995. *Puissance et limites de la raison. Le problème des valeurs*. Paris: Les Belles Lettres.

Burkert, Walter. 1985. *Greek Religion*. Translated by John Raffan. Cambridge, MA: Harvard University Press.

Canto-Sperber, Monique. 1997. *Philosophie grecque*. In collaboration with Jonathan Barnes, Luc Brisson, Jacques Brunschwig, and Gregory Vlastos. Paris: Presses Universitaires de France.

Carruthers, Peter. 2000. "The Roots of Scientific Reasoning: Infancy, Modularity and the Art of Tracking." In *The Cognitive Basis of Science*, edited by Peter Carruthers, Stephen Stich, and Michael Siegal, 73–98. Cambridge: Cambridge University Press

Causadias, José, and Kevin Korous. 2018. "How Are Genes Related to Culture? An Introduction to the Field of Cultural Genomics." In *Handbook of Culture and Biology*, edited by José Causadias, Eva Telzer, and Nancy Gonzalas, 153–77. London: John Wiley and Sons. https://doi.org/10.1002/9781119181361.ch7.

Chantraine, Pierre. 1974. *Dictionnaire étymologique de la langue grecque*. Vol. 3. Paris: Klincksieck.

Chareyron, Nicole. 2005. *Pilgrims to Jerusalem in the Middle Ages*. Translated by Donald Wilson. New York: Columbia University Press.

Christensen, Joel P. 2020. *The Many-Minded Man: The Odyssey, Psychology, and the Therapy of Epic*. Ithaca, NY: Cornell University Press.

Cicero, Marcus Tullius. 1933. *On the Nature of the Gods*. Translated by H. Rackham. Loeb Classical Library. Cambridge MA: Harvard University Press.

Cohen, A.B. 2009. "Many Forms of Culture." *American Psychologist* 64 (3): 194–204.

Creanza, Nicole, Oren Kolodny, and Marcus W. Feldman. 2017. "Cultural Evolutionary Theory: How Culture Evolves and Why It Matters." *PNAS* 114 (30): 7782–9. https://doi.org/10.1073/pnas.1620732114.

Damasio, Antonio. 2010. *The Self Comes to Mind: Constructing the Conscious Brain*. New York: Vintage Books.

Dawkins, Richard. 1976. *The Selfish Gene*. Oxford: Oxford University Press.

Dediu, Dan, and Stephen C. Levinson. 2013. "On the Antiquity of Language: The Reinterpretation of Neandertal Linguistic Capacities and Its Consequences." *Frontiers in Psychology* 4 (397): 1–17. https://doi.org/10.3389/fpsyg.2013.00397.

Descola, Philippe. 2014. *Beyond Nature and Culture*. Translated by Janet Lloyd. London: Blackwell.

Detienne, Marcel. 1979. "The Orphic Dionysos and Roasted Boiled Meat." In *Dionysos Slain*. Translated by Mireille and Leonard Muellner. Baltimore: Johns Hopkins University Press.

– 1980. "Une mythologie sans illusion." In *Le temps de la reflection*, edited by Marcel Detienne, 44–60. Paris: Gallimard.

Diès, Auguste. (1927) 1972. *Autour de Platon. Essai de critique et d'histoire*. Paris: Les Belles Lettres.

Donald, Merlin. 1991. *Origins of the Modern Mind: Three Stages in the Evolution of Culture and Cognition*. Cambridge, MA: Harvard University Press.

Dor, Daniel. 2015. *The Instruction of Imagination: Language as a Social Communication Technology*. Oxford: Oxford University Press.

Dor, Daniel, and Eva Jablonka. 2014. "Why We Need to Move from Gene-Culture Co-evolution to Culturally Driven Co-evolution." In *The Social Origins of Language*, edited by Chris Knight and Jerome Lewis, 14–30. Oxford: Oxford University Press. https://doi.org/10.1093/acprof:oso/9780199665327.003.0002.

Dumont, Louis. 1970. *Homo Hierarchicus: The Caste System and Its Implications*. Translated by Mark Sainsbury, Louis Dumont, and Basa Gulati. London: Weidenfeld and Nicolson.

– 1977. *From Mandeville to Marx: The Genesis and Triumph of Economic Ideology*. Chicago: University of Chicago Press.

Dunbar, R.I.M., and J.A.J. Gowlett. 2014. "Fireside Chat: The Impact of Fire on Hominin Socioecology." In *Lucy to Language: The Benchmark Papers*, edited by R.I.M. Dunbar, Clive Gamble, and J.A.J. Gowlett, 277–96. Oxford: Oxford University Press. https://doi.org/10.1093/acprof:osobl/9780199652594.003.0012.

Edelman, Gerald M. 2004. *Wider than the Sky: The Phenomenal Gift of Consciousness*. London: Allen Lane.

Everett, Daniel. 2017. *How Language Began: The Story of Humanity's Greatest Invention*. New York: Liveright.

Frankfort, Henri, H.A. Groenewegen-Frankfort, John A. Wilson, Thorkild Jacobsen, and William A. Irwin. 1946. *Before Philosophy: The Intellectual Adventure of Ancient Man*. Chicago: Penguin Books.

Fuentes, Agustín. 2017. *The Creative Spark: How Imagination Made Humans Exceptional*. New York: Penguin Random House.

Gill, Chris. 1996. *Personality in Greek Epic, Tragedy and Philosophy: The Self in Dialogue*. Oxford: Oxford University Press.

Goody, Jack, and Ian Watt. 1963. "The Consequences of Literacy." *Comparative Studies in Society and History* 5 (3): 304–45. https://doi.org/10.1017/S0010417500001730.

Graham, Daniel. 2013. *Science before Socrates: Parmenides, Anaxagoras, and the New Astronomy*. Oxford: Oxford University Press.

Hadot, Pierre. 2009. *The Present Alone Is Our Happiness: Conversations with Jeannie Carlier and Arnold I. Davidson*. Translated by Marc Djaballah. Cambridge, MA: Harvard University Press.

Harvati, Katrina, Carolin Röding, Abel M. Bosman, Fotios A. Karakostis, Rainer Grün, Chris Stringer, Panagiotis Karkanas, Nicolas C. Thompson, Vassilis Koutoulidis, Lia A. Moulopoulos, Vassilis G. Gorgoulis, and Mirsini Kouloukoussa. 2019. "Apidima Cave Fossils Earliest Evidence of *Homo sapiens* in Eurosia." *Nature*, no. 517, 500–4. https://www.nature.com/articles/s41586-019-1376-z.

Havelock, Eric. 1982. *Literate Revolution in Greece and Its Cultural Consequences*. Princeton, NJ: Princeton University Press.

Heisenberg, Werner. 1958. *Physics and Philosophy: The Revolution in Modern Science*. New York: Harper.

Heller, Agnes. 2003. "Five Approaches to the Phenomenon of Shame." *Social Research* 70 (4): 1015–30. https://doi.org/10.1353/sor.2003.0056.

Henrich, Joseph. 2011. "A Cultural Species: How Culture Drove Human Evolution." *Psychological Science Agenda* 25 (11). https://www.apa.org/science/about/psa/2011/11/human-evolution.

– 2016. *The Secret of Our Success: How Culture Is Driving Human Evolution, Domesticating Our Species, and Making Us Smarter*. Princeton, NJ: Princeton University Press.

– 2020. *The WEIRDest People in the World: How the West Became Psychologically Peculiar and Particularly Prosperous*. New York: Picador.

– 2023. "How Culture Made Us Uniquely Human." *Zygon* 58 (2): 405–24. https://doi.org/10.1111/zygo.12894

Henshilwood, Christopher. 2004. "Ancient Jewellery Found in African Cave." *Nature*, 16 April 2004. https://doi.org/10.1038/news040412-9.

Henshilwood, Christopher, Francesco D'Errico, Karen L. van Niekert, Laure Dayet, Alain Queffelec, and Luca Pollarolo. 2018. "An Abstract Drawing from the 73,000-Year-Old Levels at Blombos Cave, South Africa." *Nature*, no. 562, 115–18. https://doi.org/10.1038/s41586-018-0514-3.

Hesiod. 2006. *Theogony, Works and Days, Testimonia*. Edited and translated by Glenn W. Most. Loeb Classical Library. Cambridge, MA: Harvard University Press.

Homer. 1924. *The Iliad*. Translated by A.T. Murray. 2 vols. Loeb Classical Library. Cambridge, MA: Harvard University Press.

– 1919. *The Odyssey*. Translated by A.T. Murray. 2 vols. Loeb Classical Library. Cambridge, MA: Harvard University Press.

Hublin, Jean-Jacques. 2021. "How Old Are the Oldest *Homo Sapiens* in Far East Asia?" *PNAS* 118 (10): e2101173118. https://doi.org/10.1073/pnas.2101173118.

Hublin, Jean-Jacques, Abdelouahed Ben-Ncer, Shara E. Bailey, Sarah E. Fridline, Simon Neubauer, Matthew M. Skinner, Inga Bergmann, Adeline Le Cabec, Stefano Benazzi, Katerina Harvati, and Philipp Gunz. 2017. "New Fossils from Jebel Irhoud, Morocco and the Pan-African Origin of *Homo sapiens*." *Nature*, no. 546, 289–92. https://doi.org/10.1038/nature22336.

Huntington, Richard, and Peter Metcalf. 1979. *Celebrations of Death: The Anthropology of Mortuary Ritual*. Cambridge: Cambridge University Press.

Isocrates. 1928. *Volume I: To Demonicus. To Nicocles. Nicoles of the Cyprians. Panegryricus. To Phillip. Archidamus*. Translated by George Norlin. Loeb Classical Library. Cambridge, MA: Harvard University Press.

Jaynes, Julian. 1976. *The Origin of Consciousness in the Breakdown of the Bicameral Mind*. New York: Houghton Mifflin.

Jeremiah, Edward. 2012. *The Emergence of Reflexivity in Greek Language and Thought*. Leiden: Brill.

Kobe, Zdravko. 2018. "Reason Reborn: Pietistic Motifs in Kant's Moral Philosophy." *Problemi International*, no. 2, 57–88. https://problemi.si/issues/p2018-2/problemi_international_2018_2.pdf.

La Boétie, Étienne. (1576) 2004. *The Politics of Obedience: The Discourse of Voluntary Servitude*. Translated by Harry Kurz. Whitefish, MT: Kessinger Publishing.

Laurin, Camille. 1978. "Ethnic Minorities in the New Quebec." *Canadian Ethnic Studies* 10 (1): 5–11.

Lewis, Jerome. 2014. "BaYaka Pygmy Multi-modal and Mimetic Communication Traditions." In *The Social Origins of Language*, edited by Daniel Dor, Chris Knight, and Jerome Lewis, 77–91. Oxford: Oxford University Press. https://doi.org/10.1093/acprof:oso/9780199665327.001.0001.

Lloyd, G.E.R. 2012. *Being, Humanity, and Understanding*. Oxford: Oxford University Press.

Longrich, Nick. 2022a. "Here Is When and How Humans Attained 'Behavioural Modernity.'" Genetic Literacy Project, 26 October 2022. https://geneticliteracyproject.org/2022/10/26/here-is-when-and-how-humans-attained-behavioral-modernity.

– 2022b. "Stone Age Innovators: How Technology Exchange between Modern Humans, Archaic *Homo sapiens*, and Neanderthals Drove Progress." Nicklongrich.com, 7 November 2022. https://www.nicklongrich.com/blog/stone-age-innovators.

MacIntyre, Alasdair. 1981. *After Virtue: A Study in Moral Theory*. Notre Dame, IN: University of Notre Dame Press.

Madden, Andrew, Joe Palimi, and Jared Bryson. 2005. "Information Behavior in Pre-literate Societies." In *New Directions in Human Information Behavior*, edited by Amanda Spink and Charles Cole, 33–53. Oxford: Oxford University Press. https://doi.org/10.1007/1-4020-3670-1_3.

Mauss, Marcel. (1920) 2000. *The Gift: The Form and Reason for Exchanges in Archaic Societies*. Translated by W.D. Halls. New York: W.W. Norton and Company.

McIntyre, Lee. 2021. *How to Talk to a Science Denier: Conversations with Flat Earthers, Climate Deniers, and Others Who Defy Reason*. Cambridge, MA: Harvard University Press.

Meisner, Dwayne. 2018. *Orphic Tradition and Birth of the Gods*. Oxford: Oxford University Press.

Mizumura, Minae. 2015. *The Fall of Language in the Age of English*. Translated by Mari Yoshihara and Juliet Winters Carpenter. New York: Columbia University Press.

Naddaf, Gerard. 2002. "Hesiod as a Catalyst for Western Political Paideia." *The European Legacy: Toward New Paradigms* 7 (3): 343–61. https://doi.org/10.1080/10848770220132357.

– 2003. "Anthropogony and Politogony in Anaximander of Miletus." In *Anaximander in Context: New Studies in the Origins of Greek Philosophy*, edited by Dirk Couprie, Robert Hahn, and Gerard Naddaf, 7–69. Albany: State University of New York Press.

– 2005. *The Greek Concept of Nature*. Albany: State University of New York Press.

– 2009. "Allegory and the Origins of Philosophy." In *Logos and Mythos: Philosophical Essays on Greek Literature*, edited by Willian Wians, 99–131. Albany: State University of New York Press.

– 2012. "L'historia comme genre littéraire dans la pensée grecque archaïque." In *Lire les Présocratiques*, edited by Luc Brisson, Arnaud Macé, and Anne-Laure Therme, 61–78. Paris: Presses Universitaires de France. An English version can be found at https://www.academia.edu/37980043/Historia_in_Early_Greek_Writing_and_Thought.

– 2016a. "Poetic Myths of the Afterlife: Plato's Last Song." *Reflections on Plato's Poetics: Essays from Beijing*, edited by Rick Benitez and Keping Wang, 111–36. Berrima, AU: Academic Printing and Publishing.

– 2016b. Review of *Science before Socrates: Parmenides, Anaxagoras, and the New Astronomy*, by Daniel Graham. *Mind* 125 (499): 942–52.

– 2019. "Revisiting the Religion of the Early Greek Philosophers, and Socrates' Contribution to the Controversy." *Ápeiron. Estudios de filosofía, monográfico "Presocráticos,"* no. 11, 65–97.

– 2023. "Discovering φύσις: Reductive Materialism, the Emergence of Reflexivity, and the First Secular Theories of Everything." In *Studies in Ancient Greek Philosophy: In Honor of Professor Anthony Preus*, edited by David M. Spitzer, 18–36. New York: Routledge.

– Forthcoming. "Cosmological Models and the *Peri Phuseos* Tradition." In *The Edinburgh Critical History of Western Philosophy*, vol. 1, *Greek and Roman Philosophy*, edited by Giuseppe Cambiana and Alexandra Lianeri. Edinburgh: Edinburgh University Press. The penultimate version is available at https://www.academia.edu/25128934/COSMOLOGICAL_MODELS_AND_THE_PERI_PHUSEOS_TRADITION.

Nagel, Thomas. 2012. *Mind and Cosmos*. Oxford: Oxford University Press.

Nagy, Gregory. 1982. "Hesiod." In *Ancient Writers*, edited by T. James Luce, 43–74. New York: Scribner.

Neubauer, Simon, Jean-Jacques Hublin, and Phillip Gunz. 2018. "The Evolution of the Modern Human Brain Shape." *Science Advances* 4 (1). https://doi.org/10.1126/sciadv.aao5961.

Oglesby, Nathan Dufour. 2018. "Footnotes to Footnotes: Whitehead's Plato." PhD diss., City University of New York. https://academicworks.cuny.edu/cgi/viewcontent.cgi?article=3489&context=gc_etds.

Onians, R.B. 1951. *The Origins of European Thought*. Cambridge: Cambridge University Press.

Ophuls, William. 2013. *Plato's Revenge: Politics in the Age of Ecology*. Cambridge, MA: MIT Press.

Peterson, Merrill, ed. 1974. *The Portable Thomas Jefferson*. New York: Viking.

Pettitt, Paul. 2013. *The Palaeolithic Origins of Human Burial*. London: Routledge.

Phillips, Steven. 2010. *Classical Indian Metaphysics: Refutation of Realism and the Emergence of "New Logic."* Chicago: Open Court Publishing.

Polletta, Francesca, Pang Ching Bobby Chen, Beth Gharrity Gardener, and Alice Motes. 2011. "The Sociology of Storytelling." *Annual Review of Sociology* 37: 109–30. https://doi.org/10.1146/annurev-soc-081309-150106.

Popper, Karl. 1945a. *The Open Society and It's Enemies*. Vol. 1, *The Spell of Plato*. London: Routledge.

– 1945b. *The Open Society and It's Enemies*. Vol. 2, *The High Tide of Prophecy: Hegel, Marx, and the Aftermath*. London: Routledge.

Purzycki, Benjamin G., Coren Apicella, Quentin D. Atkinson, Emma Cohen, Rita Ann McNamara, Aiyanna K. Willard, Dimitris Xygalatas, Ara Norenzayan, and Joseph Henrich. 2016. "Moralistic Gods, Supernatural Punishment, and the Expansion of Human Society." *Nature*, no. 530, 327–30. https://doi.org/10.1038/nature16980.

Reich, David. 2018. *Who We Are and How We Got Here: Ancient DNA and the New Science of the Human Past*. New York: Pantheon Books.

Rovelli, Carlo. 2011. *Anaximander*. Translated by M.L. Rosenberg. Yardley, PA: Westholme.

Schlebusch, Carina M., Pontus Skoglund, Per Sjödin, Lucie M. Gattepaille, Flora Jay, Michael de Jongh, Andrew Singleton, Michael G.B. Blum, Himla Soodyall, and Mattias Jakobsson. 2012. "Genomic Variation in Seven Khoe-San Groups Reveals Adaptation and Complex African History." *Science* 338 (6105): 374–9. https://doi.org/10.1126/science.1227721.

Seaford, Richard. 2004. *Money and the Early Greek Mind: Homer, Philosophy, Tragedy*. Cambridge: Cambridge University Press.

– ed. 2011. *Universe and Inner Self in Early Indian and Early Greek Thought*. Edinburgh: University of Edinburgh Press.

– 2017. "*Psychê* from Homer to Plato: A Historical Sketch." In *Self and the Soul: Essays on Ancient Thought and Literature in Honour of Christopher Gill*, edited by Richard Seaford, John Wilkins, and Matthew Wright, 11–32. Oxford: Oxford University Press.

– 2020. *The Origins of Philosophy in Ancient Greece and Ancient India: A Historical Comparison*. Cambridge: Cambridge University Press.

Simonton, Dean. 1999. *The Origin of Genius*. Oxford: Oxford University Press.

Smith, Daniel, Philip Schlaepfer, Katie Major, Mark Dyble, Abigail E. Page, James Thompson, Nikhil Chaudhary, Gul Deniz Salali, Ruth Mace, Leonora Astete, Marilyn Ngales, Lucio Vinicius, and Andrea

Bamberg Migliano. 2017. "Cooperation and the Evolution of Hunter-Gatherer Storytelling." *Nature Communications* 8 (1853). https://doi.org/10.1038/s41467-017-02036-8.

Smith, Karl. 2012. "From Dividual and Individual Selves to Porous Subjects." *Australian Journal of Anthropology* 23 (1): 50–64. https://doi.org/10.1111/j.1757-6547.2012.00167.x.

Snell, Bruno. 1953. *The Discovery of Mind*. Translated by T.G. Rosenmeyer. Oxford: Oxford University Press.

Sorabji, Richard. 2006. *Self: Ancient and Modern Insights about Individuality, Life, and Death*. Chicago: University of Chicago Press.

Spink, Amanda, and Charles Cole, eds. 2005. *New Directions in Human Information Behavior*. Oxford: Oxford University Press

Stepka, Zane, Liora Kolska, and Filipe Natalio. 2022. "Hidden Signatures of Early Fire at Evron Quarry (1.0 to 0.8 Mya)." *PNAS* 119 (25): e2123439119. https://doi.org/10.1073/pnas.2123439119.

Stetka, Bret. 2014. "What Do Great Musicians Have in Common? DNA." *Scientific American*, 5 August 2014. https://www.scientificamerican.com/article/what-do-great-musicians-have-in-common-dna.

Sugiyama, Michelle Scalise. 2011. "The Forager Oral Tradition and the Evolution of Prolonged Juvenility." *Frontiers in Psychology*, 23 August 2011. https://doi.org/10.3389/fpsyg.2011.00133.

Suzman, James. 2017a. *Affluences without Abundance: What We Can Learn from the World's Most Successful Civilization*. New York: Bloomsbury.

– 2017b. "When a 200,000-Year-Old Culture Encountered the Modern Economy." *The Atlantic*, 24 July 2017. https://www.theatlantic.com/business/archive/2017/07/hunter-gatherers-modern-economy/534522.

Taylor, Charles. 1989. *Sources of the Self: The Making of the Modern Identity*. Cambridge: Cambridge University Press.

Tomasello, Michael. 1995. *The Cultural Origin of Human Cognition*. Cambridge, MA: Harvard University Press.

Tominson, Gary. 2018. *A Million Years of Music: The Emergence of Human Modernity*. New York: Zone Books.

Van Gulick, Robert. 2022. "Consciousness." In *Stanford Encyclopedia of Philosophy* (Winter 2022). https://plato.stanford.edu/entries/consciousness.

Vlastos, Gregory. (1952) 1993. "Theology and Philosophy in Early Greek Thought." In *Studies in Greek Philosophy*, vol. 1, *The Presocratics*, 3–31, edited by Daniel W. Graham. Princeton, NJ: Princeton University Press.

– 1975. *Plato's Universe*, Seattle: University of Washington Press.

Waring, T.M., and Z.T. Wood. 2021. "Long-Term Gene–Culture Coevolution and the Human Evolutionary Transition." *Proceedings of the Royal Society B: Biological Sciences* 288 (1952): 20210538. https://doi.org/10.1098/rspb.2021.0538.

West, M.L. 1993. *Greek Lyric Poetry*. Oxford: Clarendon Press.

Whitehead, Alfred North. (1929) 1985. *Process and Reality: An Essay on Cosmology*. New York: Free Press.

Wiessner, Polly W. 2014. "Embers of Society: Firetalk among the Ju/'hoansi Bushman." PNAS 111 (39): 14027–35. https://doi.org/10.1073/pnas.1404212111.

Williams, Bernard. 1993. *Shame and Necessity*. Berkeley: University of California Press.

Wilson, Edward O. 2017. *The Origins of Creativity*. New York: Liveright.

Wrangham, Richard. 2009. *Catching Fire: How Cooking Made Us Human*. New York: Basic Books.

– 2019. *The Goodness Paradox: The Strange Relationship between Virtue and Violence in Human Evolution*. New York: Pantheon Books.

Index